THE TAMING OF THE SHREW

Edited by
ANN THOMPSON
Senior Lecturer in English, University of Liverpool

CAMBRIDGE
UNIVERSITY PRESS

PUBLISHED BY THE PRESS SYNDICATE OF THE UNIVERSITY OF CAMBRIDGE
The Pitt Building, Trumpington Street, Cambridge, United Kingdom

CAMBRIDGE UNIVERSITY PRESS
The Edinburgh Building, Cambridge CB2 2RU, UK
40 West 20th Street, New York, NY 10011–4211, USA
10 Stamford Road, Oakleigh, VIC 3166, Australia
Ruiz de Alarcón 13, 28014 Madrid, Spain
Dock House, The Waterfront, Cape Town 8001, South Africa

http://www.cambridge.org

First published 1984
Reprinted 1985, 1988, 1995, 1998, 1999, 2000

Printed in the United Kingdom at the University Press, Cambridge

Library of Congress Catalogue card number: 83–7856

British Library Cataloguing in Publication data
Shakespeare, William
The Taming of the Shrew. — (The New Cambridge Shakespeare)
I. Title   II. Thompson, Ann
822.3′3 PR2832

ISBN 0 521 22195 1 hardback
ISBN 0 521 29388 X paperback

UP

THE NEW CAMBRIDGE SHAKESPEARE

The *New Cambridge Shakespeare* succeeds *The New Shakespeare* which began publication in 1921 under the general editorship of Sir Arthur Quiller-Couch and John Dover Wilson, and was completed in the 1960s, with the assistance of G. I. Duthie, Alice Walker, Peter Ure and J. C. Maxwell. *The New Shakespeare* itself followed upon *The Cambridge Shakespeare,* 1863–6, edited by W. G. Clark, J. Glover and W. A. Wright.

The New Shakespeare won high esteem both for its scholarship and for its design, but shifts of critical taste and insight, recent Shakespearean research, and a changing sense of what is important in our understanding of the plays, have made it necessary to re-edit and redesign, not merely to revise, the series.

The *New Cambridge Shakespeare* aims to be of value to a new generation of playgoers and readers who wish to enjoy fuller access to Shakespeare's poetic and dramatic art. While offering ample academic guidance, it reflects current critical interests and is more attentive than some earlier editions have been to the realisation of the plays on the stage, and to their social and cultural settings. The text of each play has been freshly edited, with textual data made available to those users who wish to know why and how one published text differs from another. Although modernised, the edition conserves forms that appear to be expressive and characteristically Shakespearean, and it does not attempt to disguise the fact that the plays were written in a language other than that of our own time.

Illustrations are usually integrated into the critical and historical discussion of the play and include some reconstructions of early performances by C. Walter Hodges. Some editors have also made use of the advice and experience of Maurice Daniels, for many years a member of the Royal Shakespeare Company.

Each volume is addressed to the needs and problems of a particular text, and each therefore differs in style and emphasis from others in the series.

PHILIP BROCKBANK
Founding General Editor

For SUSANNA AND JUDITH

CONTENTS

ILLUSTRATIONS

PREFACE

Like all other editors of Shakespeare I must express a heavy debt to my predecessors. I have made particular use of the previous Cambridge edition of *The Taming of the Shrew* edited by Sir Arthur Quiller-Couch and John Dover Wilson in the New Shakespeare series (1928), and of the excellent New Penguin edition by G. R. Hibbard (1968). I have also found much of interest in R. Warwick Bond's Arden edition (1904) and in the Riverside edition (1974). Brian Morris's Arden edition (1981) was published when my own work was already well advanced, and I am especially grateful to the editor for letting me see the proofs in advance of publication and for encouraging me at a time when I felt that my efforts had become redundant. H. J. Oliver's edition in the Oxford Shakespeare (1982) also appeared at a very late stage, just before this edition went to press, but I have tried to take his findings into account.

I should like to express my thanks to the General Editors of this series and in particular to Robin Hood, who has commented on my work most promptly and thoroughly at every stage, offering innumerable fruitful suggestions and saving me from a world of errors. Others who have read drafts and commented very helpfully on all aspects of the edition are Philip Edwards, Kenneth Muir, Richard Proudfoot and my husband, John Thompson. In addition I have had expert advice from Gary Taylor on textual matters, from Tom Craik, C. Walter Hodges and Marion Lomax on questions of staging, from Maurice Daniels and Russell Jackson on stage history and from Helen Wilcox on music. All errors that remain are of course my own responsibility and I should be grateful to be told about them.

Although this edition is published at Cambridge it is very much a product of Liverpool. I should like to thank the University for a number of research grants over the last three years, as well as for a period of study leave at the beginning of the project. I am grateful to the students who took the optional Shakespeare course in 1980-1 and 1981-2 for providing me with a lively series of discussions on the play. And I must once again express my gratitude for the endless patience and skill of the English Department secretaries, especially Catherine Rees and Joan Welford.

Finally, I am grateful to Liverpool University Library, the British Library, Birmingham Reference Library, the Shakespeare Centre Library in Stratford-upon-Avon and the Henry E. Huntington Library in California for the use of their resources and the helpfulness of their staff.

A. T.

University of Liverpool

ABBREVIATIONS AND CONVENTIONS

1. Shakespeare's plays

The abbreviated titles of Shakespeare's plays have been modified from those used in the *Harvard Concordance to Shakespeare*. All quotations and line references to plays other than *The Taming of the Shrew* are to G. Blakemore Evans (ed.), *The Riverside Shakespeare*, 1974, on which the *Concordance* is based.

Ado	*Much Ado about Nothing*
Ant.	*Antony and Cleopatra*
AWW	*All's Well That Ends Well*
AYLI	*As You Like It*
Cor.	*Coriolanus*
Cym.	*Cymbeline*
Err.	*The Comedy of Errors*
Ham.	*Hamlet*
1H4	*The First Part of King Henry the Fourth*
2H4	*The Second Part of King Henry the Fourth*
H5	*King Henry the Fifth*
1H6	*The First Part of King Henry the Sixth*
2H6	*The Second Part of King Henry the Sixth*
3H6	*The Third Part of King Henry the Sixth*
H8	*King Henry the Eighth*
JC	*Julius Caesar*
John	*King John*
LLL	*Love's Labour's Lost*
Lear	*King Lear*
Mac.	*Macbeth*
MM	*Measure for Measure*
MND	*A Midsummer Night's Dream*
MV	*The Merchant of Venice*
Oth.	*Othello*
Per.	*Pericles*
R2	*King Richard the Second*
R3	*King Richard the Third*
Rom.	*Romeo and Juliet*
Shr.	*The Taming of the Shrew*
STM	*Sir Thomas More*
Temp.	*The Tempest*
TGV	*The Two Gentlemen of Verona*
Tim.	*Timon of Athens*
Tit.	*Titus Andronicus*
TN	*Twelfth Night*
TNK	*The Two Noble Kinsmen*

Tro.	*Troilus and Cressida*
Wiv.	*The Merry Wives of Windsor*
WT	*The Winter's Tale*

2. Editions

Editions of Shakespeare are abbreviated under the name of the editor unless they are the work of more than one editor, when an abbreviated series name is used, e.g. Cam., Riverside. When more than one edition by the same editor is cited, later editions are discriminated by a raised figure, e.g. *Rowe*³. This list includes all editions referred to in the collation and Commentary. It is not a complete list of editions collated.

Alexander	*William Shakespeare, The Complete Works*, ed. Peter Alexander, 1951
Bond	*The Taming of the Shrew*, ed. R. Warwick Bond, 1904; rev. edn, 1929 (Arden Shakespeare)
Cam.	*The Works of William Shakespeare*, ed. William George Clark and John Glover, 1863–6 (Cambridge Shakespeare)
Capell	*Mr William Shakespeare his Comedies, Histories, and Tragedies*, ed. Edward Capell, 1768
Collier	*The Works of William Shakespeare*, ed. J. Payne Collier, 1842–4
Dyce	*The Works of William Shakespeare*, ed. Alexander Dyce, 1857
F	*Mr William Shakespeares Comedies, Histories, and Tragedies*, 1623 (First Folio)
F2	*Mr William Shakespeares Comedies, Histories, and Tragedies*, 1632 (Second Folio)
F3	*Mr William Shakespeares Comedies, Histories, and Tragedies*, 1664 (Third Folio)
F4	*Mr William Shakespeares Comedies, Histories, and Tragedies*, 1685 (Fourth Folio)
Gentleman	*Bell's Edition of Shakespeare's Plays*, ed. F. Gentleman, 1774
Halliwell	*The Complete Works of Shakespeare*, ed. James O. Halliwell, 1852
Hanmer	*The Works of Shakespear*, ed. Thomas Hanmer, 1744
Hibbard	*The Taming of the Shrew*, ed. G. R. Hibbard, 1968 (New Penguin Shakespeare)
Hudson	*The Complete Works of William Shakespeare*, ed. H. N. Hudson, 1881 (Harvard Shakespeare)
Irving	*The Works of William Shakespeare*, ed. Henry Irving and F. A. Marshall, 1888–90 (Irving Shakespeare)
Johnson	*The Plays of William Shakespeare*, ed. Samuel Johnson, 1765
Keightley	*The Plays of William Shakespeare*, ed. Thomas Keightley, 1864
Kittredge	*The Complete Works of Shakespeare*, ed. George Lyman Kittredge, 1936
Knight	*The Pictorial Edition of the Works of Shakspere*, ed. C. Knight, 1839–42

Malone	*The Plays and Poems of William Shakespeare*, ed. Edmond Malone, 1790
Morris	*The Taming of the Shrew*, ed. Brian Morris, 1981 (Arden Shakespeare)
NS	*The Taming of the Shrew*, ed. Sir Arthur Quiller-Couch and John Dover Wilson, 1928 (New Shakespeare)
Neilson	*The Complete Dramatic and Poetic Works of William Shakespeare*, ed. W. A. Neilson, 1906
Oliver	*The Taming of the Shrew*, ed. H. J. Oliver, 1982 (Oxford Shakespeare)
Pelican	*William Shakespeare: The Complete Works*, ed. A. Harbage, 1956 (Pelican Shakespeare)
Pope	*The Works of Shakespear*, ed. Alexander Pope, 1723–5
Pope²	*The Works of Shakespear*, ed. Alexander Pope, 2nd edn, 1728
Q	*A Wittie and Pleasant Comedie Called The Taming of the Shrew* 1631 (quarto)
Rann	*The Dramatic Works of Shakespeare*, ed. Joseph Rann, 1786–94
Reed	*The Plays of William Shakespeare*, ed. Isaac Reed, 1803
Riverside	*The Riverside Shakespeare*, textual ed. G. Blakemore Evans, 1974
Rowe	*The Works of Mr William Shakespear*, ed. Nicholas Rowe, 1709
Rowe²	*The Works of Mr William Shakespear*, ed. Nicholas Rowe, 2nd edn, 1709
Rowe³	*The Works of Mr William Shakespear*, ed. Nicholas Rowe, 3rd edn, 1714
Singer	*The Dramatic Works of William Shakespeare*, ed. Samuel Weller Singer, 1826
Sisson	*William Shakespeare: The Complete Works*, ed. C. J. Sisson, 1954
Steevens	*The Plays of William Shakespeare*, ed. Samuel Johnson and George Steevens, 1773
Stockdale	*Stockdale's Edition of Shakespeare*, ed. J. Stockdale, 1784
Theobald	*The Works of Shakespeare*, ed. Lewis Theobald, 1733
Warburton	*The Works of Shakespeare*, ed. William Warburton, 1747

3. Other works, periodicals, general references

Abbott	E. A. Abbott, *A Shakespearian Grammar*, 1869 (references are to numbered paragraphs)
Bullough, *Sources*	Geoffrey Bullough (ed.), *Narrative and Dramatic Sources of Shakespeare*, 8 vols., 1957–75
conj.	conjecture
ELR	*English Literary Renaissance*
ES	*English Studies*
Greg	W. W. Greg, *The Shakespeare First Folio*, 1955
Hinman	Charlton Hinman, *The Printing and Proof-Reading of the First Folio of Shakespeare*, 2 vols., 1963
HLQ	*Huntington Library Quarterly*

Hosley, 'Sources and analogues'	Richard Hosley, 'Sources and analogues of *The Taming of the Shrew*', *HLQ* 27 (1963–4), 289–308
JEGP	*Journal of English and Germanic Philology*
Kökeritz, *Pronunciation*	Helge Kökeritz, *Shakespeare's Pronunciation*, 1953
MLQ	*Modern Language Quarterly*
MLR	*Modern Language Review*
MLS	*Modern Language Studies*
Muir, *Sources*	Kenneth Muir, *The Sources of Shakespeare's Plays*, rev. edn, 1977
N&Q	*Notes and Queries*
OED	*Oxford English Dictionary*
Partridge, *Bawdy*	Eric Partridge, *Shakespeare's Bawdy*, 1948
PMLA	*Publications of the Modern Language Association of America*
REL	*Review of English Literature*
RES	*Review of English Studies*
SB	*Studies in Bibliography*
SD	stage direction
SEL	*Studies in English Literature*
SH	speech heading
Sisson, *New Readings*	C. J. Sisson, *New Readings in Shakespeare*, 1956
SJ	*Shakespeare Jahrbuch*
SQ	*Shakespeare Quarterly*
S.St.	*Shakespeare Studies*
S.Sur.	*Shakespeare Survey*
subst.	substantively
Tilley	M. P. Tilley, *A Dictionary of the Proverbs in England in the Sixteenth and Seventeenth Centuries*, 1950 (references are to numbered proverbs)
Tillyard	E. M. W. Tillyard, 'Some consequences of a lacuna in *The Taming of the Shrew*', *ES* 43 (1962), 330–5
TLS	*Times Literary Supplement*
Tyrrwhitt	Thomas Tyrrwhitt, *Observations and Conjectures upon some Passages of Shakespeare*, 1766
Vickers, *Prose*	Brian Vickers, *The Artistry of Shakespeare's Prose*, 1968
Walker	W. S. Walker, *A Critical Examination of the Text of Shakespeare*, 1860
Wells	Stanley Wells and Gary Taylor, *Modernizing Shakespeare's Spelling, with Three Studies in the Text of 'Henry V'*, 1979

INTRODUCTION

Date and theatrical context

It is generally agreed that *The Taming of the Shrew* is among Shakespeare's earliest comedies, but to date it more precisely we need to examine the surviving references to its first publication and performance. Enquiry is complicated by the existence of two closely related plays: *The Taming of the Shrew*, printed in the Shakespeare Folio of 1623, and *The Taming of a Shrew*, a different version whose connection with the Folio play remains puzzling; it is convenient to refer to them as *The Shrew* and *A Shrew*. While the distinction between the two is important to us, however, it is not clear that it was consistently made in the early references. The preliminary evidence can be set out as follows:

1   On 2 May 1594 a play was entered to Peter Short in the Stationers' Register as 'A plesant Conceyted historie called the Tamyinge of a Shrowe'.[1]

2   A play was printed in a quarto edition in the same year with the following information on its title page: 'A Pleasant Conceited Historie, called The taming of a Shrew. As it was sundry times acted by the Right honorable the Earle of Pembrook his servants. Printed at London by Peter Short and are to be sold by Cutbert Burbie, at his shop at the Royall Exchange, 1594'. A single copy of this edition survives. It is the play known today as *A Shrew*.[2]

3   On 11 June 1594 a performance of a play called 'the tamyng of A shrowe' at the Newington Butts theatre is recorded in Henslowe's diary.[3] Henslowe does not mark the play 'ne' (meaning 'new'). Both the Admiral's Men and the newly formed Chamberlain's Men (Shakespeare's company from this time onwards) seem to have been playing in this theatre in 1594.

4   In 1596 Peter Short and Cuthbert Burby reprinted the quarto of *A Shrew* with a few minor modifications.

5   On 22 January 1607 three plays, 'The taming of a Shrewe', 'Romeo and Juliett' and 'Loves Labour Loste', were entered in the Stationers' Register to 'Master Linge by direccon of A Court and with consent of Master Burby under his handwrytinge'. A third quarto of *A Shrew* appeared immediately with the imprint 'Printed at London by V.S. for Nicholas Ling and are to be sold at his shop in Saint Dunstons Church-yard in Fleet street. 1607.' This edition again had a few minor modifications.[4] In the same year Ling transferred his rights in *A Shrew* to John Smethwick.

[1] Edward Arber (ed.), *The Stationers' Registers, 1554–1640*, 2 vols., 1875, II, 648. See also the discussion of the descent of the copyright in this play from 1594 to 1623 in Greg, p. 62.
[2] Quotations from *A Shrew* throughout this edition are from the text given in Bullough, *Sources*, I, 69–108.
[3] R. A. Foakes and R. T. Rickert (eds.), *Henslowe's Diary*, 1961, p. 22.
[4] For details of the variants between these early editions, see F. S. Boas (ed.), *The Taming of a Shrew*, 1908.

6 In 1623 *The Shrew* was printed in the First Folio of Shakespeare's plays.

7 In 1631 John Smethwick printed a quarto edition, not of *A Shrew* as one might expect, but of *The Shrew*, with a text clearly deriving from the First Folio.

It appears that Smethwick, owning the rights of *A Shrew* but printing *The Shrew*, did not discriminate between the plays. Neither, apparently, did Burby, when he consented to the association of *A Shrew* with *Romeo and Juliet* and *Love's Labour's Lost*. It seems clear, however, that both Pembroke's Men and the Chamberlain's Men had *Shrew* plays in their respective repertories by 1594.

A close estimate of the date of *The Shrew* depends upon our interpretation of (1) the relationships between the two versions, (2) theatre-company history in the 1590s, and (3) connections with other relevant plays of the time. The relationship between *A Shrew* and *The Shrew* has been vigorously debated; it was once thought that *A Shrew* was the source for *The Shrew*, but it is now generally agreed that *A Shrew* is some kind of memorial reconstruction of *The Shrew* itself,[1] and it would therefore follow that *The Shrew* was performed before 1594. The troubled theatre history of the period leads us to suppose that it was at least two years before. A severe outbreak of the plague closed the theatres, apart from one short interlude, from June 1592 right on into 1594. The companies dispersed, some splitting into smaller groups and some reorganising under new patrons. Shakespeare's career at that time is not known with any certainty, but there are indications that he was with the Queen's Men before 1592, left with others to join Pembroke's Men in the same year, and finally joined the newly established Chamberlain's Men in 1594.[2]

Shakespeare's association with Pembroke's Men, which may have been co-extensive with the life of that company, may help to explain the existence of *A Shrew* and of two other abbreviated and reconstructed plays of this period: *The First Part of the Contention betwixt the Two Famous Houses of York and Lancaster* (a version of *2 Henry VI*), printed in 1594, and *The True Tragedy of Richard Duke of York* (a version of *3 Henry VI*), printed in 1595, naming Pembroke's Men on its title page. Behind these garbled plays, it has been claimed, we can detect 'good acting versions', deliberately (and perhaps even authorially) cut and rearranged for performance by a cast slightly smaller than originally intended.[3] It has been shown that all three 'bad' texts, including *A Shrew*, can be performed by a company of eleven adult actors, four boys and about five supernumeraries playing soldiers, attendants and so on. Certain actors' names ('Tom', 'Sander', 'Will') appear in speech headings and stage directions in all three texts, making it appropriate to treat them as a group. The relationship of *A Shrew* to *The Shrew*, however, is not quite like that of the *Henry VI* derivatives to the Folio texts. Although *A Shrew* contains evidence of memorial reconstruction

---

[1] For a full discussion of the relationship between *The Shrew* and *A Shrew*, see Textual Analysis, pp. 155–74 below.

[2] See Scott McMillin, 'Casting for Pembroke's Men: the *Henry 6* quartos and *The Taming of a Shrew*', *SQ* 23 (1972), 141–59; G. M. Pinciss, 'Shakespeare, Her Majesty's Players, and Pembroke's Men', *S.Sur.* 27 (1974), 129–36; and Karl P. Wentersdorf, 'The origin and personnel of the Pembroke company', *Theatre Research International* 5 (1980), 45–68.

[3] McMillin, 'Pembroke's Men', p. 148. Gary Taylor has reached similar conclusions about the 1600 'bad' quarto of *Henry V*: see Stanley Wells and Gary Taylor, *Modernizing Shakespeare's Spelling, with Three Studies in the Text of 'Henry 5'*, 1979.

and of cutting, it is much more freely rewritten. The Folio text of *The Shrew* itself, moreover, appears to have been cut, since Sly and his companions disappear at the end of 1.1 instead of staying, as they do in *A Shrew*, to watch the play and conclude the action. Neither surviving text, therefore, seems wholly to preserve the play as it was performed before the closing of the theatres.[1]

Two further pieces of peripheral evidence tend to support a date before 1592. At one point in *A Shrew* we find the stage direction *Enter Simon, Alphonsus, and his three daughters*. Since the play's character 'Simon' is already on stage, it has been suggested that this was also the name of the actor who played 'Alfonsus', and therefore to be identified as Simon Jewell, of either the Queen's or Pembroke's Men, who died (probably from the plague) in August 1592.[2] Another intimation of an early performance of *The Shrew* is found in an allusion in Antony Chute's poem *Beawtie Dishonoured written under the title of Shores Wife*: 'He calls his *Kate* and she must come and kisse him'; *A Shrew* does not have the kissing sequences of *The Shrew* 5.1 and 5.2.[3]

Verbal parallels with non-Shakespearean plays may be adduced to confirm a date before 1592, perhaps as early as 1590. A number have been noted between the anonymous play *A Knack to Know a Knave* and both *Shrew* plays.[4] *A Knack* was first performed by Strange's Men at the Rose on 10 June 1592 and marked 'ne' (meaning 'new') in Henslowe's diary. It was printed in 1594. While we cannot be sure that the published text of *A Knack* was the same as that acted in 1592, any detectable borrowings from the *Shrew* plays must date back to pre-plague performances. If we assume from the borrowings from *A Shrew* that a performance of the derivative text intervened between the original performance of *The Shrew* and the first of *A Knack*, the date of *The Shrew* is pushed back even earlier. Parallels with Thomas Kyd's *The Spanish Tragedy* are of interest but do not give much help with the precise dating of *The Shrew*, as the date of Kyd's play itself cannot be established with certainty within the range 1582–92. Recent scholars, however, favour a date towards the end of the period. A trace of the old play *King Leir* may be left at 4.1.58–9; it belonged to the Queen's Men and it has been argued that Shakespeare acted in it.[5]

The evidence so far suggests, therefore, that Shakespeare originally wrote his play, complete with all the Sly material, for a large company (possibly the Queen's Men) either in the season ended by the closing of the theatres in June 1592 or in the preceding season. During the turbulent years 1592–4 two companies came to possess cut versions of the play – *The Shrew*, which remains close to the original, and *A Shrew*, a memorial reconstruction of the original. It remains possible that *The Shrew* was among the first of Shakespeare's plays and dates back to 1590, but since there is no controlling external evidence, such a speculation depends upon a judgement of the play's maturity in relation to Shakespeare's other early work.

---

[1] For a fuller discussion of the origins of the Folio text, see Textual Analysis, pp. 155–74 below.

[2] See Mary Edmond, 'Pembroke's Men', *RES* 25 (1974), 129–36; Scott McMillin, 'Simon Jewell and the Queen's Men, *RES* 27 (1976), 174–7; and Wentersdorf, 'Pembroke company', pp. 48 and 63.

[3] See William H. Moore, 'An allusion in 1593 to *The Taming of the Shrew?*' *SQ* 15 (1964), 55–60.

[4] See G. R. Proudfoot (ed.), *A Knack to Know a Knave*, Malone Society Reprints, 1963, and Ann Thompson, 'Dating evidence for *The Taming of the Shrew*', *N&Q* 29 (1982), 108–9.

[5] See Kenneth Muir (ed.), *Lear*, 1952, pp. xxiv–xxix, and Pinciss, 'Her Majesty's Players', p. 133.

1 A possible staging of Induction 2 with the use of a gallery, by C. Walter Hodges. The scene is played 'aloft', as in a playhouse of the 1590s provided with a spacious upper stage. It is here suggested that the musicians, if seen at all, need not be placed above. The Messenger is shown announcing the performance from the acting-area below

The Shrew in the context of Shakespeare's own work

Among Shakespeare's comedies, *The Shrew* has particularly close affinities with *The Comedy of Errors* and *The Two Gentlemen of Verona*. It is generally agreed that these three plays are Shakespeare's earliest comedies but the order in which they were written has not been definitely established. In the absence of other arguments it has seemed logical to suppose that Shakespeare progressed away from writing plays directly based on classical or Italian models towards the less plot-bound mode of romantic comedy which he subsequently developed from *Love's Labour's Lost* to *Twelfth Night*. If we accept this view, *The Comedy of Errors*, which is most heavily dependent on classical sources, would come first, *The Taming of the Shrew*, with its mixture of classical and romantic materials, would follow, and *The Two Gentlemen of Verona*, Shakespeare's first attempt at fully romantic comedy, would be the latest of the three.

There are obvious objections to this theory: one might claim, for example, that the ending of *The Two Gentlemen of Verona* is comparatively weak and that

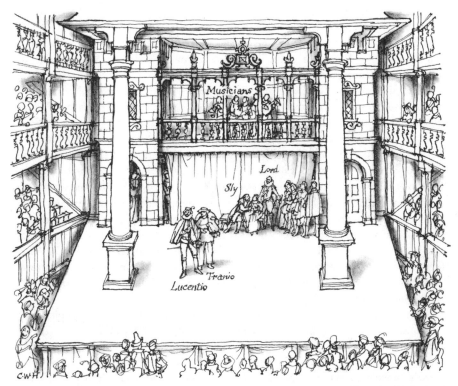

2 A possible staging of Induction 2 on the main stage, by C. Walter Hodges. The scene is all placed below, as in a playhouse with a restricted upper stage. The Messenger has just withdrawn and the first players have entered

Shakespeare could hardly have written it after dealing competently with much more complicated dénouements in *The Comedy of Errors* and *The Shrew*,[1] or one might object that Shakespeare did not in fact jettison classical motifs after *The Shrew* but continued to use them throughout his career.[2] Marco Mincoff has argued that *The Shrew* must precede *The Comedy of Errors* on the grounds that it is stylistically more primitive,[3] and Brian Morris has gone so far as to suggest that *The Shrew* 'might be not simply Shakespeare's first comedy: it might be his first play'. He draws our attention to the evocation of Warwickshire in the Induction, suggesting that Shakespeare is here 'recalling a countryside he had quite recently left', and he proposes a date of 1589.[4] Another recent editor, H. J. Oliver, agrees that *The Shrew* must have been written at least as early as 1592 but supposes on internal evidence that *The Two Gentlemen* came first.[5] The whole question of the dating of Shakespeare's

[1] In Clifford Leech (ed.), *TGV*, 1969, pp. xxi–xxxv, it is argued that the first draft of that play preceded *The Shrew* but that the present (revised) text is later.
[2] This is well demonstrated by Richard Hosley in 'The formal influence of Plautus and Terence', in J. R. Brown and B. Harris (eds.), *Elizabethan Theatre*, 1966, pp. 131–45.
[3] M. Mincoff, 'The dating of *The Taming of the Shrew*', *ES* 54 (1973), 554–65.
[4] Morris, pp. 50–65.   [5] Oliver, pp. 29–33.

earliest plays has been reopened recently by E. A. J. Honigmann, who draws our attention to the number of independent arguments that have been advanced for pushing back the dates of various early plays, thus giving greater weight to the theory that Shakespeare began his career as a dramatist in the 1580s and not around 1590 as traditionally accepted.[1]

The links between *The Shrew* and *The Comedy of Errors* are most obvious in *The Shrew*'s sub-plot, though they are not confined to it. In both plays we find the plot-device of the threat to the life of an innocent merchant: *The Comedy of Errors* opens dramatically with the Duke of Ephesus telling the Syracusan merchant Egeon that his life and goods are forfeit because of newly begun hostilities between the two dukedoms (1.1.1–22), and Tranio invents a similar situation in *The Shrew* when the hapless merchant he has chosen for the role of 'supposed Vincentio' says he comes from Mantua (4.2.72–87). Both plays also have a comic scene in which a man is refused entry to a house (either his own or his son's) because another man masquerading as him is already inside and is accepted as the genuine character by the other occupants: this happens to Antipholus of Ephesus in *Errors* (3.1) and to Vincentio in *The Shrew* (5.1). These two plot-devices derive ultimately from Roman comedy but Shakespeare's immediate source for both of them was probably George Gascoigne's *Supposes*, which served him for most of *The Shrew*'s sub-plot.[2]

There are several other similarities between *Errors* and *The Shrew*. Both plays have a 'framing action' outside the main narrative: the Egeon story in *Errors* and the Sly material in *The Shrew*. The Egeon story has a simple narrative link with the main plot of *Errors*, since Egeon is the father of the twins whose mistakes and adventures constitute the main action, while the Sly story is related to the main plot of *The Shrew* in a more indirect thematic way, particularly in its concern with deception and transformation. Sly's confusion as to which part of his experience is dream and which part is reality comes to a head when he is presented with a 'wife':

> Am I a lord, and have I such a lady?
> Or do I dream? Or have I dreamed till now? (Induction 2.64–5)

Antipholus of Syracuse undergoes a similar confusion when his twin brother's wife addresses him as her husband:

> To me she speaks, she moves me for her theme:
> What, was I married to her in my dream?
> Or sleep I now and think I hear all this? (2.2.181–3)[3]

Both men decide to accept the 'dream' since it appears so agreeable, but for Antipholus of Syracuse the experience becomes frightening and nightmarish and a potentially cruel 'awakening' awaits Sly. *Errors* develops the darker side of the mistaken-identity theme which is only hinted at in *The Shrew*, but in both cases the potentially disturbing 'man denied entry' scene discussed above may have suggested these developments.

[1] E. A. J. Honigmann, *Shakespeare's Impact on his Contemporaries*, 1982, pp. 53–90.
[2] For a fuller discussion of Shakespeare's use of *Supposes* in *The Shrew*, see pp. 9–17 below.
[3] Quotations and line references to plays other than *The Shrew* are from Riverside.

Both plays have two contrasted heroines, one of whom in each case is a shrew. Antipholus of Ephesus complains of the shrewish behaviour of his wife Adriana and she is reproved by her sister Luciana, who argues the case for male supremacy and female obedience in terms similar to those used by Katherina *(The Shrew* 5.2.136–79, *Errors* 2.1.10–31). Like Hortensio's Widow in *The Shrew*, Adriana rejects this 'fool-begged patience' but finally confesses her fault when she is severely scolded by the Abbess in the last scene. Mincoff and Morris consider that the reproof of shrewishness in *Errors* represents a moral and artistic advance on that in *The Shrew*, but this seems debatable, since Adriana is publicly humiliated despite the fact that in her husband's behaviour she has far more provocation for her attitude than Katherina. Even if one did accept that *Errors* was more sophisticated in this respect, it seems dubious to use the comparison for dating evidence as Mincoff and Morris do: one might as well argue that the treatment of jealousy in *Othello* is more sophisticated than that in *The Winter's Tale*, so *Othello* must be the later play.

The setting of *The Shrew* in Padua may be a deliberate contrast with the setting of *Errors* in Ephesus since Padua was renowned in the Renaissance as 'a citadel of common sense against the new mythology [of witchcraft]' typically associated with Ephesus.[1] Shakespeare exploits the reputation of Ephesus for superstition and sorcery in *Errors*, while in *The Shrew* there are several suggestions that Katherina is possessed by a 'devil' (the archetypal shrew being 'the devil's dam') and hence that the taming process is a kind of exorcism. Padua was also famous as an ancient university town, so it is appropriate that Lucentio should go there to pursue 'A course of learning and ingenuous studies' (1.1.9). He sees the move as an important part of his education and of his initiation into adult life:

> for I have Pisa left
> And am to Padua come as he that leaves
> A shallow plash to plunge him in the deep.   (1.1.21–3)

Petruchio also seems to have 'left home' in a significant sense, as he tells his friend Hortensio that he has been blown from Verona to Padua by

> Such wind as scatters young men through the world
> To seek their fortunes farther than at home
> Where small experience grows.   (1.2.47–9)

This theme provides a strong link with *The Two Gentlemen of Verona* where the plot is similarly activated by young men travelling from one part of Italy to another for education and general profit. Valentine departs on his travels with the remark that 'Home-keeping youth have ever homely wits' (1.1.2) and there is some concern that his friend and cousin Proteus is not going to have the same opportunities (1.3.4–16). Of course the chief result of all this educational travel, as in the Roman comedies which again lie behind this motif, is romantic involvement with the women in the new location. As Tranio points out in 1.1 of *The Shrew*, the advanced study of Ovid (meaning the pursuit of amorous adventures) is a major reason for leaving home. The

[1] See H. R. Trevor-Roper, *The European Witch-Craze of the Sixteenth and Seventeenth Centuries*, 1969, pp. 58–61.

romantic rhetoric of both plays is similarly influenced by Lylyan rhetorical patterning, and Shakespeare makes good comedy out of the swearing and forswearing of the young lovers.[1]

All three of these early comedies contain comic scenes between masters and servants: Dromio of Ephesus genuinely mistakes the commands of Antipholus of Syracuse in *Errors* 1.2, but he gets beaten for it just as Grumio does for pretending to misunderstand Petruchio in *The Shrew* 1.2. Speed in *The Two Gentlemen* also pretends to misunderstand commands (2.1), and he can be compared with Tranio and Biondello (*The Shrew* 4.2 and 4.4) when he finds himself in the position of explaining the situation to his rather slow employer (2.1). Launce in *The Two Gentlemen* is a more original comic character who is allowed to reveal his wit in lengthy speeches (as in his two scenes with his dog, 2.3 and 4.4) as well as in repartee. In this he is more like the Grumio who describes the journey home from Padua in 4.1 of *The Shrew*.

Clearly these three comedies are closely related to each other in various ways, though the similarities may not help to establish the order of composition. *The Shrew* has more surprising links with the early history plays: the outrageous courtship scene between Petruchio and Katherina in 2.1 would surely have been compared by contemporary audiences with the similar confrontations between Suffolk and Margaret in *1 Henry VI* 5.3 and between Richard and Anne in *Richard III* 1.2, if we accept the conventional dating of those plays as 1589–90 and 1592 respectively. Possibly the three female roles were written with the same forceful boy actor in mind. The characterisation of Petruchio as a bluff, rather engaging man who encourages the audience to appreciate his 'performance' by telling us in advance how he is going to manipulate people (2.1.165–76, 4.1.159–82) is unusual among Shakespeare's comedies but reminds us of Richard III himself and of the Bastard in *King John*, which may have been written as early as 1590. A further link between *The Shrew* and *Richard III* is suggested by Sly's odd error when he claims 'we came in with Richard Conqueror' (Induction 1.4), which recalls the story recorded by John Manningham in his diary in 1601 as told to him by his fellow law student Edward Curle:

Upon a time when Burbidge played Richard 3 there was a citizen grew so far in liking with him that, before she went from the play, she appointed him to come that night unto her by the name of Richard the Third. Shakespeare, overhearing their conclusion, went before, was entertained and at his game ere Burbidge came. Then, message being brought that Richard the Third was at the door, Shakespeare caused return to be made that William the Conqueror was before Richard the Third.

Manningham helpfully adds 'Shakespeare's name William'.[2] It might not be too far-fetched to see the line in *The Shrew* as a joke for those who knew this contemporary anecdote.

Finally, one can see in *The Shrew* examples of the strong Ovidian influence which affected much of Shakespeare's work in the early 1590s. Tranio encourages his master to read Ovid in 1.1 and we duly find him reading the *Heroides* with Bianca in 3.1

---

[1] Compare, for example, the repetitions in *The Shrew* 1.1.148–9 and 207–8 with Proteus's soliloquy in *TGV* 2.6.1–22; and see 4.2.26 n. below.

[2] This anecdote is related and discussed by Samuel Schoenbaum in *Shakespeare's Lives*, 1970, pp. 37–8.

and joking with her about the *Ars Amatoria* in 4.2. The Ovidian influence on the Induction is even stronger, since the 'wanton pictures' described to Sly represent various erotic encounters from Ovid's *Metamorphoses* (Induction 2.45–56); this passage has been criticised for over-decorativeness and for being 'direct imitation of Marlowe',[1] but it is clearly relevant to the theme of transformation through trickery (in the case of Sly) and love (in the case of Katherina). The Elizabethan fashion for writing Ovidian erotic narrative poems began when Thomas Lodge published *Scylla's Metamorphosis* in 1589, and Shakespeare was one of the first of many poets to essay this genre when he published *Venus and Adonis* in 1593. His earliest classical play, *Titus Andronicus* (usually dated 1593–4), is even more heavily Ovidian than *The Shrew*, drawing on the story of Tereus and Philomel for its plot and requiring a copy of the *Metamorphoses* to appear on stage in 4.1. It has also been remarked that the language of *Titus* is Ovidian, particularly in its tendency to elaborate pictorial effects.[2]

Comparison with Shakespeare's other works, therefore, while it cannot establish any clear sequence, suggests that the play belongs to the earliest phase of his development and leaves us free to suppose that it was written in or about 1590.

Sources

Discussion of Shakespeare's sources for *The Shrew* has been confused, firstly by the existence of *A Shrew* and secondly by the reluctance of literary scholars to deal with folktale and oral tradition.

As I have said above (p. 2), it was formerly held that *A Shrew* was quite simply Shakespeare's direct source-play for *The Shrew* but this position has become untenable for the following reasons: (1) There is considerable evidence for believing that *A Shrew* is not an independent text at all but a rather unusual kind of 'bad' quarto deriving from Shakespeare's *The Shrew*.[3] (2) Recent work on the folktale origins of both plays supports the likelihood that *A Shrew* derives from *The Shrew* rather than *vice versa*.[4] (3) The structural and thematic sophistication of *A Shrew* (which contains all three of the plot-strands of *The Shrew*) is so outstanding that even those few scholars who reject the 'bad' quarto theory resort to suggestions like '*A Shrew* may not be so much the source-play as Shakespeare's first shot at the theme.'[5] The alternative, as Richard Hosley says, is 'to assume around 1593 [or 1590] the existence of a dramatist other than Shakespeare who was capable of devising a three-part structure more impressive than the structure of any extant play by Lyly, Peele, Greene, Marlowe or Kyd'.[6] Even without the textual evidence, this assumption is so dubious that it seems wisest to assume that it was Shakespeare who was responsible for the complex structure and interweaving of materials that we find in both *Shrew* plays.

[1] Mincoff, 'Dating', p. 560.   [2] See J. C. Maxwell (ed.), *Tit.*, 1953, pp. xxxi–xl.
[3] See Textual Analysis, pp. 155–74 below.
[4] J. H. Brunvand, '*The Taming of the Shrew*: A Comparative Study of Oral and Literary Versions', unpublished Ph.D. thesis, Indiana University, 1961. See also Brunvand's article, 'The folktale origin of *The Taming of the Shrew*', *SQ* 17 (1966), 345–59.
[5] Bullough, *Sources*, I, 58.
[6] Richard Hosley, 'Sources and analogues of *The Taming of the Shrew*', *HLQ* 27 (1963–4), 289–308.

The three-part structure comprises the Christopher Sly framing action (referred to hereafter as the frame), the courtship and taming of Katherina by Petruchio (the main plot) and the courtship of her sister Bianca (the sub-plot). It is unanimously accepted that the sub-plot derives from George Gascoigne's play *Supposes* (1566), a prose version of Ariosto's *I Suppositi* (1509). The situation is straightforward and free from argument because we have a clear literary tradition with specific texts to compare. In the case of the main plot and the frame the situation is more complicated because both derive from folktale and oral tradition. We can cite *The Arabian Nights* and sundry English translations and derivatives as precedents for the trick played on Sly, and we can scour jest-books, ballads and collections of fabliaux for shrew-taming stories, but the best we can find will be general analogues rather than precise sources in the literary sense. It has even been argued that such literary analogues as have been discovered for the shrew-taming story have been misleading rather than helpful, since they have been overemphasised by scholars unwilling to explore the less familiar terrain of folklore and oral tradition.[1]

In deciding to have a framing action or Induction Shakespeare seems to have been following a contemporary theatrical fashion since several plays dating from around 1590 exhibit this kind of structure, notably Kyd's *Spanish Tragedy* (if we accept the later dating), Peele's *The Old Wives' Tale*, Greene's *James IV*, Greene and Lodge's *Looking Glass for London and England* and the anonymous *Histrio-mastix* (which was later touched up by Marston).[2] The personnel and subject-matter of these inductions vary considerably, from supernatural figures watching a revenge plot in *The Spanish Tragedy* to rustics telling fairy tales to while away a night when they are stranded in a wood in *The Old Wives' Tale*. The basic type of narrative Shakespeare uses – the story of a beggar transported into luxurious surroundings and tricked into believing he is a lord – can be found in *The Arabian Nights* where Haroun Al Raschid plays the trick on someone he finds sleeping. A European version occurs in the exploits of Philip the Good of Burgundy, who repeated the trick, according to Heuterus who tells the story in his *De Rebus Burgundicis* (1584). Goulart translated this version into French in the *Thrésor d'histoires admirables et memorables* around 1600 and Edward Grimeston translated Goulart into English in 1607.[3] Although this version is an attractive analogue of Shakespeare's play since the abducted artisan is entertained with 'a pleasant Comedie', the French and English translations are too late for Shakespeare to have used them and there is no evidence that he read Heuterus in Latin. There is, however, some reason to believe that the story was also printed in a lost jest-book compiled by Richard Edwards and published in 1570 and this could have been Shakespeare's source.[4]

[1] See Brunvand, 'Folktale origin', pp. 348–53, and 'Comparative Study', pp. 263–84.

[2] See Thelma N. Greenfield, *The Induction in Elizabethan Drama*, 1969, for a complete list of such plays. Critical discussion can also be found in Anne Righter, *Shakespeare and the Idea of the Play*, 1962, and Leo Salingar, *Shakespeare and the Traditions of Comedy*, 1974, pp. 267–72. See also Appendix 2, pp. 181–5 below, on the staging of the Induction.

[3] Bullough reprints Grimeston's version in *Sources*, I, 109–10.

[4] Thomas Warton records having seen the story in a copy of this book in his *History of English Poetry*, 1775, Section 52.

Shakespeare may not have needed a literary source at all for this story, and he certainly did not for other elements of the Induction. The whole atmosphere of rural Warwickshire with its hunting lords, drunken tinkers and fat alewives is clearly drawn (perhaps somewhat rosily) from his own youthful experience. It may even have been the case that Shakespeare, like Christopher Sly, first encountered the art of the theatre when a group of travelling players like those in Induction 1 arrived at some large country house in Warwickshire and put on a performance for the family and the locals. These players are no London company on tour with the latest offering from the University Wits but a local group who provide more homely fare: 'This fellow I remember', says the Lord,

> Since once he played a farmer's eldest son –
> 'Twas where you wooed the gentlewoman so well.   (Induction 1.79–81)

As C. R. Baskervill pointed out, this sounds like a scene from a typical mummers' wooing play in which a number of men representing the different levels of society compete for the favours of the heroine: 'A seasonal lord and his eldest son and heir – sometimes the farmer's eldest son or merely the farmer's son – frequently appear, and the "Eldest Son" is a fairly constant figure among the rivals of the mummers' wooing plays.'[1] Thus the Lord of *The Shrew*'s Induction prepares a double entertainment for himself in the deception of Sly, which he says will be 'pastime passing excellent' (Induction 1.63), and the presentation of the play – which does of course turn out to be one about wooing.

While Sly is the butt of the Lord's joke, he can also be seen as a kind of Lord of Misrule presiding over a brief period of holiday from everyday conventions. The folk festival of misrule was widely celebrated in Elizabethan England though deplored by churchmen (along with much of the popular drama) for its connections with the pagan past. During such periods, usually associated with Christmas or May Day, there would be a festive abolition of social inequalities and a playful exchange of roles between masters and servants.[2] Probably Shakespeare is thinking of the licence and drunkenness for which these festivals were notorious when he makes his Lord stress three times within seventy lines (Induction 1.64, 90–5, 132–4) the need for modesty and sobriety in carrying out his plan. Comic incongruity ensues, since Sly is eager to drink ale and go to bed with his 'wife' while the Lord's servants offer him the more refined pleasures of sack and 'wanton pictures' of scenes from Ovid.

This juxtaposition of earthiness and sophistication, folktale and Ovid, is of course prominent in the play that Sly watches. When the two heroines first appear, Lucentio and Tranio give us thumbnail sketches of them: 'That wench is stark mad, or wonderful froward', says Tranio of Katherina, while Lucentio looks at Bianca and replies, 'But in the other's silence do I see / Maid's mild behaviour and sobriety.' The 'wench', aptly enough, is out of the native folktale tradition while the 'maid' derives from classical comedy.

---

[1] C. R. Baskervill, *The Elizabethan Jig and Related Song Drama*, 1929, pp. 249–50.
[2] See W. B. Thorne, 'Folk elements in *The Taming of the Shrew*', *Queen's Quarterly* 75 (1968), 482–96, and the more general discussions of misrule in C. L. Barber, *Shakespeare's Festive Comedy*, 1959, and Robert Weimann, *Shakespeare and the Popular Tradition in the Theater*, translated and rev. edn, 1978.

That the shrew-taming story has a long ancestry in the literary traditions of western Europe has often been recognised; one can only too readily find general analogues in our large heritage of classical and medieval misogynistic literature. Shakespeare was certainly familiar with Chaucer's representation of a shrewish wife in the Wife of Bath,[1] and he may have seen similar figures on stage in the traditional representation of Noah's wife in the medieval mystery plays and the anti-heroines of Tudor shrew-plays like John Heywood's *Merry Play between John John the Husband, Tyb his Wife and Sir John the Priest* and the anonymous *Tom Tyler and his Wife*.[2] Claims for more specific influence on Shakespeare's play have been made by Richard Hosley and Valerie Callies on behalf of the mid-sixteenth-century ballad called *A Merry Jest of a Shrewde and Curste Wyfe, Lapped in Morrelles Skin, for Her Good Behavyour*[3] and by John W. Shroeder on behalf of Caxton's translation of the tale of Queen Vastis in the *Book of the Knight of La Tour Landry*.[4] These claims tend, however, to be more ingenious than convincing, and are rendered irrelevant by Jan Harold Brunvand's conclusive demonstration that 'Shakespeare's taming plot, which has not been traced successfully in its entirety to any known printed version, must have come ultimately from oral tradition.'[5]

Brunvand's thesis consists of a very careful and thorough examination of Tale Type 901 (in the Aarne–Thompson *Types of the Folk-Tale*) which is widely distributed throughout the Indo-European area. He finds that 'the wealthy father with good and bad daughters, the warnings to the suitor about the shrew, the bizarre wedding behaviour, the trip to the father's home where a wager is laid are all traits commonly found in the folktales'. And he claims from his own experience that 'if one were to read several hundred miscellaneous versions of Type 901 and then for the first time come upon Shakespeare's play, he would probably assume either that the playwright had constructed his plot from details in different oral versions or that he had found an especially full text to rework'.[6] Shakespeare shows his intimate familiarity with the folktale in many apparently inconsequential details such as Curtis's desire to know whether Petruchio and Katherina rode home from the wedding on a single horse (4.1.50), which does indeed happen in many folktale versions. The basic taming plot in *The Shrew* differs from the folktales in only two respects: (1) Shakespeare adapts unstageable action or relegates it to dialogue. He uses Grumio, for example, to describe the trip home on horseback with the beginning of the taming process (4.1.38–62) which is an important element of the folktales, and he has Petruchio make absurd statements about the sun and the moon (4.5.2–22) rather than about birds or

---

[1] See David M. Bergeron, 'The Wife of Bath and Shakespeare's *Taming of the Shrew*', *University Review* 35 (1969), 279–86, and Ann Thompson, *Shakespeare's Chaucer*, 1978, p. 84.

[2] *John John* and *Tom Tyler* are both discussed as analogues of *The Shrew* in M. C. Bradbrook, 'Dramatic role as social image: a study of *The Taming of the Shrew*', *SJ* 94 (1958), 132–50.

[3] Hosley, 'Sources and analogues'; Valerie Callies, 'Misogyny and humanism: the sources of *The Taming of the Shrew*' (unpublished paper). In this ballad the husband beats his wife severely and wraps her in the salted skin of an old horse ('Morel') in order to tame her.

[4] Shroeder, 'A new analogue and possible source for *The Taming of the Shrew*', *SQ* 10 (1959), 251–5.

[5] Brunvand, 'Folktale origin', p. 346. See also 'Comparative Study', *passim*.

[6] 'Folktale origin', p. 347, and Annti Aarne and Stith Thompson, *The Types of the Folk-Tale: A Classification and Bibliography*, Helsinki, 1928.

animals seen on the road. (2) The play expands and elaborates elements which have a particular comic or dramatic appeal, such as the episode with the tailor and the haberdasher[1] and the final scene where Katherina's lecture to the other wives is an innovatory addition to the traditional wager climax. The fact that *The Shrew* contains at least six traits or narrative elements from the folktales which are not found in *A Shrew* can be taken as further evidence of the derivative nature of the latter, since it seems more likely that the author(s) of *A Shrew* simply missed some significant traits out of the reconstruction (for example, the arrival of the groom at the wedding on an old, sick horse, and the account of the journey home) than that Shakespeare revised *A Shrew* with such detailed and pervasive reference back to the original tradition.[2]

The folk background of the taming story is manifested in other ways in addition to the basic dramatisation of Tale Type 901. This part of the plot is full of traditional beliefs and superstitions, folk wisdom, proverbs and snatches of popular ballads. Katherina shows herself familiar with popular lore about old maids when she cries out to her father against Bianca, 'I must dance barefoot on her wedding day / And, for your love to her, lead apes in hell' (2.1.33–4), but Petruchio's courtship of her becomes a kind of mating dance that will release her from this fate. There are many references to the songs and dances of traditional courtship rituals. On Petruchio's first appearance he tells his friend Hortensio 'I have thrust myself into this maze [an Elizabethan dance pattern], / Happily to wive and thrive as best I may' (1.2.52–3), and he goes on to claim 'wealth is burden [refrain or musical accompaniment] of my wooing dance' (1.2.65). Later he alludes to popular wooing ballads such as 'I cannot come every day to woo' (see 2.1.111) and 'I mun be married a' Sunday' (see 2.1.313).[3] Together with the play's many bird and animal metaphors, these references give the central relationship a frank sensuality that is conspicuously lacking in the sub-plot; despite the Paduan setting, Petruchio and Katherina's marriage seems to take place in a world of country courtship practices and sports (hunting, falconry) readily comprehensible to a Warwickshire tinker.

A more intellectual or philosophical vein is nevertheless apparent in Shakespeare's approach to the debate on the nature of marriage that arises from the taming plot. Kenneth Muir has noted parallels with two of the *Colloquies* of Erasmus and Richard Hosley has suggested the general relevance of Juan Vives' works in this area, *The Office and Duetie of an Husband* (translated by Thomas Paynell, 1553) and *A Very Fruteful and Pleasant Boke Callyd the Instruction of a Christen Woman* (translated by Richard Hyrde, 1529).[4] One of Muir's parallels, although it comes from the colloquy translated as *A Mery Dialogue, Declaringe the Propertyes of Shrowde Shrewes and Honest Wyves* (1557) is a fairly incidental combination of references to a three-legged stool being used as a weapon and a woman 'putting the finger in the eye' and weeping (*The Shrew*

---

[1] An analogue for this scene has been spotted in Gerard Legh's *Accedens of Armory* (1562), where a tailor is berated for cutting a gown in a fantastical fashion. See Hosley, 'Sources and analogues'.

[2] Brunvand, 'Comparative Study', pp. 284–8.

[3] See Baskervill, *Elizabethan Jig*, pp. 193–4, 214, and Michael West, 'The folk background of Petruchio's wooing dance: male supremacy in *The Taming of the Shrew*', *S.St.* 7 (1974), 65–73.

[4] Muir, *The Sources of Shakespeare's Plays*, 1977, pp. 20–1; Hosley, 'Sources and analogues'.

1.1.63–4, 78–9, *Mery Dialogue* Sig. A3ᵛ, A9), but the other is of greater importance. Erasmus writes in the person of a woman comparing the lot of women with that of men:

our Condition is much preferable to theirs: For they, endeavouring to get a Maintenance for their Families, scamper thro all the Parts of the Earth by Land and Sea. In times of War they are call'd up by the Sound of the Trumpet, stand in Armour in the Front of the Battle; while we sit at home in Safety.[1]

In the same way Katherina tells the other wives that a husband is one who

> cares for thee
> And for thy maintenance; commits his body
> To painful labour both by sea and land...
> Whilst thou li'st warm at home, secure and safe.   (5.2.147–51)

There were, of course, many sermons and tracts on the subordination of women to their husbands but this seems particularly close.[2]

Thus the taming plot of *The Shrew* is largely dependent on oral tradition, though Shakespeare was clearly not unaware of related literary materials. Almost the opposite is true of the sub-plot, which can be traced back beyond its immediate Renaissance sources in Gascoigne's *Supposes* and Ariosto's *I Suppositi* to Roman comedy: it is in fact one of the standard plots in the drama of Plautus and Terence. Gascoigne explains in the prologue to the printed version of his play that 'this our Suppose is nothing else but a mystaking or imagination of one thing for an other',[3] and the marginal notes draw our attention to no less than twenty-five 'supposes' occasioned by the numerous disguises and deceptions of the story. Shakespeare took over the whole narrative of intrigue and misunderstanding as well as some stock characters (the ingenious servant Tranio, the elderly suitor Gremio), but characteristically he altered the effect by telling the story in chronological order (beginning with Lucentio's first sight of Bianca, instead of plunging in just before the crisis as all his classical and Renaissance predecessors do) and by giving greater importance to Bianca and to the romantic feelings associated with her.[4] He increased the confusion by giving Bianca an extra admirer in Hortensio but he omitted the final twist to the story whereby the elderly suitor (whose motive all along has been to replace his lost heir) turns out to be the father of the witty servant (Tranio) – perhaps because he had recently used a very similar ending in *The Comedy of Errors*.

Sometimes *The Shrew* is very close to *Supposes*, as in the 'man denied entry' scene (5.1) discussed above, where not only the basic situation but the details of the staging with characters 'looking out of the window' are taken over. Elsewhere Shakespeare invents additional comic business like the lesson scene (3.1), which has no known source.[5] The names but not the characters of Petruchio and Litio are taken from

---

[1] From *Senatulus* (trans. N. Bailey, 1725). This colloquy does not seem to have been translated earlier.
[2] See also pp. 28–30 below for a discussion of the influence of the Homily on Marriage on Katherina's last speech.
[3] Quotation from the complete text of *Supposes* in Bullough, *Sources*, I, 111–58.
[4] Shakespeare's adaptation of the *Supposes* plot is analysed in Hosley, 'Formal influence'.
[5] There is a similar mock Latin lesson scene in R. W.'s play *The Three Lords and Three Ladies of London*, but this could derive from *The Shrew* itself rather than *vice versa* since both plays are dated around 1590.

Supposes, and those of Tranio and Grumio from Plautus's *Mostellaria*. To some extent the stock characters of Roman comedy are mingled with those of Italian comedy: Gremio is described as a 'pantaloon' both in stage direction (1.1.45) and dialogue (3.1.35), and Biondello is a cheeky page in the Italian tradition. The general romantic atmosphere is heightened by references to Ovid, as when Bianca is seen as 'Minerva' (1.1.84), 'Agenor's daughter' (1.1.159) and 'Leda's daughter' (1.2.237), picking up the literary equivalents of the Lord's 'wanton pictures' in the Induction.[1]

It is apparent, then, that both the main plot and the sub-plot of *The Shrew* present stories which would have been familiar to Shakespeare's audience either from oral tradition or from previous books and plays. The novelty and daring lie in the combination of two such different strands, the comparatively hard, dry classical plot and the more rumbustious earthy folktale. The way in which Shakespeare combines these two strands is itself interesting, especially as it is being done at such an early stage in his career. In *The Comedy of Errors* (if that is indeed the earlier play) he had shown his skill in doubling the complications of a standard plot in the Roman–Italian style but in *The Shrew* he added something quite different. The methods he used to link the two actions are, as Leo Salingar points out, typical of the Elizabethan theatre but very different from the Italian practice:

In an Italian double plot, the events in each plot are so arranged as to interfere causally with those in the other, and the actions shown on the stage follow a strictly temporal sequence, so that each plot can react on the other at exactly the right moment...Italian learned comedy is one of the first artistic expressions of a civilisation regulated by clocks. But Shakespeare adopts this principle of plot-interaction more loosely and intermittently, alongside of another principle which could be described as thematic alternation, whereby scenes from one part of his total plot react on scenes from another by way of latent psychological parallels or repetitions of imagery, without any strict temporal or causal connexion.[2]

This 'thematic alternation' tends in the case of *The Shrew* to promote a critical or ironic attitude to the sub-plot: by comparison with the straightforward approach of Petruchio, Lucentio appears bookish and naïve, depending too much on ingenious servants and complicated deceptions, and Bianca seems spoilt and calculating (especially in 3.1). It is not surprising that they seem to know each other so little at the end since they have both been more interested in the literary trappings of courtship all along. Shakespeare constantly undermines the romantic pretensions of Paduan bourgeois society through the contrast between the two plots. For example, it is Petruchio ostensibly who has the mercenary motive for marriage, but it is Bianca's suitors who are really obsessed with money: Hortensio says of Bianca 'For in Baptista's keep my treasure is. / He hath the jewel of my life in hold' (1.2.112–13), combining a kind of literary romanticism with a view of Bianca as 'treasure'or money, and Baptista himself is clearly prepared to sell her to the highest bidder:

> 'Tis deeds must win the prize, and he of both
> That can assure my daughter greatest dower
> Shall have my Bianca's love.   (2.1.331–3)

---

[1] For a summary of scattered classical references, see Niall Rudd, '*The Taming of the Shrew*: notes on some classical allusions', *Hermathena* 129 (University of Dublin, 1980), 23–8.

[2] Salingar, *Traditions of Comedy*, p. 223.

3 Holman Hunt's painting of *Bianca, Patroness of Heavenly Harmony*

Again, the mercenary nature of the transaction is cloaked by the language, in this case the vaguely heroic reference to 'deeds'. Similarly, the references to music in both plots emphasise the hypocrisy and superficiality of the sub-plot: Petruchio is serious about his 'wooing dance' and has the satisfaction of discovering a worthy partner in the notoriously 'discordant' Katherina, while Bianca's music tutor is an imposter who barely manages to tune his instrument. It has been demonstrated by other critics that the two plots are linked thematically by Shakespeare's interest in disguise and metamorphosis,[1] and there again one can see a kind of critique of *Supposes* in the resulting juxtapositions, since the psychological transformation of Katherina is a deeper, more internalised 'suppose' than any of the costume-changes in the sub-plot.

The Taming of the Shrew on stage

When the Royal Shakespeare Company staged *The Shrew* in Stratford in 1978, Michael Billington, reviewing the production in *The Guardian* on 5 May, was very anxious to let his readers know that, although he had found the evening theatrically successful in many ways, he had not enjoyed himself at all. He had in fact found the experience so distasteful that he ended by advocating censorship, questioning 'whether there is any reason to revive a play that seems totally offensive to our age and our society' and recommending that 'it should be put back firmly and squarely on the shelf'. Nevertheless he praised the director, Michael Bogdanov, for the honesty of his approach to this 'barbaric and disgusting' play: 'Instead of softening its harsh edges like most recent directors, he has chosen to emphasize its moral and physical ugliness.' This 'ugliness' is particularly apparent to modern audiences, especially when, as on this occasion, the play is performed in modern dress, but the stage history of the play shows that its 'barbaric and disgusting' quality has always been an important part of its appeal and that from the very beginning it has been disturbing as well as enjoyable. In what follows, given the limitations of space, I intend to concentrate on this problem and to examine how adapters and directors have dealt with it. This inevitably involves a stress on the taming plot to the exclusion of the rest of the play, but such an imbalance is not inappropriate since the Induction and the sub-plot were entirely banished from the stage for a hundred years while Garrick's *Catharine and Petruchio* was preferred; even now when they are performed they are often ignored by reviewers, whereas the crises of the taming plot, especially the wooing scene (2.1) and the last scene, are usually described in detail.

Other accounts of the stage history of *The Shrew* can be found in NS and Morris; both of these concentrate on pre-twentieth-century productions and adaptations. In what follows I have also made use of Tori Haring-Smith's unpublished Ph.D. thesis, 'A Stage-History of *The Taming of the Shrew*', University of Illinois at Urbana, 1980, George C. Odell's *Shakespeare from Betterton to Irving*, 2 vols., 1921, and Arthur Colby Sprague's *Shakespeare and the Actors*, 1944. My information about twentieth-century productions comes mainly from the collections of newspaper cuttings in the Birmingham Reference Library and the Shakespeare Centre Library, Stratford-upon-Avon. Musical and cinematic adaptations are listed in Phyllis Hartnoll (ed.), *Shakespeare and Music*, 1964, and Peter Morris, *Shakespeare on Film*, 1972.

Alone among Shakespeare's plays, *The Shrew* provoked a theatrical 'reply' in his

---

[1] See especially C. C. Seronsy, '"Supposes" as the unifying theme in *The Taming of the Shrew*', *SQ* 14 (1963), 15–30.

lifetime in the form of Fletcher's *The Woman's Prize, or The Tamer Tamed*, written and performed around 1611, a sequel in which Petruchio, now a widower, marries again and is himself tamed by his second wife. In writing this sequel Fletcher was in effect putting the play into its traditional context of the war of the sexes, a context in which normally, as in the stories of Boccaccio and Chaucer, a story about a husband outwitting or triumphing over his wife is capped or balanced by one in which a wife outwits her husband, the overall moral being that, despite a theoretical and practical male supremacy, the best marriages are those based on equality and mutual respect, as Fletcher claims in his epilogue:

> The Tamer's tam'd, but so, as nor the men
> Can find one just cause to complain of, when
> They fitly do consider in their lives,
> They should not reign as Tyrants o'er their wives.
> Nor can the Women from this president
> Insult, or triumph; it being aptly meant,
> To teach both Sexes due equality;
> And as they stand bound, to love mutually.[1]

If played straight, with a minimum of interpretative direction, Shakespeare's play contains no such indication of a comfortable, egalitarian compromise but rather leaves its audience with the impression that a woman's role consists in graceful submission. Perhaps this is one reason why, despite a long and vigorous stage tradition, it has probably been played straight less often than any other play in the canon. From *The Taming of a Shrew* in 1594 up to the 'free adaption' made by Charles Marowitz in 1975 it has been constantly altered and adapted. Until the middle of the nineteenth century the adaptations involved drastic cutting and wholesale rewriting, whereas in more recent times the overt meaning of the text has been undercut or contradicted by details of performance and stage business – what Michael Billington calls 'softening the edges'.

Of course, the adaptation has not all been in one direction. Many versions have actually played up the brutality, a tradition which began as early as *A Shrew* with its stage direction *Enter Ferando [Petruchio] with a peece of meate uppon his daggers point* in the equivalent of 4.3, where the author apparently draws on Marlowe's *Tamburlaine* (Part 1, 4.4) to emphasise the savagery. In the late seventeenth century, John Lacey's *Sauny the Scott, or The Taming of the Shrew (c. 1667)*, which supplanted Shakespeare's text on stage until it was replaced in 1754 by David Garrick's version called *Catharine and Petruchio*, inserts an additional scene in which the husband pretends to think that his wife's refusal to speak to him is due to toothache and sends for a surgeon to have her teeth drawn. This episode is repeated with relish in the eighteenth century in James Worsdale's adaptation, *A Cure for a Scold* (1735).[2] In

---

[1] Quoted from A. R. Waller (ed.), *The Works of Francis Beaumont and John Fletcher*, 10 vols., 1910, VIII. Another contemporary play, Dekker's *Patient Grissil (c. 1600)*, achieves the desired balance by setting the shrewish Gwenthyan of its sub-plot against the submissive heroine of the main plot.

[2] *A Shrew* quoted from the text in Bullough, *Sources*, I. *Sauny the Scott, Catharine and Petruchio* and *A Cure for a Scold* quoted from the facsimile texts printed by Cornmarket Press in 1969.

Garrick's version, which held the stage until the mid nineteenth century, we find an ominous addition to the dialogue when one of Petruchio's servants says his master 'shook his Whip in Token of his Love' (p. 24). When John Philip Kemble performed Garrick's text in 1788 he wrote the words 'whip for Petruchio' opposite the hero's entrance in the wedding scene,[1] and it is possible that Garrick also used a whip from this point. At all events it became an almost obligatory stage property for countless subsequent productions.

Curiously, we find that this exaggeration of the play's brutality is often being done at the same time as an attempt is made to soften it, illustrating the thoroughly ambiguous appeal of the whole business. The role of Katherina is constantly adjusted: she is given more motivation for her behaviour in accepting Petruchio in the first place, and her major speech in the last scene is cut, rewritten or apologised for. Even *A Shrew* motivates her somewhat clumsily by giving her an aside in the wooing scene:

> *She turnes aside and speakes*
> But yet I will consent and marrie him,
> For I methinkes have livde too long a maid,
> And match him too, or else his manhoods good.   (scene v, 40–2)

Thus it is made explicit that (a) Katherina can see some positive advantage in marrying Petruchio, and (b) she is going to relish competing with him. It is interesting that Garrick's additions to this scene are very similar:[2] his Catharine also has an aside in the midst of the insults:

> A Plague upon his Impudence! I'm vexed –
> I'll marry my Revenge, but I will tame him.   (p. 14)

Then at the end of the scene she confirms this hint of a reversal of roles and adds further motivation in her closing soliloquy:

> Sister *Bianca* now shall see
> The poor abandon'd *Cath'rine*, as she calls me,
> Can hold her Head as high, and be as proud,
> And make her Husband stoop unto her Lure,
> As she, or e'er a Wife in *Padua*.
> As double as my Portion be my Scorn;
> Look to your Seat, *Petruchio*, or I throw you.
> *Cath'rine* shall tame this Haggard; – or if she fails,
> Shall tye her Tongue up, and pare down her Nails.   (pp. 16–17)

What Garrick has done here is to transfer some of Petruchio's taming rhetoric ('stoop unto her Lure', 'tame this Haggard') to Catharine in an attempt to redress the balance between them.

More drastic alterations are made to the last scene. In *Sauny the Scott* the heroine's forty-four-line speech on the subordination of women is cut to two lines after a much

---

[1] See Arthur Colby Sprague, *Shakespeare and the Actors*, 1944, p. 57. See also illustration 5.
[2] It does not seem very likely that Garrick knew *A Shrew*, though *Sauny the Scott* apparently takes its name from Saunder, *A Shrew*'s equivalent of Grumio, perhaps originally played by Alexander Cooke, so it must have been known in the Restoration period.

abbreviated wager scene, in which her husband commends her 'for being so good natur'd to come when I send for you' (p. 47). *A Cure for a Scold* (which clearly derives in large part from *Sauny the Scott*) has a similarly brief climax, and after the heroine has declared 'You have taught me what 'tis to be a Wife, and I shall make it my Study to be obliging and obedient', the hero gallantly replies 'My best *Peg*, we will exchange Kindness, and be each others Servants' (p. 57). Even after this, the author felt sufficiently uncomfortable about the proceedings to add an apologetic epilogue to be spoken by the actress who played the heroine, beginning

> Well, I must own, it wounds me to the Heart
> To act, unwomanly, so mean a Part.
> What – to submit, so tamely – so contented,
> Thank Heav'n! I'm not the Thing I represented.

Garrick's treatment of the heroine's big speech is also interesting. Catharine speaks the first nineteen lines of the speech (as written by Shakespeare) with a few brief interruptions from Petruchio ('Why, well said *Kate*') and Bianca ('Sister, be quiet – '), but then Petruchio makes his own submission:

> Kiss me, my Kate; and since thou art become
> So prudent, kind, and dutiful a Wife,
> *Petruchio* here shall doff the lordly Husband;
> An honest Mask, which I throw off with Pleasure.
> Far hence all Rudeness, Wilfulness, and Noise,
> And be our future Lives one gentle Stream
> Of mutual Love, Compliance and Regard. (p. 56)

Finally, Petruchio '*Goes forward with* Catharine *in his Hand*' and delivers the next section of her speech himself (Shakespeare's 5.2.155–64), ending the play on the statement that women are 'bound to love, to honour and obey', significantly altered from Shakespeare's 'bound to serve, love and obey'. When Kemble played Garrick's text he restored these lines to Catharine, but the general effect either way was that the play as staged made a gesture towards an ethic of balance or equality between the sexes which is simply not present in the original text.

Garrick's version (which omits the Induction altogether and disposes of the sub-plot by presenting Bianca as one 'new-married to *Hortensio*' at the beginning) proved so popular that the full text had to wait for performance until 1844 in England and 1887 in the United States. It was in fact the last of Shakespeare's plays to be restored to the stage in its original form when J. R. Planché produced it in an Elizabethan style for Benjamin Webster at the Haymarket Theatre, London, in 1844. It is interesting that when Augustin Daly did stage the original play in New York in 1887, despite much publicity about the fullness and purity of the text, his two major alterations (apart from some cutting and considerable rearrangement) were in the wooing scene and the last scene. In both cases he followed Garrick, inserting Katherina's threat to tame Petruchio in 2.1 and Petruchio's promise to 'doff the lordly Husband' in 5.2. He cut Katherina's speech as Garrick had done and he ended the play on the same line, though Katherina spoke it, as she had done in Kemble's production.[1]

[1] See Marvin Felheim, *The Theater of Augustin Daly*, 1956, pp. 238–43.

Since the late nineteenth century the movement for the liberation of women has done for *The Shrew* what reaction to the anti-semitism of our time has done for *The Merchant of Venice*: turned it into a problem play. It is no longer fashionable to rewrite the text or interpolate lines, so modern directors and reviewers have had to grapple with the 'barbaric' original delivered more or less as it stands. (Film directors, however, have allowed themselves more liberty with the text: Sam Taylor's 1929 film uses Garrick's version and Franco Zeffirelli's 1966 one modernises freely and adds some new dialogue.) As in earlier centuries, the tone of the play has proved to be difficult, and the last scene in particular has become something of a touchstone for the liberal (or otherwise) sympathies of all concerned since at least 1897, when George Bernard Shaw wrote

No man with any decency of feeling can sit it out in the company of a woman without being extremely ashamed of the lord-of-creation moral implied in the wager and the speech put into the woman's own mouth.[1]

Several directors have tried to overcome the problem by insisting on a jolly, farcical atmosphere throughout, but Katherina's final speech is simply too long and too serious to be buried under a welter of comic stage business, and has even been thrown uncomfortably into relief by such attempts. This apparently happened when Edith Evans played Katherina in 1937 and again when Peggy Ashcroft played her in 1960. When performed relatively seriously the play has inevitably provoked topical references, especially in the 1920s and 30s and again in the 1970s and 80s. When Eileen Beldon played Katherina in modern dress in 1928, for example, she is said to have delivered her speech with 'a beautiful sincerity',[2] but one reviewer was moved to comment

It was, I thought, a severe criticism of the modern dressing that while one was listening to the lady announcing her shame, one's mind instantly reverted to the proposal that the word 'obey' should be abolished from the Marriage Service.[3]

When Sybil Thorndike gave a similarly 'sincere' performance in 1927, *The Stage* commented on her 'air of conviction' in the last scene

which would obviously not commend itself to the out-and-out feminists of the Women's Federation League or the generality of the shingled and Eton-cropped sisterhood.[4]

And one mid-1930s reviewer came up with an interesting explanation for the great popularity of the play in the years immediately preceding the First World War:

That *The Taming* was presented [at Stratford] for eight years in succession from 1909 onwards may perhaps be accounted for in some measure as being due to the activities of the vote-hungry viragoes who from 1910 to the eve of the War were breaking windows, setting fire to churches, chaining themselves to railings, and generally demonstrating their fitness to be endowed with Parliamentary responsibility. Katherina's 'purple patch' concerning the duty of women...was

[1] *Saturday Review*, 6 November 1897. Reprinted in Edwin Wilson (ed.), *Shaw on Shakespeare*, 1961, p. 198.
[2] *Birmingham Post*, 1 May 1928.
[3] *The Observer*, 6 May 1928.
[4] *The Stage*, 15 September 1927.

a smashing rejoinder to the militant Furies who were making fools of themselves in the ways indicated.[1]

A different kind of topical reference was evoked in 1939 when the *Glasgow Herald*'s reviewer commented on Wolfit's production, 'If the whip and starvation business has a distasteful touch, it has also the saving grace of being applied with an un-Nazi sense of fun.'[2] The play seems to have been 'saved' by a sense of fun rather frequently in the 1970s, as for example in 1973 when, despite a serious programme note by the well-known feminist Germaine Greer, most critics found Clifford Williams's production farcical and jolly, and one newspaper headlined its review 'And never a whisper of Women's Lib'.[3]

As in earlier centuries, the play is still 'softened' by careful, but by now more subtle, adjustments in the wooing scene and the last scene. Twentieth-century actresses restricted to the authentic text in the wooing scene have often motivated Katherina by making it abundantly obvious that she falls in love with Petruchio at first sight. Sometimes, however, it has been difficult for reviewers to agree on whether this happened or not. Janet Suzman's 1967 performance, for example, was apparently ambiguous in this scene, with some reviewers convinced that she was attracted to Petruchio from the beginning but others claiming that love blossomed out of initial antipathy. If Kate does fall in love in the wooing scene (2.1), the director and actress can achieve the same effect as earlier generations achieved by interpolating lines; it may undermine the tension of the next two acts but it helps to make the taming process more tolerable for the audience. At the same time, it has often seemed necessary for Katherina to undercut her speech in the last scene in some way. When Mary Pickford played the part in the 1929 film version of the play (the first sound film of any of Shakespeare's plays) we are told that 'the spirit of Katherina's famous advice to wives was contradicted with an expressive wink',[4] beginning (apparently) a new tradition of ironic or ambiguous performances. These could be executed with varying degrees of good humour: when Sian Phillips played the role in 1960 'her delivery of the concluding sermon on how good wives should submit to their husbands was made with tongue slightly in cheek',[5] a limited qualification of a basically generous submission, but when Joan Plowright played it in 1972 one reviewer commented

I certainly didn't believe a word of it [the final speech] when uttered by Joan Plowright with a slightly sarcastic inflection to her voice which undermines totally any possible virtue the entire exercise might have had – that the two in the end find real love and understanding.[6]

The nadir of bitterness and resentment was perhaps reached in Paola Dionisotti's performance in 1978:

Kate's famous speech...is delivered in a spiritless, unreal voice and received without much appreciation by the men, and with smouldering resentment by the women. The main feeling is of shame – and that the systematic deformation of Kate's character (the deformity of submission on top of spite) is being revenged in the weariness and boredom of the men. When

---

[1] *East Anglian Times*, 11 November 1933.   [2] *Glasgow Herald*, 8 November 1939.
[3] *Leicester Mercury*, 26 September 1973.   [4] *Daily News*, 15 November 1929.
[5] *Oxford Mail*, 27 April 1960.   [6] *Morning Star*, 7 July 1972.

4 Douglas Fairbanks as Petruchio in the wedding scene, Act 3, Scene 2. A publicity still from the 1929
film version, directed by Sam Taylor

Petruchio says 'we'll to bed' it sounds as if they have been married for years. It is an interesting
and courageous (not to say feminist) way to interpret the play.[1]

This was another time when the critics disagreed. Michael Billington wrote that
Dionisotti delivered the speech 'with a tart, stabbing irony' (The Guardian, 5 May
1978), but I saw this production three times myself and agree with the TLS reviewer,
Lorna Sage, that the tone was 'spiritless' and 'unreal'. Many reviewers felt on this

[1] Times Literary Supplement, 19 May 1978.

occasion that it might have been more logical not to present Shakespeare's text at all (one review was headlined 'The Shaming of the True'),[1] but to put on an adaptation such as that of Charles Marowitz (1975), in which the text is cut, rearranged and interspersed with scenes from a modern courtship in order to transform it into a treatise on sadism and brainwashing. In this version Petruchio drives Katherina mad and finally rapes her. She enters in the last scene wearing 'a shapeless institutional-like garment' and delivers her speech 'mechanically' and as if she has 'learnt it by rote'.[2]

Of course not all modern Katherinas have been bitter, but it has often seemed the case that a straightforward and apparently sincere delivery of the final speech has provoked as much topical thoughtfulness in reviewers (and presumably audiences) as the more subversive mode. Barbara Jefford apparently 'comes as near as any Katherina ever will to making the final abject speech of the changed shrew sound plausible',[3] while Jane Lapotaire 'gives the speech full value, touches us deeply, and leaves us to sort out our feelings about women's lib as best we may'.[4] Vanessa Redgrave's performance seems to have been a complex one, enabling one reviewer to remark

The delicious touch of irony which she adds to this speech amplifies the suggestion that she submits to Petruchio, not because woman must submit to man as her natural master, but because she loves him.[5]

Another critic thought, however, that 'she shows us a woman discovering that the delivery of a grovelling and submissive speech can actually give her a special new sensual kick'.[6] Obviously the interpretation of this speech can lie as much in the mind of the reviewer as in the intention of the director or the performance of the actress.

Thus throughout its stage history *The Taming of the Shrew* has probably received fewer completely straight performances than any other Shakespearean play of comparable popularity on the stage. The apparently unrelieved ethic of male supremacy has proved unpalatable, and generation after generation of producers and directors have altered and adapted the text in more or less flagrant ways in order to soften the ending. Of course, responses to the play are bound to be affected by the status of women in society at any given time and by the way that status is perceived by both men and women. Reading through the reviews, one sees the play acting as a kind of litmus paper, picking up worried and embarrassed reactions from men who were probably just as committed to male supremacy as they take the play's hero to be but whose methods of oppressing their women were less obvious and more socially acceptable. Productions of the play have frequently attracted whatever thoughts were in the air on the perennially topical subjects of violence and sexual politics, and this tendency can hardly fail to increase in our own time. The play may indeed become less popular on the stage than it has been in previous centuries as it becomes, rightly, more and more difficult to put on productions of it which are simply rollicking good fun.

---

[1] *Stratford-upon-Avon Herald*, 12 May 1978. [2] Charles Marowitz, *The Shrew*, 1975, p. 77.
[3] *Western Daily Press*, 3 June 1954. [4] *Plays and Players*, February 1971.
[5] *Time and Tide*, 21 September 1961. [6] *Sunday Express*, 17 September 1961.

Critical approaches

In comparison with its popularity on stage, *The Taming of the Shrew* has been somewhat neglected by critics. Why should this be so? The apparently incomplete nature of the text and the uncertain status of *A Shrew* may have deterred a few potential critics but they can hardly account for the positive conspiracy of silence which runs from Anna Jameson's *Shakespeare's Heroines* in 1832 to C. L. Barber's *Shakespeare's Festive Comedy* in 1959 and beyond. A more likely explanation is that literary critics have concurred in the opinion of theatrical critics from George Bernard Shaw to Michael Billington that the play is 'disgusting' and 'barbaric', and, having a greater freedom of choice in regard to their subject-matter, have simply censored it by omission. Those who cannot choose to ignore the play, notably its editors, take an apologetic stance, admitting the problem but attempting to excuse the author. R. Warwick Bond, for example, writing in 1904, finds Petruchio's order to Katherina in the last scene to throw off her cap and tread on it particularly offensive: 'Though not intended to humiliate her, but rather to convince his sceptical friends, it always strikes me as a needless affront to her feelings...offered at the very moment when she is exhibiting a voluntary obedience.' Fortunately his conviction that *A Shrew* was the source for *The Shrew* allows him to argue that this is a piece of 'retention from the old play' which Shakespeare would have been wiser to omit.[1] Sir Arthur Quiller-Couch, writing in 1928, adopts a rather arch tone: 'There have been shrews since Xantippe's time...and it is not discreet perhaps for an editor to discuss, save historically, the effective ways of dealing with them...but...one cannot help thinking a little wistfully that the Petruchian discipline had something to say for itself.' At the same time he excuses Shakespeare by reference to the primitive era in which he lived: if Petruchio's method 'was undoubtedly drastic and has gone out of fashion...Let it suffice to say that *The Taming of the Shrew* belongs to a period, and is not ungallant, even so.'[2] Almost universally, scholars and critics who enter the fray at all assume a necessity to defend the play even though the attack is rarely articulated; it is just taken for granted that *The Shrew* will 'normally' be read and performed as a piece of bluff brutality in which a man marries a spirited woman in order to torture and humiliate her.

The relationship between Petruchio and Katherina is obviously the heart of the problem; in no other Shakespearean comedy does a single relationship dominate the play so thoroughly, but critics have always found it difficult to decide how seriously we should view these particular characters. When John Russell Brown made a survey of criticism of Shakespeare's comedies from 1900 to 1953 he remarked that the popularity of character studies had led to the neglect of *The Comedy of Errors, The Shrew* and *The Merry Wives* as 'mere farces'.[3] The assumption here is that Petruchio and Katherina, vivid as they might seem in comparison to, say, Valentine and Silvia in *The Two Gentlemen of Verona* or Lysander and Hermia in *A Midsummer Night's*

[1] Bond, p. lviii.
[2] NS, pp. xxxvi–xxxvii.
[3] 'The interpretation of Shakespeare's comedies: 1900–1953', *S.Sur.* 8 (1955), 1–13, p. 7.

Dream, are somehow not seen as 'characters' at all in the usual dramatic sense because they exist in a farce rather than in a comedy. Farce is defined as a superficial sub-species of comedy which depends heavily on stage business, usually of a knockabout variety. It is more concerned with the manipulation of social conventions than with the development of individual characters and hence is inclined to treat love as an intrigue or a game. If we classify *The Shrew* as a farce we can stop apologising for it: as Robert B. Heilman said of farce, its essential procedure is to deal with people 'as if they lack, largely or totally, the physical, emotional, intellectual and moral sensitivity that we think of as "normal"'. Thus the apparently outrageous elements of the play can be made acceptable:

Petruchio's order to Kate to bring out the other wives is like having a trained dog retrieve a stick. The scene is possible because one husband and three wives are not endowed with full human personalities; if they were, they simply could not function as trainer, retriever and sticks.[1]

This line of argument could of course be made to serve as the justification for almost any piece of sadistic pornography: if the characters are 'not endowed with full human personalities' it ceases to matter how much they are abused or tortured.[2]

Much modern criticism has in fact been concerned more or less explicitly with finding ways of 'softening' *The Taming of the Shrew* and incorporating it more comfortably into the *oeuvre* of a Shakespeare whom we would prefer to see as a liberal humanitarian. He was clearly prepared to challenge the stereotyped attitudes of his time towards Jews in *The Merchant of Venice* and towards blacks in *Othello*, but he seems more equivocal on women. If, like so many others, we set aside *The Shrew*, the comedies allow us to take a relatively optimistic view of Shakespeare-as-feminist. From *The Two Gentlemen of Verona* and *Love's Labour's Lost* onwards, Shakespeare's women seem absolutely (and at times mysteriously) superior to his men; they seem to know all about love and they make wise and witty remarks about the antics of their admirers. They are often in the position of teachers, initiating the courtship games and responsible for their outcome; Rosalind is the supreme example in *As You Like It*. When their love is unrequited, they are pathetic where men are ridiculous; they rarely alter in the objects of their affection (*A Midsummer Night's Dream* is a characteristic display of female constancy and male fickleness), and they usually have warm friendships with other women even when the plot makes them rivals in love, as in the case of Julia and Silvia in *The Two Gentlemen of Verona* and Viola and Olivia in *Twelfth Night*.

Yet idealisation is not the whole of Shakespeare's attitude to women, and his representation of them is not limited by it. The sonnets to the Dark Lady, written at much the same time as the comedies, are bitter and cynical about women and full of disgust at the idea of 'lust in action'. The woman is 'black', cruel, 'tyrannous', a corrupting influence which men cannot resist but which leads them to destruction and despair. This more sinister kind of woman emerges strongly in the plays at two periods in Shakespeare's writing career, in the later tragedies from 1606 and 1608

[1] 'The "Taming" untamed, or the return of the shrew', *MLQ* 27 (1966), 147–61, p. 154.
[2] Oliver, pp. 51–7, offers a more complex account of the 'farce or comedy' issue.

5   Petruchio shows an alarmed Katherina the treatment she can expect at his 'taming-school'. A tapestry of *The Rape of Europa* provides an ominous background. From the painting by Sir John Gilbert

(Lady Macbeth, Cleopatra, Volumnia in *Coriolanus*), and, more significantly for our purpose, in the earliest histories and tragedies up to 1593: Tamora in *Titus Andronicus* and Joan of Arc, the Countess of Auvergne and Margaret in the *Henry VI* plays are all strong destructive women, 'witches' who betray men and reject their authority.[1] Is Katherina, whose role was probably played by the same talented boy actor who played Tamora and Margaret, another potentially 'black' woman who can only be 'redeemed' from her witch-like status by an unconditional acceptance of masculine supremacy? In the early scenes of the play she is presented as a 'devil' (1.1.66), a 'fiend of hell' (1.1.88), a 'hilding of a devilish spirit' (2.1.26) and 'the devil's dam' (3.2.146) as if the task undertaken by Petruchio is as much the exorcism of an evil spirit as the curing of an excess of choleric humour. Modern critics tend to shy away from the sheer monstrosity of Shakespeare's notion of shrewishness, giving us instead a watered-down Katherina who is merely a bad-tempered woman jealous of her spoilt younger sister. In an article entitled 'Shakespeare's romantic shrews' published in 1960, for example, Charles Brooks tries to humanise Katherina, claiming that her 'spirited conduct' is not so very unlike that of 'Shakespeare's best-loved heroines' such as Rosalind and Portia, and that it is positively 'healthy' for a woman to 'burn out' her masculine desire to dominate as part of the process of maturing from girl to wife.[2]

---

[1] Leslie Fiedler discusses this type of female character in *The Stranger in Shakespeare*, 1972, pp. 37–68.
[2] *SQ* 11 (1960), 351–6.

As for Petruchio's behaviour, it has frequently been pointed out that his methods of taming his shrew are positively kindly compared with what happens in most of the other medieval and Renaissance versions of the shrew-taming plot where sadistic violence is commonplace. As Anne Barton puts it

By comparison with the husband who binds his erring spouse, beats her, bleeds her into a state of debility or incarcerates her inside the salted skin of a dead horse...Petruchio – although no Romeo – is almost a model of intelligence and humanity.[1]

Pace stage tradition, Shakespeare's Petruchio does not carry a whip and, in so far as he deprives his wife of food and sleep, he imposes the same deprivations on himself.[2] Further, Shakespeare rejects that other principal weapon of the shrew-tamer or male supremacist: theology. If we turn to *A Shrew* we see that the author(s) of this play, knowing that a long speech was required for Katherina's final display of submission but unable to remember the details of Shakespeare's version, replaced it with what is in fact a much more conventional statement of the relationship between men and women:

> Th'eternall power that with his only breath,
> Shall cause this end and this beginning frame,
> Not in time, nor before time, but with time, confusd,
> For all the course of yeares, of ages, moneths,
> Of seasons temperate, of dayes and houres,
> Are tund and stopt, by measure of his hand,
> The first world was, a forme, without a forme,
> A heape confusd a mixture all deformd,
> A gulfe of gulfes, a body bodiles,
> Where all the elements were orderles,
> Before the great commander of the world,
> The King of Kings the glorious God of heaven,
> Who in six daies did frame his heavenly worke,
> And made all things to stand in perfit course.
> Then to his image he did make a man,
> Olde *Adam* and from his side asleepe,
> A rib was taken, of which the Lord did make,
> The woe of man so termed by *Adam* then,
> Woman for that, by her came sinne to us,
> And for her sin was *Adam* doomd to die,
> As *Sara* to her husband, so should we,
> Obey them, love them, keepe, and nourish them,
> If they by any meanes doo want our helpes,
> Laying our handes under theire feete to tread,
> If that by that we, might procure there ease,
> And for a president Ile first begin,
> And lay my hand under my husbands feete.[3]

---

[1] Riverside, p. 106. Similar arguments are mounted by M. C. Bradbrook, 'Dramatic role as social image: a study of *The Taming of the Shrew*', *SJ* 94 (1958), 132–50, and by Winifred Schleiner, 'Deromanticizing the shrew: notes on teaching Shakespeare in a "Women in Literature" course', in Walter Edens *et al.* (eds.), *Teaching Shakespeare*, 1977, pp. 79–92.

[2] See 4.1.148 n. and 4.1.170–8 n. below.

[3] Bullough, *Sources*, scene xviii, 17–43.

Thus women should submit to men because they were created by God as inferior beings and were moreover responsible for the Fall of man from Paradise.

Shakespeare does not mention God at all in his version of this speech. His view of marriage is a purely secular one where the relationship between man and wife is a civil contract. The husband is still superior, of course, but he has obligations to perform:

> Thy husband is thy lord, thy life, thy keeper,
> Thy head, thy sovereign; one that cares for thee
> And for thy maintenance; commits his body
> To painful labour both by sea and land,
> To watch the night in storms, the day in cold,
> Whilst thou li'st warm at home, secure and safe,
> And craves no other tribute at thy hands
> But love, fair looks and true obedience –
> Too little payment for so great a debt.   (5.2.146–54)

The woman, too, has positive qualities to offer, 'love, fair looks and true obedience', in return for the man's contribution as bread-winner. Her position in relation to her husband is like that of the subject in relation to the ruler; she is firmly beneath him but she has a residual right to judge his conduct:

> Such duty as the subject owes the prince,
> Even such a woman oweth to her husband.
> And when she is froward, peevish, sullen, sour,
> And not obedient to his honest will,
> What is she but a foul contending rebel
> And graceless traitor to her loving lord?   (5.2.155–60)

The implication here is that, like the subject, she is obliged to obey only as long as her husband's will seems 'honest'; the way is left open for declarations of independence such as that of Emilia in *Othello* who sees, too late, that her husband Iago's will has not been honest and who thereupon disobeys quite deliberately his order to her to go home:

> 'Tis proper I obey him; but not now.
> Perchance, Iago, I will ne'er go home.   (*Oth.* 5.2.196–7)

Emilia's disobedience here is of course totally endorsed by the author and the audience, and Shakespeare's statement of the role of the wife in *The Shrew* allows for such an eventuality, unlike the theological argument in *A Shrew* which implies that, because they are intrinsically inferior and sinful, all women should obey all men at all times.

It is possible to relate Shakespeare's comparatively advanced views on marriage to a general shift in thinking on such matters which occurred in this period, mainly as a result of various waves of religious dissent. The medieval Catholic church had been largely anti-feminist, stressing the attitude of St Paul and the church fathers which is repeated in the Anglican Homily on Marriage (one of many homilies which all vicars were ordered by the Crown to read in church from 1562 onwards) when it says 'ye wives be in subjection to your husbands...for the husband is the head of the woman, as Christ is the head of the Church'.[1] Juliet Dusinberre has, however, argued that a number of influential writers were beginning to take a more liberal view of marriage, giving greater dignity to the woman and making her the man's friend and partner, if not his absolute equal. This attitude begins with the Catholic humanists Vives and Erasmus (one of whose *Colloquies* is quoted above, p. 14, as a possible source for the 'civil contract' view of marriage in Katherina's final speech) and continues with Protestant and Puritan reformers. As Dusinberre puts it, 'The Puritans' gift to their world lay in the replacing of the legal union of the arranged marriage with a union born of the spirit.'[2] If women were to be men's spiritual companions, then marriage partners had to be freely chosen, so this shift in opinion went along with a gradual relaxing of the tradition of strictly arranged marriages for the propertied classes. But one can take a less sanguine view of the influence of the dissenting tradition on the liberation of women. Lawrence Stone points out that in practice Protestantism gave husbands even more power than before; as heads of their households they took over some of what had previously been the priest's responsibilities for the moral and spiritual welfare of the family, and the Protestant emphasis on the individual's reading of the Bible as the key to salvation naturally favoured men who were far more likely to be educated (or even literate) than women.[3]

On the whole, however, it has not been difficult to demonstrate that, even if *The Shrew*'s final statement on marriage seems offensive to modern sensibilities, it is quite enlightened when we compare it with analogous literary texts or with theologically sanctioned views of intrinsic feminine inferiority.

Thematic approaches to the play have also been dominated, consciously or not, by a desire to 'soften' it and make it more acceptable. This is manifested in a concentration on *The Shrew*'s manipulation of notions to do with 'acting', 'supposing', 'dreaming' and 'games-playing'. If we take any of these as the dominant or unifying theme, the more problematic aspects of the taming plot can be seen as being presented in a deliberately 'distanced' or 'playful' way and we can perhaps claim that Shakespeare himself shared our uneasiness about regarding Petruchio's actions as a desirable model for how to treat women in the real world. Such approaches can evade the play's moral issues and misrepresent its theatrical appeal. Sometimes, however, they have the genuine advantage of obliging us to attend to the Sly frame and the sub-plot as well as to the main plot, and encouraging us to see the play as a coherent whole.

There has always been considerable admiration for the skills of dramatic construction displayed in *The Shrew*; as I have said earlier, the complexity of its structure has been used as an argument that Shakespeare, not the anonymous author of *A Shrew*, must have been responsible for the original conception, on the grounds that no other known

[1] Quoted by Lawrence Stone in *The Family, Sex and Marriage in England 1500–1800*, 1977, p. 198. Chaucer has a vigorous summary of medieval anti-feminist attitudes in the Prologue to the 'Wife of Bath's Tale'.
[2] *Shakespeare and the Nature of Women*, 1975, p. 104. This argument is also developed by John C. Bean, 'Comic structure and the humanizing of Kate in *The Taming of the Shrew*', in Carolyn Ruth Swift Lenz *et al.* (eds.), *The Woman's Part: Feminist Criticism of Shakespeare*, 1980, pp. 65–78.
[3] Stone, *The Family*, pp. 154–5.

dramatist would have been capable of devising such an ambitious scheme. The use
of the Induction in itself can be seen as an ingeniously self-conscious device raising
questions about the relationship of the theatre to the world and the nature of 'reality'
itself. G. K. Hunter uses *The Shrew* to demonstrate how Shakespeare's attitude to
these matters is more complicated and serious than that of John Lyly, who sometimes
uses similar effects, and Anne Righter and Leo Salingar have explored the subtleties
of the play-within-the-play ramifications.[1] The use of Sly seems to have encouraged
Shakespeare to make extensive use of other 'stage audiences' in this play so that layers
of illusion are built up as one group of characters after another 'stand aside' and watch
the next group perform. At the beginning the Lord and his men devise for themselves
a performance of something that might be called 'The Gulling of Christopher Sly',
but this entertainment is superseded when the Players arrive and Sly joins the Lord
as 'audience' rather than performer. Hardly have the first players, Lucentio and
Tranio, begun their scene than they too are interrupted by the arrival of another group
consisting of Baptista, his two daughters and Bianca's suitors. Greeting this as 'some
show to welcome us to town' and 'good pastime', Lucentio and Tranio in their turn
stand aside to enjoy the performance. A similar effect but in reverse is achieved at
the end of 5.1 when the stage swiftly clears, leaving Katherina and Petruchio, who
have themselves been standing aside 'to see the end of this controversy', alone for
their first kiss. If, as Karl P. Wentersdorf argues, another scene with Sly originally
followed at this point, the effect of dissolving the layers would be even more complete.[2]

   In the body of the play, the sub-plot provides most of the 'stage audience' effects
with such complicated deceptions as the lesson scene (3.1) and the overheard courtship
scene (4.2). This is hardly surprising since the sub-plot contains most of the play's
use of intrigue and disguise. Bertrand Evans goes so far as to claim that the taming
plot itself is the only comic plot ever developed by Shakespeare 'without use of gaps
between awarenesses'; it is unique because 'no participant stands in a position of
unawareness, none has a fuller view of the situation than another, and we ourselves
[as audience or readers] occupy a vantage-point equal to that of the actors'.[3]
Nevertheless, all this takes place in such an elaborate play-within-the-play framework
that Shakespeare does not after all sacrifice his customary complexity. Indeed, it can
be argued that he achieves an unusual open-endedness, leaving us asking such
questions as 'Is Katherina's performance as a dutiful wife nearer to "the real
Katherina" than her performance as a shrew?' or 'Do we ever see "the real
Petruchio" as opposed to Petruchio playing the role of the shrew-tamer?' or even
'Is the whole thing a dream or fantasy in the mind of Christopher Sly?'

   The proposition that the three strands of action in *The Shrew* are united by the
'supposes' theme seems first to have been put forward by Donald Stauffer in 1949.
He points out that there is confusion of appearance and reality, shadow and substance,

[1] G. K. Hunter, *John Lyly: The Humanist as Courtier*, 1962, pp. 309–10; Righter, *Shakespeare and the
Idea of the Play*, pp. 94–6; Salingar, *Traditions of Comedy*, pp. 271–2.
[2] 'The original ending of *The Taming of the Shrew*: a reconsideration', *SEL* 18 (1978), 201–15.
[3] *Shakespeare's Comedies*, 1960, p. 25. Technically, Evans is correct on this point since Petruchio plainly
tells Kate in 2.1 that he is going to tame her, but it still often feels as if he has 'a fuller view of the
situation' than she.

in all three strands of the plot, and he remarks on the difference between the relatively superficial disguisings of the Sly frame and the sub-plot on the one hand and the greater subtlety of the theme in the main plot where Petruchio's apparently wilful supposition that Katherina is affable, witty, modest and so on becomes the truth by the end of the play.[1] This view was developed more thoroughly in 1963 by Cecil C. Seronsy in what has been one of the most influential of modern essays on the play, '"Supposes" as the unifying theme in *The Taming of the Shrew*'.[2] He elevates into the governing principle of the play Shakespeare's transformation of the taming plot and the Induction under the influence of *Supposes*.

In the version of *Supposes* printed in 1575, Gascoigne offered a brief prologue in which he commented on his title and explained that

this our Suppose is nothing else but a mystaking or imagination of one thing for another. For you shall see the master supposed for the servant, the servant for the master: the freeman for a slave, and the bondslave for a freeman: the stranger for a well knowen friend, and the familiar for a stranger.[3]

Shakespeare elaborates the 'supposes' game even in this limited sense in his sub-plot by adding the disguising of Hortensio and all its confusing consequences. In the Induction it is of course Sly who is 'supposed' to be what he is not, namely a lord rather than a tinker, and Seronsy claims that this theme is the major link between Sly and the rest of the play. Comparing *The Shrew* with *A Shrew* he points out that the Sly in *A Shrew* is explicitly linked to the taming plot by references to his own shrewish wife and by the early announcement of the title of the play to be performed,[4] but that Shakespeare eschewed such references and 'deliberately chose to dissociate [Sly] from the shrew plot altogether', relying instead on the 'supposes' theme for his coherence.

When it comes to the main plot, however, this emphasis on the 'supposes' theme helps to rehabilitate Petruchio as a sympathetic hero, since his method is to 'suppose' Katherina a more promising candidate for wifehood than she seems to be. Even before he meets her he is prepared to think better of her than her father, sister and neighbours do, and after they are married his programme of domination and deprivation can be seen as merely a way of drawing out what Seronsy calls 'her really fine qualities: patience, practical good sense, a capacity for humor, and finally obedience',[5] from behind the shrewish mask she has assumed. Thus Petruchio becomes a benevolent educator and a figure to whom all academic critics can warm. Education is clearly important in the play, as it is elsewhere in Shakespeare. Frequently a Shakespearean father will devote considerable time to teaching his daughter, as in the cases of Portia in *The Merchant of Venice*, Helena in *All's Well That Ends Well* (in both these plays the teaching has finished and the father has died before the play begins) and Miranda in *The Tempest*. This ideal does not seem to have been practised in real-life Warwickshire (there is some doubt as to whether Shakespeare's daughter Judith could

---

[1] *Shakespeare's World of Images*, 1949, pp. 43–6.
[2] *SQ* 14 (1963), 15–30.   [3] Bullough, *Sources*, I, 112.
[4] See the additional Sly scenes printed here in Appendix 1, pp. 175–80 below.
[5] Seronsy, 'Supposes', p. 19.

"small
compass'd
cape"

"Demi-cannon"
sleeves attached
separately to
bodice under
gown.

loose-bodied
gown over
bodice and
skirt.

6   Elizabethan fashions: Kate's cap and gown (Act 4, Scene 3) and Tranio's copatain hat (Act 5, Scene 1). Drawings by C. Walter Hodges

even write her name) or in the Padua depicted in *The Shrew*, where Baptista has no intention of teaching his daughters himself but proposes to hire tutors for them. This provides the opportunity for all the comic disguisings of the sub-plot and also allows Shakespeare to set up a contrast between the spurious education of Bianca, who could not learn anything from these pretenders even if she wanted to, and the less conventional but more effective education of Katherina.

Petruchio is indeed a teacher, not only in respect of his role in the taming plot but also in his tendency to deliver moral lessons on more general topics. He is particularly interested in the significance of clothing, as when he responds to criticisms of his manifestly inappropriate wedding garments by saying

> To me she's married, not unto my clothes.
> Could I repair what she will wear in me
> As I can change these poor accoutrements,
> 'Twere well for Kate and better for myself.   (3.2.107–10)

Later he tells Kate not to worry about going back to her father's house in her old clothes

> For 'tis the mind that makes the body rich,
> And as the sun breaks through the darkest clouds,
> So honour peereth in the meanest habit.
> What, is the jay more precious than the lark
> Because his feathers are more beautiful?   (4.3.166–70)

In both cases he is straightforwardly moralising on the lack of any necessary congruity between the clothing and the person underneath it – another aspect of the 'appearance and reality' theme which has ironic reference to the many costume-changes of the sub-plot.

The view of Petruchio as a clever and benign educator who helps Katherina out of her shrewishness by 'supposing' a more positive view of her is pushed even further and updated somewhat by Ruth Nevo, who sees Petruchio as more a psychotherapist than a teacher and one whose speciality is homoeopathy: as Peter puts it in the play, 'He kills her in her own humour' (4.1.151). Practising this kind of therapy,

subtle Dr Petruchio...speaks at once to the self [Kate] has been and the self she would like to be; the self she has made of herself and the self she has hidden. The exchange of roles, with herself now at the receiving end of someone else's furies, takes her, as we say, out of herself; but she also perceives the method of his madnesses. Petruchio's remedy is an appeal to Kate's intelligence. These are not arbitrary brutalities but the clearest of messages.[1]

Again the critic excuses the 'arbitrary brutalities' perceived by so many audiences and readers. There is even evidence in the text for comedy itself as a kind of therapy: Sly is assured that his doctors recommend him to hear a play as a cure for sadness and melancholy (Induction 2.124–30).

Brian Morris, however, questions the widespread assumption that all education is unambiguously benign. Indeed, he sees much of the controversy about the play as stemming from 'the dichotomy which underlies all educative processes', namely that

---

[1] *Comic Transformations in Shakespeare*, 1980, pp. 48–9.

On the one hand, education is designed to liberate and to bring to full fruition the innate capabilities of the pupil. On the other, it is a means of reducing the individual to social conformity through the imparting of approved knowledge and acceptable skills. To some extent it is always a taming procedure, at odds with the very human desire for liberty.[1]

By the same token, the educational process raises questions about which is the 'true' self and there is clearly a difference in kind between the 'supposes' of the main plot and those of the other plots: we cannot determine quite so confidently which is the appearance and which is the reality with Katherina as we can with Sly or Tranio.

But Sly himself has considerable difficulty in making this distinction. 'Am I a lord, and have I such a lady?' he asks, 'Or do I dream? Or have I dreamed till now?' (Induction 2.64–5). He suspects, sensibly enough, that he is now dreaming, but the Lord and his servants manage to convince him that he is awake and it is his former life which should be rejected as a dream. The first onslaught of Petruchio's taming programme has a similar effect on Katherina: soon after their arrival at Petruchio's house we are told that he is in her chamber

> Making a sermon of continency to her
> And rails and swears and rates, that she, poor soul,
> Knows not which way to stand, to look, to speak,
> And sits as one new-risen from a dream.   (4.1.154–7)

The confused state of the awakening dreamer is of course explored with considerable pathos by Shakespeare later on in *King Lear* (4.7) and *Cymbeline* (4.2). Pathos is not aroused in *The Shrew*, but the suggestion of dreaming, taken together with the atmosphere of deliberate deception and the constant references to acting and performing, contributes to the general undermining and questioning of reality. As Marjorie B. Garber puts it

The formal device of the induction has a considerable effect upon the play as a whole, and its importance is closely linked with the fact that it purports to tell a dream. The frame performs the important tasks of distancing the later action and of insuring a lightness of tone – significant contributions in view of the real abuse to which Kate is subjected by Petruchio. Its most important single advantage, however, is the immediacy with which it establishes the deliberate metaphorical ambiguity of reality and illusion.[2]

It does not seem strictly accurate to say that the Induction 'purports to tell a dream', given that the audience is perfectly well aware that Sly is awake but is being imposed upon by various levels of fiction. He does fall asleep later, though, and it has been argued ingeniously if somewhat fancifully that the 'inner play' from the end of 1.1 onwards should be played as Sly's dream with Sly himself taking the part of Petruchio and acting out a sort of wish-fulfilment fantasy about how wives should submit to their husbands.[3] Such an interpretation has been staged, most recently by the Royal Shakespeare Company in 1978, when the same actor, Jonathan Pryce, played both Sly and Petruchio, and the final scene was overlooked by a rather glum double for Pryce dressed in his Sly costume and indicating a sense of distaste and rejection of

---

[1] Morris, p. 133.
[2] *Dream in Shakespeare*, 1974, p. 28.
[3] Sears Jayne, 'The dreaming of *The Shrew*', *SQ* 17 (1966), 41–56.

his fantasy now that he had seen it acted out. Such an interpretation would of course run completely counter to the theory that Shakespeare 'deliberately dissociated Sly from the shrew plot' and it requires major and essential information to be conveyed by mime or other stage business.

Although it is debatable how far *The Taming of the Shrew* can be seen as a dream, there is no doubt that there are many references which encourage us to see much of the action as 'sport' or 'game'. The Lord who discovers Sly enters 'from hunting', full of judicious remarks about his dogs, and the trick he proposes to play on the beggar seems just another piece of sporting fun. As a supposed lord, Sly is offered his choice of three different kinds of blood sports to help him pass the time:

> Dost thou love hawking? Thou hast hawks will soar
> Above the morning lark. Or wilt thou hunt?
> Thy hounds shall make the welkin answer them
> And fetch shrill echoes from the hollow earth.
> Say thou wilt course, thy greyhounds are as swift
> As breathèd stags, ay, fleeter than the roe. (Induction 2.39–44)

The courtship of Bianca in the sub-plot is seen as a competitive sporting event from the beginning – 'He that runs fastest gets the ring', as Hortensio tells Gremio (1.1.132–3) – to the end when Tranio explains his role in the affair to Petruchio:

> O sir, Lucentio slipped me like his greyhound,
> Which runs himself and catches for his master. (5.2.52–3)

In Paduan society, however, it is natural that these aristocratic and rural metaphors from hunting should be combined with more bourgeois and urban references to gambling and card games: 'Gremio is out-vied', claims Tranio triumphantly when the two of them are bidding for Bianca in 2.1, though he admits in soliloquy at the end of the scene that he has 'outfaced it with a card of ten'. Katherina is seen as an animal to be tamed, and especially as a hawk or falcon, as in Petruchio's explanatory soliloquy at the end of 4.1:

> My falcon now is sharp and passing empty,
> And till she stoop she must not be full-gorged,
> For then she never looks upon her lure.
> Another way I have to man my haggard... (4.1.161–4)

When she begins to submit, Petruchio comments approvingly in another sporting metaphor: 'Thus the bowl should run / And not unluckily against the bias' (4.5.24–5).

The fact that in the folktale versions the shrew-taming story always comes to its climax when the husbands wager on their wives' obedience must have been partly responsible for the large number of references to sporting, gaming and gambling throughout the play. And again these metaphors can help to make Petruchio's cruelty acceptable by making it seem limited and conventionalised. As Alexander Leggatt puts it:

The taming of Katherina is not just a lesson but a game – a test of skill and a source of pleasure. The roughness is, at bottom, part of the fun: such is the peculiar psychology of sport that one is willing to endure aching muscles and risk the occasional broken limb for the sake of the challenge and the pleasure it provides.[1]

Katherina's education then consists partly in learning the rules of Petruchio's game, and ultimately she is able to take pleasure in joining in, first in the 'mistaking' of Vincentio in 4.5 and then in partnering Petruchio to win the wager in 5.2.[2] Nevertheless, it is Petruchio who lays down the rules while it is Katherina who seems more in danger of risking 'the occasional broken limb'; 'play' is all very well but ultimately patriarchy must be taken seriously. A valuable essay by Marianne L. Novy explores the complex relationship between these two concepts.[3] Patriarchy is of course important throughout the play; there are no fewer than four senior male characters – Baptista, Gremio, Vincentio and the false Vincentio (who is 'In gait and countenance surely like a father', 4.2.65) – and the younger men, Petruchio, Lucentio and even Tranio, are defined by reference to their fathers. There is no balancing phalanx of female characters, and Katherina's isolation seems the greater when we note that she is the only Shakespearean comic heroine without a female friend at any point in the play.

As Novy demonstrates, Petruchio's relationship to patriarchy seems paradoxical: he is a player of games whose favourite tactic is to violate the conventions of the social order (as he does most outrageously in his wedding scene) and yet he relies on that very society to ratify his patriarchal power. His activities seem to denote rebellion – his 'cuffing' of the priest in 3.2 and his mockery of Vincentio in 4.5 seem particularly odd behaviour for a would-be patriarch – and yet his ultimate intention is to make Katherina endorse the *status quo*. In so far as he is merely playing at rejecting the conventions, however, he constantly invites Katherina to join him in his private game, at first outrageously in his claim at the end of the wooing scene ''Tis bargained 'twixt us twain, being alone, / That she shall still be curst in company' (2.1.293–4), and in his pretence to be defending her from the attacks of the wedding guests (3.2.217–28), but finally more seriously. When she does join him in the mockery of Vincentio (4.5) her contributions are confident, even triumphant, the 'inside jokes' indicating a sense of gleeful conspiracy with Petruchio. Novy points out that this is the first of three scenes (the last three scenes in the play) in which characters ask pardon of patriarchal figures – fathers and husbands – but both here and in 5.1 the younger generation are in fact dominant, as we would expect in a comedy, and the respect for fathers and traditional values is something of an afterthought. Katherina's speech in 5.2, like her apology to Vincentio in 4.5, has a tone of paradoxical triumph; 'she holds the center stage while preaching humility' and

her energetic resilience helps distance the threatening elements of compulsion in Petruchio's past behaviour. When she concludes by offering to place her hand below her husband's foot in an hierarchical gesture of submission, his answer sounds less like an acceptance of tribute than praise for a successful performance in a game: 'Why, there's a wench! Come on and kiss me, Kate.'[4]

---

[1] *Shakespeare's Comedy of Love*, 1974, p. 56.

[2] This view of the play is endorsed by Ralph Berry, whose chapter on *The Shrew* in his *Shakespeare's Comedies*, 1972, is called 'The rules of the game'.

[3] 'Patriarchy and play in *The Taming of the Shrew*', *ELR* 9 (1979), 264–80.

[4] *Ibid.*, pp. 276–7.

But is that final speech merely 'playful', an exaggeration of a sincere attitude and an exuberant exercise of Katherina's new-found skill, or is it perhaps 'too good to be true' – a clever piece of acting from a Katherina who has seen the necessity of following Hortensio's advice ('Say as he says, or we shall never go', 4.5.11) but whose submission is merely tactical, not sincere? It seems that Margaret Webster was the first critic to argue that Katherina's delivery of this speech should be essentially ironic (thirteen years after Mary Pickford inaugurated this tradition in performance),[1] and she was supported by Harold C. Goddard, who saw the play as an early version of J. M. Barrie's *What Every Woman Knows*, the knowledge in question being that a woman can dominate her husband so long as she tricks him into believing that he is dominating her.[2] If the speech is *not* ironic, these critics argue, the play becomes totally unacceptable. A recent critic, Coppélia Kahn, has pushed this argument to its logical conclusion by claiming not only that this speech is ironic but that the whole play is a satire on the male urge to control women and the wiliness with which women respond.[3]

This satire, Kahn says, begins with Christopher Sly, whose assumption of power over his 'wife' in the world of pretence contrasts ludicrously with his real-life humiliation by the Hostess. All the male characters in the taming plot and the sub-plot are satirised for their obsession with money as well as for their ridiculously exaggerated perception of Katherina's shrewishness. Petruchio's statements of male supremacy, particularly his 'She is my goods, my chattels' speech (3.2.219–28) and his 'Thus have I politicly begun my reign' soliloquy (4.1.159–82), are so blatant that we can hardly take them seriously:

Both utterances unashamedly present the status of woman in marriage as degrading in the extreme, plainly declaring her a subhuman being who exists solely for the purposes of her husband.[4]

Thus the intention is to shock us and to draw our attention to the absurdity of male supremacy. (Whether or not this intention is plausible, Kahn has theatrical and literary history on her side here, showing that very many audiences and readers have in fact been shocked by these speeches.) The turning point in 4.5 is a further example of this deliberate absurdity: Petruchio, because he is a man, can force upon his wife the patently ridiculous 'truth' that the sun is the moon and old Vincentio is a young girl. Kahn says that Katherina responds to the latter claim 'by pretending so wholeheartedly to accept it that we know she cannot be in earnest'.[5] Here and in her final speech Katherina consciously goes too far, signalling her scepticism and her ultimate independence; she is prepared to play along with the fantasy of male supremacy but at the same time she mocks it as mere fantasy. The problem with this

[1] *Shakespeare Without Tears*, 1942, p. 142.
[2] *The Meaning of Shakespeare*, 2 vols., 1951, I, 68.
[3] *Man's Estate: Masculine Identity in Shakespeare*, 1981, pp. 104–18. An earlier version of this chapter was published as '*The Taming of the Shrew*: Shakespeare's mirror of marriage' in *MLS* 5 (1975), 88–102.
[4] Kahn, *Man's Estate*, p. 112.
[5] *Ibid.*, p. 113.

interpretation is that it gives Petruchio a hollow victory and the pair of them a potentially bitter marriage, but Kahn has a way around this:

> On the deepest level, because the play depicts its heroine as outwardly compliant but inwardly independent, it represents possibly the most cherished male fantasy of all – that woman remains *un*tamed, even in her subjection. Does Petruchio know he has been taken? Quite probably, since he himself has played the game of saying-the-thing-which-is-not. Would he enjoy being married to a woman as dull and proper as the Kate who delivers that marriage sermon? From all indications, no. Then can we conclude that Petruchio no less than Kate knowingly plays a false role in this marriage, the role of victorious tamer and complacent master? I think we can...[1]

Hence we have two characters who are, metaphorically at least, winking at the audience during the final scene; Katherina has given Petruchio the public display of obedience his male pride requires but they both know it is partly a pretence.

The ending of the play does seem to be ambiguous. Baptista sportingly comes up with another dowry for Katherina – 'Another dowry to another daughter, / For she is changed, as she had never been' (5.2.114–15) – but in the very last line of the play in the Folio text Lucentio begs leave to question the credibility of what he has just seen: ''Tis a wonder, by your leave, she will be tamed so.' Has Katherina really been tamed, or is she, as the woman in Wyatt's sonnet ('Whoso list to hunt: I know where is an hind') describes herself in a rather different context, 'wild for to hold, though I seem tame'? This poem provides a powerful illustration of a related use of the hunting and taming metaphors of the Petrarchan tradition which *The Shrew* inherits. In Wyatt it is certainly part of the woman's attraction that she is ultimately untameable, though there is tragic potential for the man who may find himself in the position of loss expressed by the speaker in another of Wyatt's poems on this theme:

> They flee from me, that sometime did me seek
> With naked foot stalking in my chamber.
> I have seen them gentle, tame, and meek
> That now are wild, and do not remember
> That sometime they put themself in danger
> To take bread at my hand; and now they range,
> Busily seeking with a continual change.[2]

Shakespeare deals with this kind of loss in *Othello* where the hero feels he must reject his wife if she is not 'tame':

> If I do prove her haggard,
> Though that her jesses were my dear heart-strings,
> I'ld whistle her off, and let her down the wind
> To prey at fortune.   (*Oth.* 3.3.260–3)

And he regrets 'That we can call these delicate creatures ours, / And not their appetites' *(Oth.* 3.3.269–70). These examples explicitly relate 'tameness' to fidelity and it would indeed be more acceptable to read the taming process in *The Shrew* as

---

[1] *Ibid.*, p. 117.
[2] *Sir Thomas Wyatt: Collected Poems*, ed. Joost Daalder, 1975, poem 37.

a teaching of fidelity, which is presumably mutual, rather than a teaching of obedience, which is one-sided.

But this leads us straight into another crucial issue in the play, which Shakespeare leaves surprisingly open, namely whether, when, and to what extent Katherina and Petruchio fall in love. Even a thoroughly feminist critic like Coppélia Kahn admits that 'what complicates the situation even more is that Kate has quite possibly fallen in love with her tamer' at some point in the procedure, and, as we have seen at pp. 17–24 above, this is a matter that directors have to take into their own hands. It is possible that Shakespeare himself was divided about his material and that his unique use of the Induction indicates a desire to distance himself and us from the outcome of the taming plot and leave us free to speculate on Kate's possible relapse to shrewishness as well as Sly's certain relapse to poverty. Marianne Novy relates this ambiguous quality in the play to its having been written at a time of 'social transition, when Renaissance England felt conflict not only between contrasting images of marriage but also between nostalgia for an older order and a new awareness of individuality, inner passions and outer chaos'.[1] A somewhat similar conclusion is reached by Marilyn M. Cooper, who tries to resolve the differences between a 'straight' reading of Katherina's final speech and a feminist one (taking Robert Heilman and Coppélia Kahn as her examples) through a linguistic approach to interpretative strategies. She finds that the text itself is in the end open to different interpretations and that the reader and the playgoer have room to choose.[2]

For the original audience the romantic climax would moreover have been crowned by the ultimate ambiguity that all the actors were male and Petruchio could no more 'bed' his Kate in the sense intended than Christopher Sly could bed his 'wife' in the Induction; the long-awaited consummation is indefinitely suspended, an impossibility in the real world.

If Shakespeare originally ended the play with an additional Sly scene this point would have received further emphasis,[3] but in any case we are constantly reminded of the theatricality of these events and, for all Hamlet's talk about 'the purpose of playing' being 'to hold as 'twere the mirror up to nature' *(Ham.* 3.2.20–2), Shakespeare himself kept the distinction between the theatre and the real world quite clear. The fact that others have been less able to do this has been a major source of negative reactions and criticism. It may be welcomed as an index of increasing sensitivity about the oppression of women that so many commentators are so nervous and apologetic about *The Shrew* – though I hope I have shown that this is not exactly a novel phenomenon[4] – but it is only sensible to talk of effectively banning the play if, as well as taking a crudely unhistorical view of this particular text, we exaggerate

---

[1] Novy, 'Patriarchy and play', p. 279.

[2] 'Implicature, convention and *The Taming of the Shrew*', *Poetics* 10 (1981), 1–14.

[3] See the 'epilogue' from *A Shrew* in Appendix 1 below, and a discussion of whether Shakespeare's play did originally end like this in the Textual Analysis, pp. 155–74 below.

[4] Modern unease about this issue is not limited to reviewers of *The Shrew* but was also apparent in the reactions to the production of Aeschylus's trilogy *The Oresteia* at the National Theatre, London, in 1981, partly because Tony Harrison's translation boldly emphasised the extent to which these plays represent the triumph of patriarchy over matriarchy.

the moral authority of all art.[1] The real problem lies outside the play in the fact that the subjection of women to men, although patently unfair and unjustifiable, is still virtually universal. It is the world which offends us, not Shakespeare.

Postscript: working on the play

One might respond to this last sentence by saying that if it is the world which offends us, then Shakespeare was rather more comfortable in that world than we might like him to have been. Must we find further excuses for him by saying that in some sense he was obliged to be orthodox in his opinions on these matters, as he was on other political issues, that he could not speak freely because of what Herman Melville called 'the muzzle that all men wore on their souls in the Elizabethan day',[2] restraining their frankness and independence? In working on the play I have found that my own problem with its overt endorsement of patriarchy does not decrease, though my pleasure in its formal qualities, the sheer craft and detail of the construction, continues to grow.

In performance I suspect that the personality of the actor playing Petruchio is crucial to the play's success, and this is a factor that Shakespeare would have been able to take into account. The man must have real stage presence, and the ability to convey an underlying intelligence and sensitivity; he must not be a loud-mouthed bully.[3] As Germaine Greer remarks, 'Kate has the uncommon good fortune to find [a husband] who is man enough to know what he wants and how to get it.'[4] By most standards, including feminist ones, Petruchio is a more interesting and challenging possibility as a husband than the Orlandos and Orsinos of this world, just as Kate is a more interesting wife than Bianca.

Finally, though, I suspect we shall have to acknowledge that we can no longer treat *The Shrew* as a straightforward comedy but must redefine it as a problem play in Ernest Schanzer's sense:

A play in which we find a concern with a moral problem which is central to it, presented in such a manner that we are unsure of our moral bearings, so that uncertain and divided responses to it in the minds of the audience are possible or even probable.[5]

---

[1] The moral authority of the drama of this period and the problems raised for modern critics have been explored by Harriett Hawkins in *Likenesses of Truth in Elizabethan and Restoration Drama*, 1972, and Joel B. Altman in *The Tudor Play of Mind*, 1978.

[2] Melville discusses what he sees as Shakespeare's self-censorship in a letter to his publisher Evert Duyckink dated 3 March 1849 and in his essay 'Hawthorne and his Mosses', 1850. Both are printed in Jay Leyda (ed.), *The Portable Melville*, 1952.

[3] One of the most satisfactory of recent Petruchios to my mind was John Cleese in the BBC television production directed by Jonathan Miller, 1980; one of the least satisfactory was Richard Burton in the 1966 film version directed by Franco Zeffirelli.

[4] Germaine Greer, *The Female Eunuch*, 1971, p. 209.

[5] Ernest Schanzer, *The Problem Plays of Shakespeare*, 1963, p. 6. The plays Schanzer discusses under this definition are *Julius Caesar, Measure for Measure* and *Antony and Cleopatra*.

NOTE ON THE TEXT

The copy-text for this edition is the 1623 First Folio (F); there is no other authoritative text. The provenance of F and its relationship to the 1594 quarto *The Taming of a Shrew* are discussed in the Textual Analysis (pp. 155–74 below). Additional passages from *A Shrew*, which can probably be seen as reported versions of lost Shakespearean originals, are given and discussed in Appendix 1 below, pp. 175–80. The collation records all significant departures from F, including variants in lineation and in the wording and placing of stage directions. It does not record corrections of misprints or modernisations of spellings except where these may be of some consequence; F's 'sacietie' for 'satiety' at 1.1.24, for example, may imply a pun on 'society', F's 'Butonios' for 'Antonio's' at 1.2.184 may help to indicate the nature of the copy (see Textual Analysis), and F's 'hapned' for 'happenèd' at 4.4.64 may indicate the pronunciation. In the format of the collations, the authority for this edition's reading follows immediately after the square bracket enclosing the quotation from the text. Other readings, if any, follow in chronological order. When, as is usually the case, the variant or emendation adopted has been used by a previous editor or suggested by a textual commentator, that authority is cited in the abbreviated form *Rowe* or *conj. Theobald*; see pp. xi–xiii above for an explanation of the abbreviations and a full list of the editions and commentaries cited. The form *Eds.* is used for insignificant and obvious editorial practices (always minor clarification of stage directions) which do not need to be ascribed to one originator, and the form *This edn* is used for innovations of my own. In addition I have regularly listed emendations and conjectures which I have not adopted in the text but which seem to have a serious claim on the reader's attention and/or have been adopted by other modern editors. In cases where there are two or more distinct twentieth-century traditions, e.g. on the question of whether to emend F's 'Brach' at Induction 1.13, or on whether to print 1.1.213–15 as prose or verse, I have illustrated this diversity by collating six significant editions: Bond (1904), NS (1928), Hibbard (1968), Riverside (1974), Morris (1981) and Oliver (1982). An asterisk in the lemma of a note in the Commentary is used to call attention to a word or phrase that has been emended in the text; the collation should be consulted for further information.

The Taming of the Shrew

LIST OF CHARACTERS

The Induction
CHRISTOPHER SLY, *a tinker*
HOSTESS *of an alehouse*
LORD
BARTHOLOMEW, *the Lord's page*
HUNTSMEN *and* SERVANTS *attending on the Lord*
PLAYERS

The Taming Plot
BAPTISTA MINOLA, *a rich citizen of Padua*
KATHERINA, *the Shrew, elder daughter of Baptista*
PETRUCHIO, *a gentleman of Verona, suitor to Katherina*
GRUMIO, *Petruchio's personal servant*
CURTIS, *Petruchio's chief servant at his country house*
TAILOR
HABERDASHER
SERVANTS *attending on Petruchio*

The Sub-plot
BIANCA, *younger daughter of Baptista*
GREMIO, *a rich old citizen of Padua, suitor to Bianca*
HORTENSIO, *a gentleman of Padua, suitor to Bianca, pretends to be Litio*
LUCENTIO, *a gentleman of Pisa, suitor to Bianca, pretends to be Cambio*
TRANIO, *Lucentio's personal servant, pretends to be Lucentio*
BIONDELLO, *Lucentio's second servant (a boy)*
VINCENTIO, *a rich old citizen of Pisa, father of Lucentio*
MERCHANT *of Mantua, pretends to be Vincentio*
WIDOW, *in love with Hortensio*
SERVANTS *attending on Baptista and Lucentio*

Notes
With normal Elizabethan doubling, this play could have been performed by a cast of ten adult actors and four boys (for the women's parts and Biondello) if Sly and his companions disappear some time after the end of 1.1 (see Appendix 2 on the staging of Induction 2), allowing the actors of Sly and the Lord to double as the Merchant, who first appears in 4.2, and Vincentio, who first appears in 4.5. The Lord's page, Bartholomew, who plays Sly's 'wife', could double as the Widow, who appears only in 5.2. In addition to these actors of major roles there should be at least five supernumeraries to play huntsmen, servants and other minor parts.

PETRUCHIO This name (but nothing else about the character) is taken from Gascoigne's *Supposes* where, in the printed text of 1575, it is spelt 'Petrucio'. Shakespeare presumably put in the 'h' to show that he intended the 'ch' to be pronounced as in 'church'. Confusion has arisen because 'ch' is pronounced hard in modern Italian, so that for example in the 1966 film version of the play directed by Franco Zeffirelli the name is pronounced 'Petrukio' throughout.

CURTIS Obviously intended to be a male servant from the cuckold joke at 4.1.20–1, but from Garrick's *Catharine and Petruchio* (1754) to at least the Royal Shakespeare Company's production in 1978 the part has very often been played by a woman.

HABERDASHER During the sixteenth century, according to *OED*, a haberdasher might be either (a) a dealer in or maker of hats or caps, or (b) a dealer in small articles appertaining to dress, as thread, tape, ribbons, etc. The former is clearly relevant.

BIANCA The word means 'white' in Italian, giving rise to Petruchio's pun at 5.2.186.

GREMIO This character is called a 'pantaloon' in the dialogue at 3.1.35 and in the stage direction for his first entrance at 1.1.45. The pantaloon was a stock figure in Italian Renaissance comedy, a ridiculous old man whose role was usually to serve as an obstacle to the young lovers.

Litio Shakespeare took the name for Hortensio's alias from Gascoigne's *Supposes*. It is spelt 'Litio' or 'Lisio' in F but many editors follow F2's 'Licio'. Richard Hosley explains that the name could be a joke in the New Comedy tradition of significant names, as 'lizio' is an old Italian word for garlic ('Sources and analogues of *The Taming of the Shrew*', *HLQ* 27 (1963–4), 289–308).

Cambio. The name for Lucentio's alias means 'exchange' in Italian.

MERCHANT *of Mantua* This character is called a Pedant rather than a Merchant in F and all subsequent editions. See 4.2.71 SD n., and Textual Analysis, pp. 157–8 below.

THE TAMING OF THE SHREW

[INDUCTION 1] *Enter* CHRISTOPHER SLY *and the* HOSTESS.

SLY I'll feeze you, in faith.

HOSTESS A pair of stocks, you rogue!

SLY Y'are a baggage, the Slys are no rogues. Look in the Chronicles; we came in with Richard Conqueror. Therefore *paucas pallabris*, let the world slide. Sessa! 5

HOSTESS You will not pay for the glasses you have burst?

SLY No, not a denier. Go by, Saint Jeronimy, go to thy cold bed and warm thee.

Induction 1] *Pope; Actus Primus. Scœna Prima.* F   0 SD *Enter...*HOSTESS] *Rowe subst.; Enter Begger and Hostes, Christophero Sly.* F   1 SH SLY] *Rowe; Begger.* F *(subsequently / Beg.)*

Induction, Scene 1

INDUCTION 1 F's act and scene divisions are incomplete; see collation. This edition follows standard practice from Steevens onwards. Pope was the first editor to call the two Sly scenes an 'Induction'; see pp. 10–11, 30–6 above for a discussion of this convention.

0 SD *Enter...*HOSTESS F reads *Enter Begger and Hostes, Christophero Sly*; see Textual Analysis, pp. 156–7 below, for the implications of this redundancy. *A Shrew*, which often has fuller stage directions than *The Shrew*, reads *Enter a Tapster, beating out of his doores Slie Droonken*, and this gives a good impression of the usual stage practice.

1 SH •SLY F reads *Begger* (centred) for Sly's first speech heading and *Beg.* for all subsequent ones in these two scenes. (See Induction 2.16–18 and n. for the accuracy of this description.) He names himself first in the swaggering, mock-Spanish form 'Christophero Sly' and then as plain 'Christopher Sly' in Induction 2.5 and 15.

1 feeze you fix you, do for you.

2 A...stocks The Hostess calls for the stocks as a suitable punishment for Sly.

3 baggage good-for-nothing woman, prostitute.

3 Look...Chronicles Sly's attempt to impress the Hostess by claiming aristocratic descent ironically anticipates the deception that is to be practised on him.

3 Chronicles A vague reference to historical chronicles such as those written by Hall (1548) and Holinshed (1577).

4 Richard Conqueror Sly's error for William. His confusion of the two names curiously recalls the

anecdote recorded by John Manningham about Richard Burbage and William Shakespeare; see p. 8 above.

4 *paucas pallabris* few words; a common corruption of the Spanish *pocas palabras*, also found in the shortened form *palabras* in *Ado* 3.5.16. Sly may be recalling in a rather befuddled way Kyd's *The Spanish Tragedy* 3.14.118 where Hieronimo (one of the most famous stage characters of the age) warns himself to be discreet about his revenge, saying '*Pocas Palabras*, mild as the Lamb'. See 7 n.

5 slide pass, go by. A sentiment repeated by Sly at Induction 2.140.

5 Sessa! Be quiet (?), be off with you (?). An expression of unknown origin used twice by Edgar in *Lear*, having apparently the former meaning at *Lear* 3.4.100 and the latter at *Lear* 3.6.74.

7 denier Small French coin of very low value.

7 Go...Jeronimy A misquotation from *The Spanish Tragedy* 3.12.31 (see 4 n.) where Hieronimo's warning to himself includes the words 'Hieronimo, beware; go by; go by.' These words became a popular catch-phrase but Sly's apparent confusion of Hieronimo with Saint Jerome (producing 'Jeronimy') is unusual.

7–8 go...thee Perhaps a reference to another famous line spoken by Hieronimo, 'What out-cries pluck me from my naked bed?' (2.5.1). Curiously, Edgar repeats Sly's line exactly at *Lear* 3.4.48 when he is disguised as Poor Tom. Hibbard suggests that the words may have had some proverbial association with beggars whose 'cold bed' would be the ground (as in 29 below).

[*He lies down.*]

HOSTESS I know my remedy; I must go fetch the thirdborough.[*Exit*]

SLY Third, or fourth, or fifth borough, I'll answer him by law. I'll not   10
budge an inch, boy. Let him come, and kindly.

He falls asleep.

Wind horns. Enter a LORD *from hunting, with his train* [*of*
HUNTSMEN *and* SERVINGMEN].

LORD Huntsman, I charge thee, tender well my hounds.
    Breathe Merriman – the poor cur is embossed –
    And couple Clowder with the deep-mouthed brach.
    Saw'st thou not, boy, how Silver made it good   15
    At the hedge corner, in the coldest fault?
    I would not lose the dog for twenty pound.

1 HUNTSMAN Why, Belman is as good as he, my lord;
    He cried upon it at the merest loss,
    And twice today picked out the dullest scent.   20
    Trust me, I take him for the better dog.

LORD Thou art a fool. If Echo were as fleet
    I would esteem him worth a dozen such.

---

8 SD *He...down*] *Eds.; not in* F   9 thirdborough] *Pope², conj. Theobald;* Headborough F, *Oliver*   9 SD *Exit*] *Rowe; not in* F   13 Breathe] *Sisson, Hibbard, Morris, Oliver;* Brach F, *Bond, Riverside;* Leech *Hanmer;* Trash *Dyce;* Broach *NS*   18, 26 SH 1 HUNTSMAN] *Capell subst.;* Hunts. F

8 SD *He...down* There is no stage direction in F at this point but the dialogue requires it. Stage directions in F are sparse and sometimes obscure: see collation, and Textual Analysis, pp. 156–8 below.

9 *thirdborough officer or constable. F's 'Headborough' has the same meaning but Sly's reply justifies the emendation suggested by Theobald in *Shakespeare Restored*, 1726. He commented 'The Author intended but a poor Witticism and even That is lost.'

10 by law in the courts (?). An uncommon usage of the phrase.

11 boy A contemptuous form of address to a servant or inferior. This is the only example in Shakespeare of it being applied to a woman, so perhaps it is another drunken error. *A Shrew* however has a male Tapster instead of a female Hostess which may indicate the original casting.

11 kindly by all means (ironic).

11 SD.2 *Wind horns* Blow the horns (imperative). There are only three other imperative stage directions in F, *Sound trumpets* at 69 below and two in 5.1, *Knock* (12) and *Kneele* (87). See Textual Analysis, p. 157 below, for a discussion of their significance.

12–25 This short discussion of hunting bears a close resemblance to *MND* 4.1.103–26. See also Induction 2.43–4 n.

13 *Breathe Give a breathing space to; see *OED* sv 13. F's 'Brach' (meaning 'bitch-hound') leaves the clause without a verb, and a dog called 'Merriman' is unlikely to be a bitch. It is easy to imagine a copyist or compositor mistakenly picking up 'brach' from the end of the following line, so I follow C. J. Sisson's suggestion that we emend to 'Breathe' (*New Readings*, p. 159). That this makes good sense in the context is supported by the following *OED* entry under Emboss *v²* 3: 'Who so hunteth unbreathed hounds...in hot weather, causeth them to imbost and surbate greatly', Sir Thomas Cokaine, *A Short Treatise of Hunting* (1590).

13 embossed foaming at the mouth as a result of hard running; see previous note.

15 made it good found the (lost) scent.

16 in...fault at the point at which the scent was most nearly lost.

19 cried...loss discovered and cried out upon the right scent when it seemed completely lost.

But sup them well, and look unto them all:
Tomorrow I intend to hunt again.   25

1 HUNTSMAN I will, my lord.

LORD What's here? One dead, or drunk? See, doth he breathe?

2 HUNTSMAN He breathes, my lord. Were he not warmed with ale,
This were a bed but cold to sleep so soundly.

LORD O monstrous beast, how like a swine he lies!   30
Grim death, how foul and loathsome is thine image!
Sirs, I will practise on this drunken man.
What think you, if he were conveyed to bed,
Wrapped in sweet clothes, rings put upon his fingers,
A most delicious banquet by his bed,   35
And brave attendants near him when he wakes –
Would not the beggar then forget himself?

1 HUNTSMAN Believe me, lord, I think he cannot choose.

2 HUNTSMAN It would seem strange unto him when he waked –

LORD Even as a flatt'ring dream or worthless fancy.   40
Then take him up, and manage well the jest.
Carry him gently to my fairest chamber
And hang it round with all my wanton pictures;
Balm his foul head in warm distillèd waters
And burn sweet wood to make the lodging sweet;   45
Procure me music ready when he wakes
To make a dulcet and a heavenly sound;
And if he chance to speak, be ready straight
And with a low submissive reverence
Say, 'What is it your honour will command?'   50

28–9 He...soundly] *As verse, Rowe; as prose,* F

31 **image** likeness. This comparison is frequent in Shakespeare; compare *Mac.* 2.3.75–7: 'Malcolm awake! / Shake off this downy sleep, death's counterfeit / And look on death itself!'

32 **practise on** play a trick on.

34 **sweet clothes** This probably means 'sweet-smelling' or 'perfumed', as in *WT* 4.4.249–50: 'Come, you promis'd me a tawdry-lace and a pair of sweet gloves.'

36 **brave** finely dressed.

42–58 This detailed evocation of the luxurious lifestyle of a country gentleman can be compared with Gremio's description of his well-furnished houses at 2.1.335–48. Sly will 'forget himself' when he is endowed with these comforts while Katherina's transformation depends on her being deprived of them (see 4.1 and 4.3).

43 **wanton pictures** See Induction 2.45–56 and n.

44 **Balm** Bathe, anoint.

44 **distillèd** concentrated, perfumed. Compare the rose-water at 52 below.

45 **sweet wood** Juniper, which gives off a sweet smell when burning, was often used for this purpose.

46 **music** Not just an entertainment but a cure for distraction, as in *Lear* 4.7 and *Per.* 5.1. See also Appendix 3, pp. 186–8 below, for a general discussion of music in this play.

47 **heavenly** To be taken literally, i.e. the music will imitate that of the spheres. Compare *MV* 5.1.60–5.

49 **reverence** bow, curtsy; see *OED sv sb²*.

Let one attend him with a silver basin
Full of rose-water and bestrewed with flowers;
Another bear the ewer, the third a diaper,
And say, 'Will't please your lordship cool your hands?'
Some one be ready with a costly suit   55
And ask him what apparel he will wear;
Another tell him of his hounds and horse,
And that his lady mourns at his disease.
Persuade him that he hath been lunatic,
And when he says he is, say that he dreams,   60
For he is nothing but a mighty lord.
This do, and do it kindly, gentle sirs.
It will be pastime passing excellent,
If it be husbanded with modesty.

1 HUNTSMAN My lord, I warrant you we will play our part   65
As he shall think by our true diligence
He is no less than what we say he is.

LORD Take him up gently and to bed with him,
And each one to his office when he wakes.

[Sly is carried off]

Sound trumpets.

Sirrah, go see what trumpet 'tis that sounds.   70

[Exit Servingman]

Belike some noble gentleman that means,
Travelling some journey, to repose him here.

Enter Servingman.

How now? Who is it?

SERVINGMAN   An't please your honour, players
That offer service to your lordship.

---

60 he is, say] F, *Bond, Riverside, Morris, Oliver;* he is poor, say *Rowe;* he's Sly, say *Johnson;* he is Sly, say *NS, Hibbard*
69 SD.1 *Sly...off*] *Theobald subst.; not in* F   70 SD *Exit Servingman*] *Theobald; not in* F

53 ewer jug, pitcher.

53 diaper towel, napkin.

58 disease disorder (in this case mental rather than physical).

60 when...is i.e. when he says he must be mad now. This F reading is awkward, but tolerable. Some editors emend to 'when he says he is poor' or 'when he says he is Sly'; see collation.

62 kindly naturally, with conviction.

63 passing surpassingly, extremely.

64 husbanded with modesty managed with moderation.

66 As So that.

69 to his office perform his duty, role.

69 SD.1 *Sly...off* Again F has no stage directions but this is clearly required by the action and *A Shrew* has *Exeunt two with Slie* at this point.

73 An't If it.

73 players i.e. an itinerant troup of actors like those who arrive in Elsinore (*Ham.* 2.2). There may be a topical reference here as the text of *The Shrew* may date from a time (1592–4) when the London acting companies were forced to tour the provinces since plague had closed the theatres.

LORD Bid them come near.

Enter PLAYERS.

                         Now, fellows, you are welcome.   75

PLAYERS We thank your honour.

LORD Do you intend to stay with me tonight?

1 PLAYER So please your lordship to accept our duty.

LORD With all my heart. This fellow I remember

      Since once he played a farmer's eldest son –   80

      'Twas where you wooed the gentlewoman so well –

      I have forgot your name, but sure that part

      Was aptly fitted and naturally performed.

2 PLAYER I think 'twas Soto that your honour means.

LORD 'Tis very true; thou didst it excellent.   85

      Well, you are come to me in happy time,

      The rather for I have some sport in hand

      Wherein your cunning can assist me much.

      There is a lord will hear you play tonight –

      But I am doubtful of your modesties,   90

      Lest over-eyeing of his odd behaviour

---

75 SD *Enter* PLAYERS] *Follows 74 in* F   78 SH 1 PLAYER] *Hibbard;* 2 *Player.* F; *A Player* / *Eds.*   84 SH 2 PLAYER] *Morris; Sincklo.* F; *Sim.* F3; *Play* / *Hanmer;* 1 *Player* / *Capell*

78 SH *1 PLAYER F allots this speech to 2.*Player* although the First Player has not spoken. See Textual Analysis, pp. 156–8 below.

78 So please If it please.

80 Since once When, the time when. Compare *MND* 2.1.148–9: 'Thou rememb'rest / Since once I sat upon a promontory.'

83 aptly fitted well suited, well played.

83 naturally performed Like Hamlet (*Ham.* 3.2.1–45), the Lord seems to favour a 'natural' style of acting. See also Induction 2.52.

84 SH *2 PLAYER F reads *Sincklo* for the speech heading here, referring apparently to John Sincklo, an actor with the King's Men, whose name also occurs in the 1600 quarto of *2H4* at 5.4.1, where he plays the Beadle, and in the Folio text of *3H6* at 3.1.1, where he plays a forester. He also played various parts in Part 2 of *The Seven Deadly Sins* (probably acted by Strange's Men, 1590–2) and he appears in the Induction added by Webster to Marston's *Malcontent* in 1604. See Allison Gaw, 'John Sincklo as one of Shakespeare's actors', *Anglia* 49 (1926), 289–303.

84 Soto In conjunction with the speech heading 'Sincklo' this is confusing because, although there is a character called Soto who is a 'farmer's eldest

son' in Fletcher's *Women Pleased*, that play was not written or acted until about 1620 by which time Sincklo, if he had not retired from the stage (his name is not included in the list of the Principal Actors of the King's Men given in the First Folio of Shakespeare in 1623), would surely have been too old for the part. This has led some editors of *Shr.* to suppose that the lines must be a late addition, but *Women Pleased* may be a red herring altogether, since in the text that we have Soto does not carry out his plan to 'woo the gentlewoman'. Either the Lord's memory is at fault (which seems unlikely if we are also to assume that this is a topical reference inserted at a later date) or the reference is to an earlier (lost) play on which Fletcher's was based; the latter assumption would be more consistent with the casting of Sincklo.

86 in happy time just at the right time.

87 The rather for More especially because.

88 cunning skill.

90 doubtful...modesties uncertain whether you can control yourselves.

91 over-eyeing observing, catching sight of. Perhaps with the sense of 'eyeing excessively', 'staring'.

(For yet his honour never heard a play)
You break into some merry passion
And so offend him; for I tell you, sirs,
If you should smile, he grows impatient.   95
1 PLAYER Fear not, my lord, we can contain ourselves
Were he the veriest antic in the world.
LORD Go, sirrah, take them to the buttery
And give them friendly welcome every one.
Let them want nothing that my house affords.   100

                    Exit one with the Players

Sirrah, go you to Barthol'mew my page
And see him dressed in all suits like a lady.
That done, conduct him to the drunkard's chamber,
And call him 'madam', do him obeisance.
Tell him from me – as he will win my love –   105
He bear himself with honourable action
Such as he hath observed in noble ladies
Unto their lords, by them accomplishèd.
Such duty to the drunkard let him do
With soft low tongue and lowly courtesy,   110
And say, 'What is't your honour will command
Wherein your lady and your humble wife
May show her duty and make known her love?'
And then with kind embracements, tempting kisses,
And with declining head into his bosom,   115
Bid him shed tears, as being overjoyed
To see her noble lord restored to health,
Who for this seven years hath esteemèd him

---

96 SH 1 PLAYER] *Capell subst.; Plai.* F   118 this] F; *twice Theobald*

---

93 merry passion fit of merriment. ('Passion' is trisyllabic.)

97 veriest antic most extreme eccentric, oddest fellow.

98 buttery pantry, kitchen store-room.

100 want lack.

100 affords offers.

101–2 The Lord is of course following the stage convention whereby all female parts were played by boys. The situation becomes multi-layered as we prepare to watch 'amateur' actors accompanying Sly at a professional performance; see p. 31 above.

102 see him dressed arrange for him to be dressed.

102 in all suits in all respects (with a pun on 'suit').

105 as...love if he wants to be sure of winning my love.

106 He...action He behave in a dignified manner (appropriate to one of honourable rank).

108 accomplishèd performed, carried out.

110 soft low tongue Compare *Lear* 5.3.273–4, 'Her voice was ever soft / Gentle and low, an excellent thing in woman.'

118 seven years A common time-span in folklore and fairy tale, with perhaps a glance at the 'seven lean years' of Pharaoh's dream. Theobald emended 'this seven' to 'twice seven' in order to achieve consistency with Induction 2.75, but this seems unnecessary.

118 esteemèd him thought himself.

No better than a poor and loathsome beggar.
And if the boy have not a woman's gift   120
To rain a shower of commanded tears,
An onion will do well for such a shift,
Which in a napkin being close conveyed
Shall in despite enforce a watery eye.
See this dispatched with all the haste thou canst;   125
Anon I'll give thee more instructions.

Exit a Servingman

I know the boy will well usurp the grace,
Voice, gait and action of a gentlewoman.
I long to hear him call the drunkard 'husband',
And how my men will stay themselves from laughter   130
When they do homage to this simple peasant.
I'll in to counsel them. Haply my presence
May well abate the over-merry spleen
Which otherwise would grow into extremes.

[Exeunt]

[INDUCTION 2] *Enter aloft* [SLY] *with* ATTENDANTS – *some with apparel, basin and ewer, and other appurtenances* – *and* LORD.

SLY For God's sake, a pot of small ale!
1 SERVINGMAN Will't please your lordship drink a cup of sack?

134 SD *Exeunt*] *Gentleman; not in* F; *exit Lord* / *Theobald*   Induction 2] *Capell; no scene division in* F
0 SD.1 SLY] *Rowe; the drunkard* F   1 SH SLY] *Rowe; Beg.* F *(throughout)*   2 lordship] Q; Lord F

121 **commanded** forced, calculated. (See
1.1.78–9 and n.)
122 **An...shift** An onion will be a suitable
expedient (for producing the tears). Perhaps onions
really were used by the less competent actors?
123 **close** secretly.
124 **in despite** i.e. against nature.
127 **usurp** assume, feign.
128 **gait and action** walk and bodily movements.
130 **And how** And (to see) how.
133 **over-merry spleen** excessive impulse to
merriment. The spleen was regarded as the seat of
mirth as well as of melancholy and other strong
emotions; compare *LLL* 3.1.75–6: 'By virtue thou
enforcest laughter – thy silly thought my spleen.'
As for why the Lord should fear excess, see p. 11
above.

Induction, Scene 2
0 SD.1 *aloft* Thus F, but it is questionable

whether Elizabethan actors would have used the
gallery over the stage for such an elaborate scene;
see Appendix 2 (pp. 181–5 below) and illustrations
1 and 2 (pp. 4–5 above).
0 SD.2 *apparel...appurtenances* The apparel,
basin and ewer are all specified by the Lord at
Induction 1.51–6. The 'other appurtenances' must
include the sack and conserves offered to Sly and
perhaps one or more of the musical instruments
required at 31.
1 **small ale** The weakest and cheapest kind of
ale.
2 *lordship Q's emendation for F's 'Lord' seems
necessary for sense as well as metre and is confirmed
by Sly's response in 5. See Textual Analysis,
pp. 158–60 below, for a general discussion of
metrical emendations in this text.
2 **sack** Imported sherry or white wine; a more
aristocratic drink. There is a comic contrast of social
levels here: Sly speaks in prose and asks for ale; the
servants reply in verse and offer him sack.

2 SERVINGMAN Will't please your honour taste of these conserves?

3 SERVINGMAN What raiment will your honour wear today?

SLY I am Christophero Sly – call not me 'honour' nor 'lordship'. I ne'er   5
drank sack in my life, and if you give me any conserves, give me
conserves of beef. Ne'er ask me what raiment I'll wear, for I have
no more doublets than backs, no more stockings than legs, nor no
more shoes than feet – nay, sometime more feet than shoes, or such
shoes as my toes look through the overleather.   10

LORD Heaven cease this idle humour in your honour!
     O that a mighty man of such descent,
     Of such possessions and so high esteem,
     Should be infusèd with so foul a spirit!

SLY What, would you make me mad? Am not I Christopher Sly, old   15
Sly's son of Burton-heath, by birth a pedlar, by education a
cardmaker, by transmutation a bear-herd, and now by present
profession a tinker? Ask Marian Hacket, the fat ale-wife of Wincot,
if she know me not. If she say I am not fourteen pence on the score
for sheer ale, score me up for the lying'st knave in Christendom.   20
What, I am not bestraught! Here's –

19 fourteen pence] *Rowe;* xiiii.d. F

3 **conserves** candied fruits.

5 **Christophero** Presumably a swaggering
(mock-Spanish) version of his name. The author of
A Shrew imitates this effect by having his Sly say
(at a later point) 'am not I *Don Christo Vary?*'
(scene xvi, 48).

7 **conserves of beef** salt-beef (contrasting with
the candied fruits as the ale does with the sack).

10 **overleather** leather uppers.

11 **idle humour** empty fantasy, vain aberration.
The Elizabethans believed that the relative propor-
tions of the four humours (blood, phlegm, choler
and melancholy or black choler) determined a
person's physical or mental health.

14 **infusèd...spirit** filled with such horrible
delusions, possessed by such an evil spirit. For other
examples of this kind of 'infusion' see *MV* 4.1.130–8
and *Mac.* 1.5.26 and 40–50. There could also be a
literal meaning, with 'foul spirit' referring to the
inferior ale Sly had been drinking.

16–18 **Burton-heath...Wincot** Barton-on-the-
Heath and Wincot are both villages near Stratford-
upon-Avon, and it seems that there were some
people called Hacket living at Wincot in 1591
(Sidney Lee, *Life of William Shakespeare*, 1898, pp.
236–7). In addition to 'Marian' here, 'Cicely
Hacket' is mentioned below at 85. Shakespeare is
establishing Sly's 'low-life' background by these

unusual direct references to his own native
Warwickshire. Modern productions sometimes
substitute their own local references.

16–18 **pedlar...tinker** Sly clearly does not see
himself as a beggar, though he has not been in very
steady employment. Autolycus in *WT* has had a
similar career in marginal occupations, since he is
a pedlar when we meet him and by his own comic
account he has been 'an ape-bearer...and married
a tinker's wife' (*WT* 4.3.95–7).

17 **cardmaker** Maker of iron 'cards' or combs
used for separating wool fibres before spinning.
(The woollen industry was very important in
Warwickshire in Shakespeare's time.)

17 **bear-herd** Man who led a performing bear
around the country.

18 **ale-wife** Woman who kept an ale-house.

19 **on the score** in debt. Originally debts would
be scored or notched up on the ale-wife's stick.

20 **sheer ale** just for ale (apart from other goods
or services).

20 **score...for** chalk me up as. Sly is punning
on the meanings of 'score'.

21 **bestraught** distracted, mad.

21 **Here's –** Sly breaks off, perhaps suddenly
realising that he cannot in fact point to any proof
of his identity.

3 SERVINGMAN O, this it is that makes your lady mourn.

2 SERVINGMAN O, this is it that makes your servants droop.

LORD Hence comes it that your kindred shuns your house

As beaten hence by your strange lunacy.   25

O noble lord, bethink thee of thy birth.

Call home thy ancient thoughts from banishment,

And banish hence these abject lowly dreams.

Look how thy servants do attend on thee,

Each in his office ready at thy beck.   30

Wilt thou have music? Hark, Apollo plays,   *Music*

And twenty cagèd nightingales do sing.

Or wilt thou sleep? We'll have thee to a couch

Softer and sweeter than the lustful bed

On purpose trimmed up for Semiramis.   35

Say thou wilt walk, we will bestrow the ground.

Or wilt thou ride? Thy horses shall be trapped,

Their harness studded all with gold and pearl.

Dost thou love hawking? Thou hast hawks will soar

Above the morning lark. Or wilt thou hunt?   40

Thy hounds shall make the welkin answer them

And fetch shrill echoes from the hollow earth.

1 SERVINGMAN Say thou wilt course, thy greyhounds are as swift

As breathèd stags, ay, fleeter than the roe.

2 SERVINGMAN Dost thou love pictures? We will fetch thee straight   45

Adonis painted by a running brook,

---

22 SH 3 SERVINGMAN The speech headings in F change from 1.*Ser.* etc. to 1.*Man.* etc. here. See general discussion of speech headings in Textual Analysis, pp. 156–8 below.

27 ancient thoughts former attitudes, i.e. original sanity.

30 beck nod, summons.

31 Apollo Greek god of music, associated especially with stringed instruments; compare *LLL* 4.3.339–40: '...as sweet and musical / As bright Apollo's lute, strung with his hair'.

35 Semiramis Legendary Assyrian queen, famous for her voluptuousness. Shakespeare refers to her only here and in *Tit.* 2.1.22 and 2.3.118.

36 bestrow scatter – presumably with rushes or flowers. Compare 4.1.32.

37 trapped covered with decorated trappings.

41–2 hounds...earth The musical quality of the cry made by a pack of hounds was clearly an important aspect of the pleasures of hunting for the Elizabethans. Compare *MND* 4.1.103–26, where Theseus describes such an effect in detail.

41 welkin sky. This term, which is perhaps

deliberately high-flown, may have prompted the author of *A Shrew* to recall the Marlovian lines about 'dimming the welkin' which he borrows for his opening scene; see Textual Analysis, p. 164 below.

43 course hunt the hare.

44 breathèd well-exercised, in good wind. See Induction 1.13 n.

45–56 These are presumably the 'wanton pictures' mentioned by the Lord at Induction 1.43. The subjects are ultimately derived from Ovid's *Metamorphoses*, a common source of erotic stimulation, as can also be seen in Marlowe's *Edward II* (1.1.50–70), where Gaveston proposes to seduce the king by having his men act out episodes from Ovid such as that of Diana and Actaeon. See pp. 8–9 above for a general discussion of Ovidian influence in this play.

45 straight immediately.

46 Adonis A beautiful youth loved by Venus (Cytherea); he was killed by a boar while hunting – see Ovid, *Met.* x, 520–739. Shakespeare's own poem on the subject was published in 1593.

And Cytherea all in sedges hid,
Which seem to move and wanton with her breath
Even as the waving sedges play wi'th'wind.

LORD We'll show thee Io as she was a maid,   50
And how she was beguilèd and surprised,
As lively painted as the deed was done.

3 SERVINGMAN Or Daphne roaming through a thorny wood,
Scratching her legs that one shall swear she bleeds,
And at that sight shall sad Apollo weep,   55
So workmanly the blood and tears are drawn.

LORD Thou art a lord, and nothing but a lord.
Thou hast a lady far more beautiful
Than any woman in this waning age.

1 SERVINGMAN And till the tears that she hath shed for thee   60
Like envious floods o'er-run her lovely face,
She was the fairest creature in the world –
And yet she is inferior to none.

SLY Am I a lord, and have I such a lady?
Or do I dream? Or have I dreamed till now?   65
I do not sleep: I see, I hear, I speak,

---

49 wi'th'wind] *Alexander;* with winde F

47 **Cytherea...hid** This incident does not occur in Ovid's account of Venus and Adonis, though there is a similar episode in his account of Salmacis and Hermaphroditus (*Met.* IV, 347–481). Hibbard suggests Spenser's *Faerie Queene*, III, 1.34–8 as a source.

49 **sedges** This repetition of the word from 47 may indicate faulty copy; see Textual Analysis, p. 161 below.

49 **wi'th'wind** For similar elisions see *Rom.* 1.3.32 'wi'th'dug' and *Temp.* 1.1.63 'wi'th'King'. Shakespeare seems to have used such forms without apostrophes; see *STM*, Hand D, 11, 17, 51, 75.

50 **Io** Io was raped by Jove who concealed himself in a dense mist. Afterwards he turned her into a heifer (Ovid, *Met.* I, 588–600).

53 **Daphne** Daphne escaped being raped by Apollo by being turned into a laurel tree as she fled from him (Ovid. *Met.* I, 452–67).

55–6 The compression here puts Apollo both inside and outside the picture. Shakespeare praises naturalistic representation of this kind in *The Rape of Lucrece* 1366 ff. and *Cym.* 2.4.72–6.

56 **workmanly** skilfully, ingeniously.

58 **a lady** The Lord cunningly introduces the topic of Sly's 'wife' as the climax of these descriptions of 'wanton pictures'.

59 **this...age** this decadent or degenerate period. It was held that all human qualities had steadily declined from the perfection of Adam and Eve; see Spenser, *Faerie Queene*, V, Proem 1–9.

61 **o'er-run** Shakespeare often uses 'run' rather than 'ran' as the past tense; compare *Mac.* 2.3.110–11.

63 **yet** still, even so.

64–71 Sly moves from prose into verse under the pressure of his companions. Brian Vickers suggests that 'the oscillations between prose and verse sensitively record the progress of Sly's waking dream' and compares this moment with Eliza Doolittle's switch into 'Received Standard English' in Shaw's *Pygmalion* (*Vickers, Prose*, pp. 13–14). G. N. Murphy has argued that Sly's use of 'thee' and 'thou' at 95 is comic because these polite forms are inappropriate for a lord to use to his servants ('Christopher Sly and the pronoun game in *The Taming of the Shrew*', *Papers on Language and Literature* (Southern Illinois University) 2 (1966), 67–70), but Shakespeare himself is often inconsistent and puzzling in his use of 'thou' and 'you' forms; see Angus McIntosh, '*As You Like It*: a grammatical clue to character', *REL* 4 (1963), 68–81.

66–7 Sly's attempt to discover whether he is awake by checking his senses can be compared with Bottom's awakening in *MND* 4.1.200–19.

I smell sweet savours and I feel soft things.
Upon my life, I am a lord indeed,
And not a tinker, nor Christopher Sly.
Well, bring our lady hither to our sight,   70
And once again a pot o'th'smallest ale.

                                        [*Exit a Servingman*]

2 SERVINGMAN Will't please your mightiness to wash your hands?
    O, how we joy to see your wit restored!
    O, that once more you knew but what you are!
    These fifteen years you have been in a dream,   75
    Or when you waked, so waked as if you slept.
SLY These fifteen years! By my fay, a goodly nap.
    But did I never speak of all that time?
1 SERVINGMAN O yes, my lord, but very idle words,
    For though you lay here in this goodly chamber,   80
    Yet would you say ye were beaten out of door,
    And rail upon the hostess of the house,
    And say you would present her at the leet
    Because she brought stone jugs and no sealed quarts.
    Sometimes you would call out for Cicely Hacket.   85
SLY Ay, the woman's maid of the house.
3 SERVINGMAN Why, sir, you know no house, nor no such maid,
    Nor no such men as you have reckoned up,
    As Stephen Sly and old John Naps of Greece,

---

69 Christopher] F, *Riverside, Oliver;* Christophero F2, *Bond, NS, Hibbard, Morris*   71 SD *Exit a Servingman*] *This edn; not in* F   89 of Greece] F; o'th'Green *Hanmer;* of Greete *conj. Halliwell*

---

69 Christopher Many editors follow F2 in printing 'Christophero' here but the metre does not really require this correction.

71 SD There is no stage direction in F here, but someone must leave at some point to fetch Sly's ale. It is possible that he has been drinking from an earlier point in the scene: Hibbard generously gives him his ale at 20 and interprets 71 as a request for a refill rather than a repetition of the original request. I assume from his remarks at 95–7 that he does not actually get it until then, though the servingmen may have been plying him with sack.

73 wit intelligence, sanity.

75 fifteen years The servingman improves boldly upon the 'seven years' suggested by his master at Induction 1.118.

77 fay faith.

78 of in.

79 idle meaningless, mad.

83 present…leet bring her to trial at the manorial (i.e. small, local) court.

84 sealed quarts Measures officially sealed as proof that they contained the correct quantity. Sly's complaint seems to be that the stone jugs held less – or perhaps that they were deceptive because they included froth.

85 Cicely Hacket See 16–18 n. We must assume that the servingmen are relying on their own local knowledge for the details here and in 89–90, or perhaps that Sly mentioned the names while he was off stage with them.

89 John Naps of Greece It has been claimed that Greek mercenary soldiers did make their way as far as England in the sixteenth century and that 'Naps', which is not an English surname, could be a corruption of Yannopoulos or Papayannopoulos (Terence Spencer, 'Three Shakespearean notes', *MLR* 49 (1954), 48–9). Many editors, however, have taken 'Greece' to be a misreading of 'Greet', the name of a village near Stratford. In this case 'John Naps' might be a pun on 'Jackanapes' meaning 'trickster' or 'ridiculous fellow'.

And Peter Turph and Henry Pimpernell,   90
And twenty more such names and men as these,
Which never were, nor no man ever saw.
SLY Now Lord be thankèd for my good amends!
ALL Amen.

Enter [BARTHOLOMEW, *a page, dressed as a*] *lady, with*
ATTENDANTS, [*one of whom gives Sly a pot of ale*].

SLY I thank thee, thou shalt not lose by it.   95
BARTHOLOMEW How fares my noble lord?
SLY Marry, I fare well, for here is cheer enough. [*He drinks.*] Where
    is my wife?
BARTHOLOMEW Here, noble lord, what is thy will with her?
SLY Are you my wife, and will not call me 'husband'?   100
    My men should call me 'lord'; I am your goodman.
BARTHOLOMEW My husband and my lord, my lord and husband,
    I am your wife in all obedience.
SLY I know it well – What must I call her?
LORD 'Madam.'   105
SLY 'Al'ce madam' or 'Joan madam'?
LORD 'Madam' and nothing else. So lords call ladies.
SLY Madam wife, they say that I have dreamed
    And slept above some fifteen year or more.
BARTHOLOMEW Ay, and the time seems thirty unto me,   110
    Being all this time abandoned from your bed.
SLY 'Tis much. Servants, leave me and her alone.

                                          [*Exeunt Servingmen*]

    Madam, undress you and come now to bed.
BARTHOLOMEW Thrice noble lord, let me entreat of you
    To pardon me yet for a night or two,   115

---

94 SD *Enter* BARTHOLOMEW...*ale*] *This edn; Enter Lady with Attendants.* F*; Enter Page as Lady, attended / Capell;
One gives Sly a pot of ale / Hibbard*   96 SH BARTHOLOMEW] *This edn; Lady.* F *(Lady. / or / La. / throughout);
Page / Capell*   97 SD *He drinks*] *Hibbard; not in* F   112 SD *Exeunt Servingmen*] NS *subst.; not in* F

93 **amends** recovery.

94 SD F's stage direction reads simply *Enter Lady
with Attendants* and the speech headings are
consistently *Lady*, but this must be 'Barthol'mew,
my page' (complete with his onion wrapped in a
napkin) as mentioned in Induction 1.101–24. *A
Shrew* has *Enter the boy in Womans attire.*

97 **cheer enough** Sly puns on 'fare' meaning
food and drink. Compare 4.3.37.

101 **goodman** husband. A homely term,
inappropriate for a lord, as the names Sly suggests

in 106, Al'ce and Joan, are inappropriate for a
lady.

103 **I...obedience** An ironic foreshadowing of
the main theme of the taming plot.

111 **abandoned** banished.

112 SD F has no stage direction here but the
servingmen should probably obey Sly's command,
leaving just the Lord and Bartholomew to watch the
play with him. Hibbard suggests that the Lord also
leaves but returns immediately in the role of the
Messenger.

Or, if not so, until the sun be set.
For your physicians have expressly charged,
In peril to incur your former malady,
That I should yet absent me from your bed.
I hope this reason stands for my excuse.   120

SLY Ay, it stands so that I may hardly tarry so long, but I would be
loath to fall into my dreams again. I will therefore tarry in despite
of the flesh and the blood.

Enter a MESSENGER.

MESSENGER Your honour's players, hearing your amendment,
Are come to play a pleasant comedy;   125
For so your doctors hold it very meet,
Seeing too much sadness hath congealed your blood
And melancholy is the nurse of frenzy –
Therefore they thought it good you hear a play
And frame your mind to mirth and merriment,   130
Which bars a thousand harms and lengthens life.

SLY Marry, I will. Let them play it. Is not a comonty a Christmas
gambold or a tumbling trick?

BARTHOLOMEW No, my good lord, it is more pleasing stuff.

SLY What, household stuff?   135

BARTHOLOMEW It is a kind of history.

---

123 SD *Enter a* MESSENGER] F; *Enter the Lord as a Messenger / Hibbard*   132 will. Let them play it. Is not] *Capell subst.*; will let them play, it is not F

118 **In…incur** Because of the danger of reviving.

120 **reason stands** Both words have sexual connotations to do with the 'raising' or erection of the penis; see Kökeritz, *Pronunciation*, p. 139, and Partridge, *Bawdy*. This meaning is confirmed by Sly's reply and is usually emphasised by stage business.

126–31 When discussing cures in *The Anatomy of Melancholy* (1621), Robert Burton says 'Dancing, Singing, Masking, Mumming, Stage-plays, howsoever they be heavily censured by some severe Catos, yet, if opportunely and soberly used, may justly be approved', though he goes on to extol study as the best recreation or distraction (ed. A. R. Shilleto, 3 vols., 1893, II, 97–100).

126 **meet** appropriate.

127–8 Melancholy was thought to result literally from a thickening of the blood; compare *John* 3.3.42–3: 'Or if that surly spirit, melancholy, / Had bak'd the blood and made it heavy, thick'. Like the

reference to Sly's 'idle humour' in 11 and to his being 'infused with so foul a spirit' in 14, the technical terms here are perhaps being used in order to blind Sly with science and convince him he really has been distracted.

128 **nurse** nourisher.

131 **bars** prevents, wards off.

132 **Marry…comonty** Capell's emended punctuation makes much better sense than F.

132 **comonty** Sly's error for 'comedy'. In *A Shrew* it is, less aptly, one of the players who says 'comoditie' for 'comedy'.

133 **gambold** game, frolic.

133 **tumbling trick** performance of balancing or acrobatics.

135 **household stuff** Literally 'furnishings', with perhaps a pun on the obscene sense of 'to stuff' meaning 'to have intercourse (with a woman)'; see Partridge, *Bawdy*.

136 **history** story (either factual or fictional).

SLY Well, we'll see't.

                                              [*Exit Messenger*]
Come, madam wife, sit by my side,
And let the world slip. We shall ne'er be younger.
             [*They sit down.*]
             [*A flourish of trumpets to announce the play.*]

[1.1] *Enter* LUCENTIO *and his man* TRANIO.

LUCENTIO Tranio, since for the great desire I had
             To see fair Padua, nursery of arts,
             I am arrived for fruitful Lombardy,
             The pleasant garden of great Italy,
             And by my father's love and leave am armed   5
             With his good will and thy good company –
             My trusty servant well approved in all –
             Here let us breathe and haply institute
             A course of learning and ingenuous studies.
             Pisa renownèd for grave citizens   10

137–9 Well...younger] *As verse,* F; *as prose, Pope*   137 SD *Exit Messenger*] *Eds.; not in* F   139 SD.1 *They...down*]
Capell subst.; not in F   139 SD.2 *A flourish...play*] *Alexander subst.; Flourish* F   **Act 1, Scene 1**   1.1] *Pope; no scene
division in* F   0 SD TRANIO] F2; *Triano* F   9 ingenuous] *This edn, conj. Johnson;* ingenious F

137–9 Lineation as in F. Some editors print as
prose (Brian Vickers comments on the appropriate-
ness of Sly's being 'left at the end of the scene in
prose', *Prose*, p. 14), but the last line seems a good
pentameter to me. See Textual Analysis, p. 155
below, for a general discussion of lineation
problems.

Act 1, Scene 1
1 **for** because of.
2 **Padua...arts** Padua was famous for its
ancient university; compare *MV* 4.1, where the
Duke sends for advice from the learned doctor
Bellario in Padua. It was also renowned as a 'citadel
of common sense against the new mythology [of
witchcraft]' (H. R. Trevor-Roper, *The European
Witch-Craze of the 16th and 17th Centuries*, 1969,
pp. 58–61), thus contrasting with Ephesus, which
had a reputation for magic and sorcery; see *Err.*
1.2.97–102, and p. 7 above.
3 **am arrived for** have arrived in.
3–4 **Lombardy...Italy** This expression may
derive from John Florio's manual for the study of
Italian, *Second Fruites* (1591), where he says 'La

Lombardia è il giardino del mondo.' It became
proverbial (Tilley L414). Shakespeare used Florio's
manuals for the Italian words and phrases in this
scene and the next (see 25 n.) and may even have
known him personally; see Mario Praz, 'Shakespeare's Italy', *S.Sur.* 7 (1954), 95–106.
7 **well...all** proved by experience to be good in
all respects.
8 **breathe** pause, settle down for a while.
8 **haply institute** perhaps begin.
9 *•ingenuous* F reads 'ingenious' here and all
editors follow, though Johnson commented 'I
rather think it was written *ingenuous studies* but of
this and a thousand such observations there is little
certainty.' His reading has recently been supported
by Stanley Wells, who points out that the two words
were spelt identically in the Elizabethan period and
that the meaning here is 'befitting a well-born
person, liberal', which *OED* gives as an obsolete
sense of 'ingenuous' (Wells, p. 12).
10 **Pisa...citizens** This line is repeated
precisely at 4.2.95. Perhaps it is a parody of this sort
of tag and, in the context, a joke: Lucentio is glad
to be away from all those *grave* citizens.

Gave me my being and my father first,
A merchant of great traffic through the world,
Vincentio, come of the Bentivolii.
Vincentio's son, brought up in Florence,
It shall become to serve all hopes conceived   15
To deck his fortune with his virtuous deeds.
And therefore, Tranio, for the time I study,
Virtue and that part of philosophy
Will I apply that treats of happiness
By virtue specially to be achieved.   20
Tell me thy mind, for I have Pisa left
And am to Padua come as he that leaves
A shallow plash to plunge him in the deep
And with satiety seeks to quench his thirst.

TRANIO *Mi perdonato*, gentle master mine,   25
I am in all affected as yourself,
Glad that you thus continue your resolve
To suck the sweets of sweet philosophy.
Only, good master, while we do admire
This virtue and this moral discipline,   30
Let's be no stoics nor no stocks, I pray,
Or so devote to Aristotle's checks
As Ovid be an outcast quite abjured.

13 Vincentio] *Hanmer;* Vincentio's F   14 brought] Q; brough F   24 satiety] *Rowe;* sacietie F   25 *Mi perdonato*]
Capell (Mi perdonate); Me Pardonato F

12 **traffic** business.

13 **Bentivolii** The real Bentivogli were powerful
in Bologna, not Pisa; see Machiavelli, *History of
Florence*, Book 6. Shakespeare abbreviates the name
to Benvolio in *Rom.*

15–16 **to serve... / To deck** to fulfil all
expectations by adorning or complementing.

17–18 **study, / Virtue** Punctuated as in F. Some
editors move the comma to after 'Virtue'.

19 **apply** pursue, apply myself to.

23 **plash** puddle. This picture of a young man
travelling from one part of Italy to another for
education and general profit has obvious similarities
with *TGV* 1.1, where Valentine sets out from
Verona for Milan telling his friend Proteus that
'Home-keeping youth have ever homely wits.'

24 **satiety** F has the obsolete form 'sacietie'
which may have permitted a pun on 'society';
compare *Venus and Adonis* 19.

25 *Mi perdonato* Pardon me (Italian). Other

Italian words and phrases occur at 189 below and
at 1.2.23–5 and 275. They come from John Florio's
First and *Second Fruites* (1578 and 1591) (see above
3–4 n.), as does the Italian sentence in *LLL* 4.2.97–8.
In this play they are confined to Act 1 (apart from
the isolated use of the word 'marcantant' at 4.2.63)
and seem intended to give 'local colour' and
convince us that this is Italy in contrast to the vivid
sketch of rural Warwickshire in the Induction.

26 **affected** disposed.

31 **stocks** blocks of wood, with pun on 'stoics'
meaning people who are indifferent to pleasure.
See Bond 1.1.31 n. for evidence that this pun was
a common one.

32 **checks** restrictions.

33 **Ovid** Not part of the official curriculum
probably. The contrast between Ovid and more
serious studies also occurs in *TGV* 1.1.21–2. See
Induction 2.45–56 n. and pp. 8–9 above for a
general discussion of Ovidian influence in this play.

Balk logic with acquaintance that you have
And practise rhetoric in your common talk;   35
Music and poesy use to quicken you;
The mathematics and the metaphysics –
Fall to them as you find your stomach serves you.
No profit grows where is no pleasure tane:
In brief, sir, study what you most affect.   40
LUCENTIO Gramercies, Tranio, well dost thou advise.
If, Biondello, thou wert come ashore,
We could at once put us in readiness
And take a lodging fit to entertain
Such friends as time in Padua shall beget.   45

Enter BAPTISTA *with his two daughters* KATHERINA *and* BIANCA;
GREMIO, *a pantaloon, and* HORTENSIO, *suitor to Bianca.*

But stay awhile, what company is this?
TRANIO Master, some show to welcome us to town.
                    Lucentio and Tranio stand by.
BAPTISTA Gentlemen, importune me no farther
For how I firmly am resolved you know –
That is, not to bestow my youngest daughter   50

---

45 SD.1 *Enter...*BIANCA] *Follows 47 in* F   45 SD.2 HORTENSIO] F2; *Hortentio* F   45 SD.2 *suitor*] F3; *sister* F
47 SD *Lucentio...by*] *Follows immediately after* SD 'Enter Baptista...Bianca' *in* F

---

34 Balk logic This has usually been taken to mean 'chop logic, engage in formal arguments' (*OED* Balk *v*[1] III 6), though 'balk' could also mean 'avoid' or 'ignore' (*OED* sv *v*[1] II 2).

36 quicken enliven, animate.

38 stomach taste, appetite. The metaphor begins with 'Fall to' which is regularly used in relation to food; compare *R2* 5.5.98: 'My lord, will't please you to fall to?'

39 tane taken. Regularly spelt thus in F and always monosyllabic. The modern editorial practice of printing 'ta'en' makes the derivation more obvious but encourages dissyllabic pronunciation.

40 affect like, prefer.

41 Gramercies Many thanks (Old French *grant merci*).

42 Lucentio addresses the absent Biondello.

42 come ashore Shakespeare implies that inland Padua is a port, like Verona in *TGV* (1.1.53–4, 2.2.14) and Milan in both *TGV* (1.1.71) and *Temp.* (1.2.144–5). Bond informs us about 'the great river-system of Northern Italy' which might have made some of these voyages possible (Bond 1.1.42 n.), but it seems more likely that Shakespeare was

influenced here by his main source for the sub-plot, Gascoigne's *Supposes* (see pp. 14–15 above), where Philogano, the equivalent of Vincentio, describes his journey 'to Ancona, from thence by water to Ravenna, and from Ravenna hither, continually against the tide' (*Supposes* 4.3). Alternatively, Shakespeare may be assuming here (as in *TGV*) the convention of Roman comedy whereby the harbour or port was assumed to be off one side of the stage. Apart from this kind of slip, Shakespeare's sense of Italian geography in this play, as shown in his knowledge of the relative positions of Padua, Mantua, Verona and Venice, is accurate; Mario Praz attributes this to the likelihood that Shakespeare had met merchants from this part of Italy in London ('Shakespeare's Italy', pp. 104–5).

45 SD.2 *pantaloon* ridiculous old man. A stock figure in Italian Renaissance comedy, his role was usually to serve as an obstacle to the young lovers.

47 show play, pageant.

47 SD *Lucentio...by* See p. 31 above for a general discussion of *The Shrew*'s use of stage audiences.

50 bestow give in marriage.

Before I have a husband for the elder.
If either of you both love Katherina,
Because I know you well and love you well,
Leave shall you have to court her at your pleasure.

GREMIO To cart her rather! She's too rough for me.   55
There, there, Hortensio, will you any wife?

KATHERINA [*To Baptista*] I pray you, sir, is it your will
To make a stale of me amongst these mates?

HORTENSIO 'Mates', maid? How mean you that? No mates for you
Unless you were of gentler, milder mould.   60

KATHERINA I'faith, sir, you shall never need to fear.
Iwis it is not halfway to her heart –
But if it were, doubt not her care should be
To comb your noddle with a three-legged stool
And paint your face and use you like a fool.   65

HORTENSIO From all such devils, good Lord deliver us!

GREMIO And me too, good Lord!

TRANIO [*Aside to Lucentio*]
Husht, master, here's some good pastime toward;
That wench is stark mad, or wonderful froward.

LUCENTIO [*Aside to Tranio*] But in the other's silence do I see   70
Maid's mild behaviour and sobriety.
Peace, Tranio.

TRANIO [*Aside to Lucentio*]
Well said, master. Mum! And gaze your fill.

BAPTISTA Gentlemen, that I may soon make good
What I have said – Bianca, get you in.   75
And let it not displease thee, good Bianca,
For I will love thee ne'er the less, my girl.

57 SD *To Baptista*] Capell; *not in* F   59–60 'Mates'...you] *Eds; as three lines in* F *divided after* that *and* for you
68 SD *Aside to Lucentio*] Theobald subst.; *not in* F   70 SD *Aside to Tranio*] Theobald subst.; *not in* F   73 SD *Aside to Lucentio*]
Theobald subst.; *not in* F

55 **cart her** treat her like a convicted prostitute
by drawing her through the streets in an open cart.
(With pun on 'court' in 54.)
58 **stale** The word means 'laughing-stock' as
well as 'prostitute'.
58 **mates** crude fellows. Hortensio in 59
pretends to think she means 'husbands'.
62 **Iwis...heart** Indeed it (marriage) is not even
a half-hearted concern of hers (i.e. mine).
64–5 A rhyming couplet, as in 68–71, 160–1 and

229–34 below; see Textual Analysis, pp. 160–1
below.
64 **comb your noddle** i.e. hit you on the head.
65 **paint** i.e. with blood.
66 Hortensio quotes the standard protective
incantation.
68 **pastime toward** entertainment coming up.
69 **froward** perverse, wilful.
73 **Mum!** Keep quiet.

KATHERINA A pretty peat! It is best put finger in the eye, and she knew
    why.

BIANCA Sister, content you in my discontent.   80
      Sir, to your pleasure humbly I subscribe.
      My books and instruments shall be my company,
      On them to look and practise by myself.

LUCENTIO [*Aside*] Hark, Tranio, thou mayst hear Minerva speak!

HORTENSIO Signor Baptista, will you be so strange?   85
      Sorry am I that our good will effects
      Bianca's grief.

GREMIO   Why will you mew her up,
      Signor Baptista, for this fiend of hell,
      And make her bear the penance of her tongue?

BAPTISTA Gentlemen, content ye. I am resolved.   90
      Go in, Bianca.

                                 [*Exit Bianca*]

      And, for I know she taketh most delight
      In music, instruments and poetry,
      Schoolmasters will I keep within my house
      Fit to instruct her youth. If you, Hortensio,   95
      Or Signor Gremio you, know any such,
      Prefer them hither; for to cunning men
      I will be very kind, and liberal
      To mine own children in good bringing up.
      And so farewell. Katherina, you may stay,   100
      For I have more to commune with Bianca.   *Exit*

KATHERINA Why, and I trust I may go too, may I not?

78–9 A pretty...why] *As prose,* F; *as verse, divided after* eye, Rowe, *after* best, Capell   84 SD *Aside*] *Theobald; not in* F   91 SD *Exit Bianca*] *Theobald; not in* F

78–9 Some editors print as verse, dividing after
'eye' or 'best'.

78 peat pet, spoilt child.

78–9 It...why The best thing she could do
would be to make herself cry if she could think of
an excuse. (The audience may well recall the
reference to 'commanded tears' as 'a woman's gift'
in Induction 1.120–1.)

81–3 Bianca's profession of obedience seems
ostentatious; compare 2.1.7 and contrast 3.1.19–20.

84 Minerva Roman goddess of wisdom.

85 strange severe, unkind.

87 mew cage, confine. The word literally means

'to moult' and the metaphorical use derives from
the practice of caging hawks when they were
moulting. For further use of metaphors from
hawking see 4.1.161–7 and n.

93 music...poetry Such subjects would have
been studied by a very few aristocratic women in
Shakespeare's time; see Lawrence Stone, *The
Family, Sex and Marriage in England, 1500–1800*,
1977, pp. 202–6.

97 Prefer Recommend.

97 cunning clever, skilful; as in 178 below.

101 commune discuss, talk about.

What, shall I be appointed hours as though, belike,
I knew not what to take and what to leave? Ha!   *Exit*

GREMIO You may go to the devil's dam! Your gifts are so good here's   105
none will hold you. There! Love is not so great, Hortensio, but we
may blow our nails together and fast it fairly out. Our cake's dough
on both sides. Farewell. Yet, for the love I bear my sweet Bianca,
if I can by any means light on a fit man to teach her that wherein
she delights, I will wish him to her father.   110

HORTENSIO So will I, Signor Gremio. But a word, I pray. Though the
nature of our quarrel yet never brooked parle, know now, upon
advice, it toucheth us both – that we may yet again have access to
our fair mistress and be happy rivals in Bianca's love – to labour
and effect one thing specially.   115

GREMIO What's that, I pray?

HORTENSIO Marry, sir, to get a husband for her sister.

GREMIO A husband? A devil!

HORTENSIO I say a husband.

GREMIO I say a devil. Think'st thou, Hortensio, though her father be   120
very rich, any man is so very a fool to be married to hell?

HORTENSIO Tush, Gremio. Though it pass your patience and mine to
endure her loud alarums – why, man, there be good fellows in the
world, and a man could light on them, would take her with all faults,
and money enough.   125

GREMIO I cannot tell. But I had as lief take her dowry with this
condition: to be whipped at the high cross every morning.

HORTENSIO Faith, as you say, there's small choice in rotten apples. But

---

103–4 What...Ha] *As two verse lines, Capell, Bond, NS, Hibbard, Riverside; as three verse lines, divided after* though *and* take, F; *as prose, Morris, Oliver*   106 There! Love] *Collier subst.; Their love* F, *Oliver;* There love Q; Our love *Rowe*   124 all faults] F; all her faults F4

105 the devil's dam the devil's mother, pro-
verbially the archetype of shrews; for further
discussion of this tradition, see Lucy de Bruyn,
Woman and the Devil in Sixteenth-Century Literature,
1979.

106 *There! Love F reads 'Their love' which
could mean 'the love of women', but 'there' / 'their'
is a common confusion and 'There' is an expression
Gremio has used at 56 above.

107 blow our nails wait patiently. Proverbial.
This conversation (up to 136) is full of proverbs and
commonplaces, beneath which Gremio and Hortensio manipulate their self-interest.

107–8 Our...sides i.e. we have both failed.
Proverbial (Tilley C12). Gremio uses this saying
again at 5.1.113.

109 light on come upon, find.

110 wish recommend (as at 1.2.57). *OED* sv v 6.

112 brooked parle allowed negotiations (between
us).

113 advice reflection.

113 toucheth concerns.

123 alarums scoldings. Literally 'calls to arms'
in a military context, as Petruchio uses it at 1.2.200.

124 and if (as often in Shakespeare).

124 with...faults A phrase from the
cattle-market.

126 had as lief would as willingly.

127 high cross i.e. market cross (at town centre).
The Italian atmosphere has slipped here: Shakespeare seems to be thinking of the traditional scene
of correction in an English country town like
Stratford.

128 small...apples Proverbial (Tilley C358).

come, since this bar in law makes us friends, it shall be so far forth
friendly maintained till by helping Baptista's eldest daughter to a   130
husband we set his youngest free for a husband – and then have
to't afresh. Sweet Bianca! Happy man be his dole! He that runs
fastest gets the ring. How say you, Signor Gremio?

GREMIO I am agreed, and would I had given him the best horse in Padua
to begin his wooing that would thoroughly woo her, wed her, and   135
bed her, and rid the house of her. Come on.

Exeunt Gremio and Hortensio

TRANIO I pray sir, tell me, is it possible
That love should of a sudden take such hold?

LUCENTIO O Tranio, till I found it to be true
I never thought it possible or likely.   140
But see! while idly I stood looking on,
I found the effect of love-in-idleness,
And now in plainness do confess to thee
That art to me as secret and as dear
As Anna to the Queen of Carthage was –   145
Tranio, I burn! I pine, I perish, Tranio,
If I achieve not this young modest girl.
Counsel me, Tranio, for I know thou canst;
Assist me, Tranio, for I know thou wilt.

TRANIO Master, it is no time to chide you now;   150
Affection is not rated from the heart.
If love have touched you, naught remains but so:
Redime te captum quam queas minimo.

136 SD *Exeunt...Hortensio*] Capell; *Exeunt ambo. Manet Tranio and Lucentio* F

129 **bar in law** legal impediment (meaning
Baptista's declaration).

131 **husband...husband** This Lylyan rhetorical trick recurs with the repetition of 'Lucentio' at
207–8 below; see also Textual Analysis, pp. 160–1
below.

132 **Happy...dole** May happiness be the winner's reward. Proverbial (Tilley M158).

132–3 **He...ring** Proverbial (Tilley R130), with
an obscene implication in 'ring'; compare *MV*
5.1.304–7. It is also one of the play's many sporting
metaphors; see pp. 36–7 above.

135–6 **woo...bed her** Proverbial (Tilley W731).

142 **love-in-idleness** Lucentio puns on the
popular name for the pansy, a flower thought to have
aphrodisiac powers; compare *MND* 2.1.155–74. He
also has in mind the proverb 'Idleness is the mother
of all evil' (Tilley I 13).

144 **secret** intimately trusted.

145 **Anna** Sister and confidante to Dido; see
Virgil, *Aeneid* IV, 8–30. Marlowe had dramatised the
scene between the two sisters in *The Tragedy of
Dido, Queen of Carthage* (printed in 1594 but
written before 1590).

146 Lucentio's rhetoric is tritely conventional.
Shakespeare often satirises such professions of love
in the early comedies, as for example in *LLL* 4.3.
See also 210–11 below.

148–9 The patterning of these lines is again
reminiscent of Lyly; see 131 n. and compare Proteus's speech in *TGV* 2.6.

151 **rated** driven away by scolding.

153 *Redime...minimo* Ransom yourself, now
you have been captured, for as low a price as you
can. A quotation from Terence's play *The Eunuch*
1.1.29–30 but, as Johnson pointed out ('that it may

LUCENTIO Gramercies, lad. Go forward. This contents;
　　　　The rest will comfort, for thy counsel's sound.　　　　　　155
TRANIO Master, you looked so longly on the maid,
　　　　Perhaps you marked not what's the pith of all.
LUCENTIO O yes, I saw sweet beauty in her face,
　　　　Such as the daughter of Agenor had,
　　　　That made great Jove to humble him to her hand　　　　160
　　　　When with his knees he kissed the Cretan strand.
TRANIO Saw you no more? Marked you not how her sister
　　　　Began to scold and raise up such a storm
　　　　That mortal ears might hardly endure the din?
LUCENTIO Tranio, I saw her coral lips to move,　　　　　　　　165
　　　　And with her breath she did perfume the air.
　　　　Sacred and sweet was all I saw in her.
TRANIO Nay, then, 'tis time to stir him from his trance.
　　　　I pray, awake, sir. If you love the maid
　　　　Bend thoughts and wits to achieve her. Thus it stands:　170
　　　　Her elder sister is so curst and shrewd
　　　　That, till the father rid his hands of her,
　　　　Master, your love must live a maid at home,
　　　　And therefore has he closely mewed her up,
　　　　Because she will not be annoyed with suitors.　　　　　175
LUCENTIO Ah, Tranio, what a cruel father's he!
　　　　But art thou not advised he took some care
　　　　To get her cunning schoolmasters to instruct her?
TRANIO Ay, marry, am I, sir – and now 'tis plotted!
LUCENTIO I have it, Tranio!
TRANIO　　　　　　　　　Master, for my hand,　　　　　　　180
　　　　Both our inventions meet and jump in one.
LUCENTIO Tell me thine first.
TRANIO　　　　　　　　　You will be schoolmaster
　　　　And undertake the teaching of the maid –
　　　　That's your device.
LUCENTIO　　　　　　　　It is. May it be done?

not be brought as an example of our author's
learning'), Shakespeare gives the inaccurate version
found in Lyly's *Latin Grammar* (1542), a work
well-known to every Elizabethan schoolboy.
　157 **pith** main issue.
　159 **daughter of Agenor** Europa. Jove trans-
formed himself into a bull to woo her and carried
her off on his back to Crete; see Ovid, *Met.* ii,
846–75.
　162 **Saw...more** It is often the role of servants

in Shakespeare (as in Roman comedy) to explain the
plot to their love-sick masters; see 4.2.66 and
4.4.80–93 below, and compare *TGV* 2.1.135–70.
　171 **curst and shrewd** bad-tempered and
perverse.
　175 **Because** In order that; see Abbott 117.
　175 **annoyed with** troubled by.
　177 **art...advised** did you not notice.
　181 **meet...one** coincide.

TRANIO Not possible. For who shall bear your part   185
          And be in Padua here Vincentio's son,
          Keep house, and ply his book, welcome his friends,
          Visit his countrymen and banquet them?
LUCENTIO *Basta!* Content thee, for I have it full.
          We have not yet been seen in any house,   190
          Nor can we be distinguished by our faces
          For man or master. Then it follows thus:
          Thou shalt be master, Tranio, in my stead;
          Keep house and port and servants as I should.
          I will some other be – some Florentine,   195
          Some Neapolitan or meaner man of Pisa.
          'Tis hatched and shall be so. Tranio, at once
          Uncase thee; take my coloured hat and cloak.
              [*They exchange clothes.*]
          When Biondello comes, he waits on thee,
          But I will charm him first to keep his tongue.   200
TRANIO So had you need.
          In brief, sir, sith it your pleasure is,
          And I am tied to be obedient –
          For so your father charged me at our parting:
          'Be serviceable to my son', quoth he,   205
          Although I think 'twas in another sense –
          I am content to be Lucentio,
          Because so well I love Lucentio.
LUCENTIO Tranio, be so, because Lucentio loves,
          And let me be a slave t'achieve that maid   210
          Whose sudden sight hath thralled my wounded eye.

              Enter BIONDELLO.

          Here comes the rogue. Sirrah, where have you been?

198 coloured] F2 (Coulord); Conlord F   198 SD They...clothes] *Theobald subst.; not in* F

187 **Keep house** Entertain guests.
187 **ply his book** pursue his studies.
189 *Basta!* Enough (Italian); see 25 n.
189 **I...full** I have worked it out completely.
194 **port** lifestyle, social station.
198 **Uncase thee** Take off your outer garments.
198 ***coloured** The meaning is that Tranio is wearing the blue uniform of a servant (compare 4.1.67) – and perhaps that Lucentio is something of a dandy.

201–2 There may be something missing from the text here, as Tranio does not explain why there is any particular need to keep Biondello quiet; he is Lucentio's own servant, after all, and his secrecy could surely be taken for granted. Tranio's 'In brief, sir' seems inconsequential and the metre of these two lines is shaky. See also 218–24 n.
205 **serviceable** eager or diligent to serve.

BIONDELLO Where have I been? Nay, how now, where are you?
    Master, has my fellow Tranio stolen your clothes or you stolen his,
    or both? Pray, what's the news?   215
LUCENTIO Sirrah, come hither. 'Tis no time to jest,
    And therefore frame your manners to the time.
    Your fellow Tranio here, to save my life,
    Puts my apparel and my count'nance on,
    And I for my escape have put on his;   220
    For in a quarrel since I came ashore
    I killed a man, and fear I was descried.
    Wait you on him, I charge you, as becomes,
    While I make way from hence to save my life.
    You understand me?
BIONDELLO   Ay, sir. Ne'er a whit.   225
LUCENTIO And not a jot of 'Tranio' in your mouth:
    Tranio is changed into Lucentio.
BIONDELLO The better for him! Would I were so too.
TRANIO So could I, faith, boy, to have the next wish after –
    That Lucentio indeed had Baptista's youngest daughter.   230
    But, sirrah, not for my sake but your master's, I advise
    You use your manners discreetly in all kind of companies.
    When I am alone, why then I am Tranio,
    But in all places else your master Lucèntio.
LUCENTIO Tranio, let's go.   235
    One thing more rests that thyself execute:

213–15 Where...news] *As prose,* F, *Bond, Hibbard, Riverside, Oliver; as verse, NS, Morris*   **225** Ay, sir] *Rowe, NS, Riverside;* I sir F, *Bond, Hibbard, Morris, Oliver*   229–34 So...Lucentio] *As verse, Capell; as prose,* F, *Oliver* **234** your] F2; you F

---

214 fellow fellow-servant (as in 218); see also 4.1.18. The frequent use of the terms 'fellow' and 'master' from here to 234 is presumably intended to help the audience to follow the plot.

217 frame...manners adapt your behaviour.

218–24 It is not clear why Lucentio should trouble to invent this story, as there is no sustained attempt to deceive Biondello. Perhaps the sheer extravagance of the fiction is part of the general satire on romantic conventions (see 146 n.), or perhaps there was once a good reason for deceiving Biondello which was cut from Tranio's speech at 201–2. See Textual Analysis, pp. 161–4 below, for a discussion of 'loose ends' in the play as a whole.

219 count'nance bearing, position.

221 ashore See 42 n.

222 descried observed.

225 *Ay, F reads 'I', as it regularly does when

'Ay' is meant, as for example in Induction 2.86, 110 and 121. 'I, sir?' is possible here and the actor is free to choose, but since the editor cannot leave it so open I have opted for 'Ay', which can be very successful on stage if the actor says 'Ay, sir' enthusiastically and then pauses before saying in a different tone 'Ne'er a whit'. (Lucentio has perhaps succeeded in his intention to 'charm' Biondello into silence (200) simply by stupefying him.)

225 Ne'er a whit Not in the least.

229–34 More couplets (see 64–5 n.). 'After' / 'daughter' is a rhyme, as in *Lear* 1.4.317–21.

229 boy The relationship between the adult servant Tranio and the boy Biondello here is similar to that between Launce and Speed in *TGV* – see especially *TGV* 3.1.280–384.

232 use your manners behave.

236 rests remains.

To make one among these wooers. If thou ask me why,
Sufficeth my reasons are both good and weighty.

Exeunt

The Presenters above speaks.

LORD My lord, you nod; you do not mind the play.
SLY Yes, by Saint Anne, do I. A good matter surely. Comes there any   240
  more of it?
BARTHOLOMEW My lord, 'tis but begun.
SLY 'Tis a very excellent piece of work, madam lady. Would 'twere done!
  They sit and mark.

[1.2] *Enter* PETRUCHIO *and his man* GRUMIO.

PETRUCHIO Verona, for a while I take my leave
  To see my friends in Padua, but of all
  My best belovèd and approvèd friend,
  Hortensio: and I trow this is his house.
  Here, sirrah Grumio, knock, I say.   5
GRUMIO Knock, sir? Whom should I knock? Is there any man has
  rebused your worship?
PETRUCHIO Villain, I say, knock me here soundly.
GRUMIO Knock you here, sir? Why, sir, what am I, sir, that I should
  knock you here, sir?   10

239 SH LORD] *Hibbard;* 1.*Man.* F   Act 1, Scene 2   1.2] *Capell; no scene division in* F

238 SD.2 *Presenters* Commentators. A term
generally used for actors representing spectators
who explain or comment on the play.
  238 SD.2 *above* See Appendix 2, pp. 181–5 below,
for a discussion of the staging.
  239 SH •LORD F reads 1.*Man.* here, but surely
the Lord (disguised as a servant) should watch the
outcome of his own plot? (See Induction 2.112 SD
n.) It is of course possible that changes were made
in the personnel available as 'Presenters' if we
assume that the Sly scenes were cut and curtailed
as part of a revision; see Textual Analysis,
pp. 164–74 below.
  239 **mind** pay attention to.
  242 SH BARTHOLOMEW Still disguised as
Sly's 'wife'; see Induction 2.94 n.
  243 SD *They...mark* These words indicate that
the 'Presenters' remain on stage (*sit*) and even
prepare for later involvement in the action (*mark*)
but F makes no further mention of them, and in most
modern productions they leave unobtrusively quite
soon after this. It would seem that Shakespeare

originally intended to make further use of Sly and
that *A Shrew* preserves a version of four later
interventions plus a final scene; see Appendix 1 and
Textual Analysis, pp. 164–74 below.

Act 1, Scene 2
  0 SD *Enter...*GRUMIO Compare the beginning of 1.1: *Enter* LUCENTIO *and his man*
TRANIO. Especially after the intervention of the
'Presenters' we may get the impression that the play
is about to 'begin' all over again. Petruchio, like
Lucentio, begins with a speech explaining where he
is and why.
  2 **of all** especially, above all.
  4 **trow** believe.
  7 **rebused** Grumio's error for 'abused'.
  8 **knock me here** Petruchio uses 'me' as an
archaic dative (= 'knock for me') but Grumio takes
it as an accusative (= 'hit me'). There may also be
a play on 'here' / 'ear', which were pronounced
alike; see Kökeritz, *Pronunciation*, p. 103, and
4.1.43–8 below.

PETRUCHIO Villain, I say, knock me at this gate,
    And rap me well, or I'll knock your knave's pate!
GRUMIO My master is grown quarrelsome. I should knock you first,
    And then I know after who comes by the worst.
PETRUCHIO Will it not be?   15
    Faith, sirrah, and you'll not knock, I'll ring it.
    I'll try how you can *sol-fa*, and sing it.
            He wrings him by the ears.
GRUMIO Help, mistress, help! My master is mad.
PETRUCHIO Now knock when I bid you, sirrah villain.

                    Enter HORTENSIO.

HORTENSIO How now, what's the matter? My old friend Grumio and   20
    my good friend Petruchio! How do you all at Verona?
PETRUCHIO Signor Hortensio, come you to part the fray?
    Con tutto il cuore ben trovato, may I say.
HORTENSIO *Alla nostra casa ben venuto*
    Molto honorato signor mio Petruchio.   25
    Rise, Grumio, rise. We will compound this quarrel.
GRUMIO Nay, 'tis no matter, sir, what he ledges in Latin. If this be not
    a lawful cause for me to leave his service – look you, sir: he bid me
    knock him and rap him soundly, sir. Well, was it fit for a servant
    to use his master so, being perhaps, for aught I see, two and thirty,   30
    a pip out?
    Whom would to God I had well knocked at first,
    Then had not Grumio come by the worst.

13–14 My...worst] *As two verse lines, thus, Theobald; as three verse lines in* F *divided after* quarrelsome *and* first
18 mistress] F; *masters Theobald, Bond, NS, Hibbard, Riverside, Morris, Oliver*   24–5 Alla...Petruchio] *As verse,*
Capell; as prose, F, *Oliver*   31 pip] *Rowe*³; peepe F   32–3 Whom...worst] *As verse, Rowe*³; *as prose,* F

13–14 **I should...worst** i.e. if I hit you first I
know you will hit me harder in return.
    16 and if.
    16 I'll ring it I'll ring the bell; with a pun on
'wring'.
    17 *sol-fa* sing a scale.
    18 mistress Many editors emend F's 'mistris' to
'masters' on the assumption that the manuscript
reading was 'mrs.', which the compositor expanded
erroneously. This does seem to be the case at 5.1.5
and 42 but I do not feel the emendation is strictly
necessary here, especially since a different compositor
is involved.
    23–5 *Con...Petruchio* With all my heart well
met. Welcome to our house, much honoured Signor
Petruchio. (Italian; see 1.1.25 n.)

26 compound settle, resolve.
    27 ledges alleges. A legal term, like 'compound'.
    27 in Latin Grumio momentarily becomes an
English servant who is ignorant of Italian; compare
the inconsistency of the Greek soldier who cannot
read all of the inscription on the tomb in *Tim.*
5.3.1–10. In that case it seems to be a genuine error
on Shakespeare's part whereas here a joke may be
intended, since Grumio is deliberately misunderstanding his master throughout this sequence.
    30–1 two...out i.e. 'slightly in error', 'a degree
out'; an allusion to the card game 'one and thirty'
(also referred to at 4.2.57). Grumio seems to mean
that Petruchio is 'not quite right in the head', but
to be 'one and thirty' could mean to be drunk; see
John Ray, *Collection of English Proverbs* (1678).

PETRUCHIO A senseless villain! Good Hortensio,
　　　　I bade the rascal knock upon your gate   35
　　　　And could not get him for my heart to do it.
GRUMIO Knock at the gate? O heavens! Spake you not these words
　　　　plain: 'Sirrah, knock me here, rap me here, knock me well, and
　　　　knock me soundly'? And come you now with 'knocking at the
　　　　gate'?   40
PETRUCHIO Sirrah, be gone, or talk not, I advise you.
HORTENSIO Petruchio, patience. I am Grumio's pledge.
　　　　Why this' a heavy chance 'twixt him and you –
　　　　Your ancient, trusty, pleasant servant Grumio.
　　　　And tell me now, sweet friend, what happy gale   45
　　　　Blows you to Padua here from old Verona?
PETRUCHIO Such wind as scatters young men through the world
　　　　To seek their fortunes farther than at home
　　　　Where small experience grows. But, in a few,
　　　　Signor Hortensio, thus it stands with me: 50
　　　　Antonio my father is deceased
　　　　And I have thrust myself into this maze,
　　　　Happily to wive and thrive as best I may.
　　　　Crowns in my purse I have, and goods at home,
　　　　And so am come abroad to see the world.   55
HORTENSIO Petruchio, shall I then come roundly to thee
　　　　And wish thee to a shrewd ill-favoured wife?

49 grows. But] *Theobald subst.; growes but* F　　　53 Happily] F, *Bond, Riverside, Oliver;* Haply *Rowe³, NS, Hibbard, Morris*

---

34 **senseless villain** Compare *Err.* 4.4.24, where Antipholus of Ephesus beats his servant Dromio, calling him a 'whoreson, senseless villain'.

39 **come you now** i.e. do you now claim to have talked of.

42 **pledge** surety. Hortensio brings the run of legal terms he and Grumio have been using to an appropriate conclusion.

43 **this'** this is. See Abbott 461.

43 **heavy chance** unfortunate occurrence.

44 **ancient** of long standing.

44 **pleasant** merry, witty.

47–9 Compare 1.1.23 and n.

49 **grows. But, in a few** F's reading could make sense ('there's small experience to be found at home and that only in a few') but all modern editors follow Theobald's emended punctuation, interpreting 'in a few' as 'in brief'.

52 **maze** uncertain (unmapped) course of action. Michael West sees this as the first of the play's many

metaphors from dancing; 'The folk background of Petruchio's wooing dance: male supremacy in *The Taming of The Shrew*', *S.St.* 7 (1974), 65–73; compare *MND* 2.1.99–100: 'And the quaint mazes in the wanton green, / For lack of tread, are undistinguishable.'

53 **Happily** Thus F. Some editors follow Rowe's emendation to 'haply' (= 'perhaps' or 'with luck') but this seems unnecessary, especially in the light of the repetition of 'happily' at 73.

53 **to...thrive** Several contemporary proverbs are relevant here: 'First thrive and then wive' (Tilley T264), 'Who weds ere he be wise shall die ere he thrive' (W229) and 'It is hard to wive and thrive both in a year' (Y12).

56 **come roundly** speak plainly.

57 **ill-favoured** This usually means 'ugly' but Hortensio describes Katherina as 'beauteous' at 82, so he must be referring to her temperament here.

> Thou'dst thank me but a little for my counsel –
> And yet I'll promise thee she shall be rich,
> And very rich. But th'art too much my friend,   60
> And I'll not wish thee to her.

PETRUCHIO Signor Hortensio, 'twixt such friends as we
> Few words suffice, and therefore, if thou know
> One rich enough to be Petruchio's wife –
> As wealth is burden of my wooing dance –   65
> Be she as foul as was Florentius' love,
> As old as Sibyl, and as curst and shrewd
> As Socrates' Xanthippe or a worse,
> She moves me not, or not removes at least
> Affection's edge in me, were she as rough   70
> As are the swelling Adriatic seas.
> I come to wive it wealthily in Padua;
> If wealthily, then happily in Padua.

GRUMIO Nay, look you sir, he tells you flatly what his mind is. Why,
> give him gold enough and marry him to a puppet or an aglet-baby 75
> or an old trot with ne'er a tooth in her head, though she have as
> many diseases as two and fifty horses. Why, nothing comes amiss,
> so money comes withal.

HORTENSIO Petruchio, since we are stepped thus far in,
> I will continue that I broached in jest.   80
> I can, Petruchio, help thee to a wife
> With wealth enough, and young, and beauteous,
> Brought up as best becomes a gentlewoman.
> Her only fault – and that is faults enough –

---

70 were she as] Q; Were she is as F; whe'er she is as *Riverside*

---

65 wealth...dance Directors and critics have often emphasised this mercenary attitude but it seems at odds with Petruchio's statements about his financial independence at 51–5 and at 2.1.112–14.

65 burden musical accompaniment, refrain. See 52 n.

66 foul ugly.

66 Florentius Name of a knight in Gower's *Confessio Amantis* (1.1407–1861) who marries an ugly old woman to save his life. Chaucer tells the same story in *The Wife of Bath's Tale* but does not give the knight a name. Shakespeare's knowledge of the *Confessio* is supported by his use of the story of Apollonius of Tyre in *Err.*; see Bullough, *Sources*, I, 10–11.

67 Sibyl Aged prophetess in classical mythology.

68 Xanthippe Notoriously bad-tempered wife of Socrates.

69 moves...removes This word-play is repeated at 2.1.190–2.

70 Affection's edge The intensity of passion or desire.

75 aglet-baby small carved figure used to weight and ornament the end of a tag or lace.

76 trot hag. According to *OED* this word is not connected etymologically with 'trot' as used of horses, but it may be by association or deliberate pun.

76–7 as...horses The Elizabethans seem to have been impressed by the number and variety of equine diseases; see 3.2.45–51. The phrase also continues the cattle-market atmosphere; see 1.1.124 n.

Is that she is intolerable curst,   85
And shrewd and froward so beyond all measure
That, were my state far worser than it is,
I would not wed her for a mine of gold!
PETRUCHIO Hortensio, peace. Thou know'st not gold's effect.
Tell me her father's name and 'tis enough,   90
For I will board her though she chide as loud
As thunder when the clouds in autumn crack.
HORTENSIO Her father is Baptista Minola,
An affable and courteous gentleman.
Her name is Katherina Minola,   95
Renowned in Padua for her scolding tongue.
PETRUCHIO I know her father, though I know not her,
And he knew my deceasèd father well.
I will not sleep, Hortensio, till I see her,
And therefore let me be thus bold with you   100
To give you over at this first encounter –
Unless you will accompany me thither?
GRUMIO I pray you, sir, let him go while the humour lasts. A' my word,
and she knew him as well as I do, she would think scolding would
do little good upon him. She may perhaps call him half a score   105
knaves or so – why, that's nothing. And he begin once, he'll rail
in his rope-tricks. I'll tell you what, sir, and she stand him but a
little, he will throw a figure in her face and so disfigure her with
it that she shall have no more eyes to see withal than a cat. You
know him not, sir.   110

85 **intolerable** intolerably.

91 **board her** woo her. Compare *AWW* 5.3.210–
11: 'Certain it is I lik'd her / And boarded her
i'th'wanton way of youth.' An aggressive
metaphor derived from naval warfare. See also
4.4.102.

92 **crack** collide together, explode.

97 **I...father** The first of many instances
whereby the social world of Italy is made to seem
unusually compact.

101 **give you over** leave you.

103 **A'** On.

104 **and** if, as in 107 and 108.

106–7 **rail...rope-tricks** An obscure expression, presumably meaning something like 'scold in
outrageous terms'. Hibbard suggests that 'rope-
tricks' is Grumio's version of 'rope-rhetorics', a
term used by Thomas Nashe in *Have with You to
Saffron-Walden* (1595) where he writes scathingly
of Gabriel Harvey's 'Paracelsian rope-rethorique',
apparently meaning 'bombastic rhetoric for which
the author deserved to be hanged'. There is also a
bawdy sense to this passage (following on from
'board her' in 91) and the use of 'ropery' to mean
'knavery' in a highly bawdy context in *Rom.* 2.4.146
seems relevant. For a discussion of both passages see
Richard Levin, 'Grumio's "rope-tricks" and the
Nurse's "ropery"', *SQ* 22 (1971), 82–6. Morris also
has a very full note on this passage.

107 **stand** withstand, oppose. The word also has
a sexual connotation; see Induction 2.120 n.

108 **throw a figure** (1) hurl a figure of speech,
(2) cast a spell (?).

108–9 **disfigure...cat** The basic meaning is that
Katherina will be so disconcerted by Petruchio's
verbal (and sexual?) onslaught that she will be
incapable of response. The pursuit of 'figure'
through the metaphorical 'disfigure' seems to
suggest to Grumio the image of two cats scratching
each other's eyes out. Partridge gives 'eye' as one
of the many euphemisms for the vagina, so perhaps
the climax of this difficult passage is a metaphor for
rape.

HORTENSIO Tarry, Petruchio, I must go with thee,
    For in Baptista's keep my treasure is.
    He hath the jewel of my life in hold,
    His youngest daughter, beautiful Bianca,
    And her withholds from me and other more –   115
    Suitors to her and rivals in my love –
    Supposing it a thing impossible,
    For those defects I have before rehearsed,
    That ever Katherina will be wooed.
    Therefore this order hath Baptista tane,   120
    That none shall have access unto Bianca
    Till Katherine the curst have got a husband.
GRUMIO 'Katherine the curst'!
    A title for a maid of all titles the worst.
HORTENSIO Now shall my friend Petruchio do me grace   125
    And offer me disguised in sober robes
    To old Baptista as a schoolmaster
    Well seen in music, to instruct Bianca,
    That so I may by this device at least
    Have leave and leisure to make love to her   130
    And unsuspected court her by herself.

Enter GREMIO, *and* LUCENTIO *disguised* [*as Cambio, a schoolmaster*].

GRUMIO Here's no knavery! See, to beguile the old folks, how the young
    folks lay their heads together. Master, master, look about you! Who
    goes there, ha?
HORTENSIO Peace, Grumio. It is the rival of my love.   135
    Petruchio, stand by a while.
GRUMIO A proper stripling, and an amorous!
        [*They stand aside.*]
GREMIO O, very well, I have perused the note.

---

115 me and other] *Hanmer subst.;* me. Other F; me, and others *Theobald*   131 SD *as...schoolmaster*] *Capell subst.;*
not in F   137 SD *They...aside*] *Capell subst.; not in* F

112 **keep** (1) keeping, (2) inaccessible stronghold. (There is a similar pun on 'hold' at 113–15.) The romanticism of this image contrasts strongly with the apparent coarseness of Petruchio and Grumio's approach; see pp. 15–17 above for a general discussion of the range of different attitudes towards love in this play.
   115 **other more** others besides (me). 'Other' was often used as a plural pronoun; see Abbott 12.
   125 **do me grace** do me a favour.

128 **seen** qualified.
   130 **make love** speak of love, woo.
   132 **Here's no knavery** Spoken sarcastically.
   136 **stand by** Compare 1.1.47 SD, and see p. 31 above.
   137 **proper stripling** handsome youth. (Sarcastic again.) From this point on we are frequently encouraged to see Gremio as a comic figure.
   138 **note** list of required books.

> Hark you, sir, I'll have them very fairly bound –
> All books of love, see that at any hand –   140
> And see you read no other lectures to her:
> You understand me. Over and beside
> Signor Baptista's liberality
> I'll mend it with a largess. Take your paper too
> And let me have them very well perfumed,   145
> For she is sweeter than perfume itself
> To whom they go to. What will you read to her?

LUCENTIO Whate'er I read to her I'll plead for you
 As for my patron, stand you so assured
 As firmly as yourself were still in place –   150
 Yea and perhaps with more successful words
 Than you, unless you were a scholar, sir.

GREMIO O this learning, what a thing it is!

GRUMIO [*Aside*] O this woodcock, what an ass it is!

PETRUCHIO [*Aside*] Peace, sirrah.   155

HORTENSIO [*Aside*] Grumio, mum.
     [*Coming forward.*]
      God save you, Signor Gremio.

GREMIO And you are well met, Signor Hortensio.
 Trow you whither I am going? To Baptista Minola.
 I promised to inquire carefully
 About a schoolmaster for the fair Bianca,   160
 And by good fortune I have lighted well
 On this young man, for learning and behaviour
 Fit for her turn, well read in poetry
 And other books – good ones, I warrant ye.

HORTENSIO 'Tis well. And I have met a gentleman   165

---

154 SD *Aside*] *Sisson; not in* F 155 SD *Aside*] *Sisson; not in* F 156 SD *Aside*] *Sisson; not in* F 156 SD *Coming forward*]
Capell subst.; not in F 157–64 And...ye] *As verse,* F; *as prose, Pope, Oliver*

139 them i.e. the books.
140 see see to.
140 at any hand on any account.
144 mend...largess improve it with a contribution or donation.
144 paper Presumably the 'note' mentioned at 138.
145 them i.e. the books.
145 perfumed A common practice, and one which Shakespeare jokes about in *AWW* 5.2.15–17: '*Parolles*: Pray you, sir, deliver me this paper. *Clown*: Foh, prithee stand away. A paper from Fortune's close-stool to give to a nobleman!'

147 To...to The repeated preposition is quite common in Shakespeare but it is usually related to the need for clarity or emphasis in a longer period; compare *Tro.* 5.1.56–7, and see Abbott 407.
149–50 stand...place The obscene sense (see Induction 2.120 n.) may be present as a joke against Gremio here.
150 still in place present all the time.
154 woodcock dupe, simpleton. The woodcock was thought to be a silly bird because it was easy to trap.
158 Trow you Do you know.

                    Hath promised me to help me to another,
                    A fine musician to instruct our mistress.
                    So shall I no whit be behind in duty
                    To fair Bianca, so beloved of me.
GREMIO Beloved of me, and that my deeds shall prove.   170
GRUMIO [*Aside*] And that his bags shall prove.
HORTENSIO Gremio, 'tis now no time to vent our love.
                    Listen to me, and if you speak me fair,
                    I'll tell you news indifferent good for either.
                    Here is a gentleman whom by chance I met,   175
                              [*Presents Petruchio.*]
                    Upon agreement from us to his liking,
                    Will undertake to woo curst Katherine,
                    Yea, and to marry her, if her dowry please.
GREMIO So said, so done, is well.
                    Hortensio, have you told him all her faults?   180
PETRUCHIO I know she is an irksome, brawling scold.
                    If that be all, masters, I hear no harm.
GREMIO No? Say'st me so, friend? What countryman?
PETRUCHIO Born in Verona, old Antonio's son.
                    My father dead, my fortune lives for me,   185
                    And I do hope good days and long to see.
GREMIO O sir, such a life with such a wife were strange.
                    But if you have a stomach, to't a God's name!
                    You shall have me assisting you in all.
                    But will you woo this wildcat?
PETRUCHIO   Will I live?   190
GRUMIO Will he woo her? Ay, or I'll hang her.
PETRUCHIO Why came I hither but to that intent?
                    Think you a little din can daunt mine ears?

---

166 help me] *Rowe*; helpe one F   171 SD *Aside*] *Capell*; *not in* F   175 SD *Presents Petruchio*] *Eds.*; *not in* F
184 *Antonio's*] *Rowe*; *Butonios* F

166 help **me** F's 'helpe one' seems a classic minim misreading, corrected by Rowe.

171 **bags** money-bags, riches.

172 **vent** express, discuss.

174 **indifferent good** equally good. ('Indifferent' is trisyllabic.)

176 **Upon...liking** If we make a (financial) agreement that is satisfactory to him. (Hortensio has just invented this.)

180 **have...faults?** Gremio, like Hortensio at 56–61 above and Baptista in the following scene,
seems strangely anxious that Petruchio should know the truth about Katherina, but the shrew's suitor is always warned about her in the folktale versions.

187 **were** would be.

191 Grumio's remark can be related to two contemporary proverbs: 'Better be half hanged than ill wed' (Tilley H130) and 'Wedding and hanging go by destiny' (W232). Shakespeare alludes to the first of these again at *TN* 1.5.19–20 and to the second at *MV* 2.9.83.

Have I not in my time heard lions roar?
Have I not heard the sea, puffed up with winds,   195
Rage like an angry boar chafèd with sweat?
Have I not heard great ordnance in the field,
And heaven's artillery thunder in the skies?
Have I not in a pitchèd battle heard
Loud 'larums, neighing steeds and trumpets' clang?   200
And do you tell me of a woman's tongue,
That gives not half so great a blow to hear
As will a chestnut in a farmer's fire?
Tush, tush, fear boys with bugs!
GRUMIO   For he fears none.
GREMIO Hortensio, hark.   205
This gentleman is happily arrived,
My mind presumes, for his own good and yours.
HORTENSIO I promised we would be contributors
And bear his charge of wooing, whatsoe'er.
GREMIO And so we will – provided that he win her.   210
GRUMIO I would I were as sure of a good dinner.

Enter TRANIO [*disguised as Lucentio*] *and* BIONDELLO.

TRANIO Gentlemen, God save you. If I may be bold,
Tell me, I beseech you, which is the readiest way
To the house of Signor Baptista Minola?
BIONDELLO He that has the two fair daughters – is't he you mean? 215
TRANIO Even he, Biondello.

---

200 trumpets'] *Capell;* trumpets F   202 to hear] F; to th'ear *Hanmer*   207 yours] F, *Hibbard, Morris, Oliver;* ours
Theobald, Bond, NS, Riverside   211 SD *disguised...Lucentio*] *Rowe subst.;* brave F   212–14 Gentlemen...Minola] *As
verse,* F; *as prose, Pope, Oliver*

194–200 Petruchio's claim to a career of travel
and martial adventure seems at odds with his
statement to Hortensio at 47–55 which implies that
this is his first venture 'abroad'. Nevertheless this
speech helps to define him as a 'romantic' hero
(compare *Oth.* 1.3.128–70), in strict contrast to the
mundane experiences of Christopher Sly (Induction
2.15–18) and the scholarly background of Lucentio.
197 **ordnance** cannon.
200 **'larums** calls to arms made with drum and
trumpet.
204 **fear...fears** frighten...is frightened by.
There is a similar play on the active and passive
meanings of 'fear' at 5.2.16–19.
204 **bugs** bugbears, hobgoblins.

207 **yours** Thus F. Some editors follow
Theobald's emendation to 'ours' (see collation) but,
as Hibbard points out, the sense may be that Gremio
is eager to shift any expense involved onto
Hortensio.
208–9 Again Hortensio insists on the 'agreement'
he invented at 176, presumably as part of a device
to get money out of Gremio.
209 **charge** expenses.
211 SD *disguised as Lucentio* F reads *Enter
Tranio brave*, i.e. finely dressed.
215 **He...mean?** Biondello, who already knows
this, is presumably helping Tranio to come quickly
to the point and emphasising it for the others.

GREMIO Hark you, sir, you mean not her to –
TRANIO Perhaps him and her, sir. What have you to do?
PETRUCHIO Not her that chides, sir, at any hand, I pray.
TRANIO I love no chiders, sir. Biondello, let's away.   220
LUCENTIO [*Aside*] Well begun, Tranio.
HORTENSIO   Sir, a word ere you go.
    Are you a suitor to the maid you talk of, yea or no?
TRANIO And if I be, sir, is it any offence?
GREMIO No, if without more words you will get you hence.
TRANIO Why, sir, I pray, are not the streets as free   225
    For me as for you?
GREMIO   But so is not she.
TRANIO For what reason, I beseech you?
GREMIO For this reason, if you'll know –
    That she's the choice love of Signor Gremio.
HORTENSIO That she's the chosen of Signor Hortensio.   230
TRANIO Softly, my masters! If you be gentlemen,
    Do me this right – hear me with patience.
    Baptista is a noble gentleman
    To whom my father is not all unknown,
    And were his daughter fairer than she is,   235
    She may more suitors have, and me for one.
    Fair Leda's daughter had a thousand wooers;
    Then well one more may fair Bianca have.
    And so she shall: Lucentio shall make one,
    Though Paris came in hope to speed alone.   240
GREMIO What, this gentleman will out-talk us all!

---

217 her to –] F; her to woo *conj. Malone*; her too *Hibbard conj. Tyrrwhitt, Morris*   221 SD *Aside*] *Hanmer; not in* F
225 streets] Q; streers F   240 came in] *Singer;* came, in F

217–30 The use of rhyme here (or from 213 if 'Minola' rhymes with 'way') is perhaps intended to make the tone more comic.

217 her to – Some editors (e.g. Hibbard and Morris) emend to 'her too?' which is how Tranio seems to understand it, but Gremio may mean to say something like 'to woo' before he breaks off or is interrupted.

218 What…do? What business is it of yours?

219 at any hand Compare 140. Perhaps Petruchio is parodying Gremio?

231 Softly Gently, take it easy.

234 To…unknown See 97 n.

234 all entirely.

237 Leda's daughter Helen of Troy. The 'thousand wooers' may derive from Marlowe's

references to her in *Tamburlaine*: 'Helen, whose beauty summoned Greece to arms, / And drew a thousand ships to Tenedos' (2.4.87–8), and *Dr Faustus*: 'Was this the face that launched a thousand ships?' (5.1.97). The author of *A Shrew* echoes the *Tamburlaine* lines closely (see Textual Analysis, p. 167 below) and Shakespeare himself remodelled the *Dr Faustus* line in *Tro.* 2.2.81–2 where Troilus says of Helen 'Why, she is a pearl, / Whose price hath launch'd above a thousand ships.'

240 Though Paris came Even if Paris (who stole Helen from her husband Menelaus) were to come.

240 speed succeed.

LUCENTIO Sir, give him head. I know he'll prove a jade.
PETRUCHIO Hortensio, to what end are all these words?
HORTENSIO Sir, let me be so bold as ask you,
   Did you yet ever see Baptista's daughter?   245
TRANIO No, sir, but hear I do that he hath two,
   The one as famous for a scolding tongue
   As is the other for beauteous modesty.
PETRUCHIO Sir, sir, the first's for me; let her go by.
GREMIO Yea, leave that labour to great Hercules,   250
   And let it be more than Alcides' twelve.
PETRUCHIO Sir, understand you this of me in sooth:
   The youngest daughter, whom you hearken for,
   Her father keeps from all access of suitors
   And will not promise her to any man   255
   Until the elder sister first be wed.
   The younger then is free, and not before.
TRANIO If it be so, sir, that you are the man
   Must stead us all, and me amongst the rest,
   And if you break the ice and do this feat –   260
   Achieve the elder, set the younger free
   For our access – whose hap shall be to have her
   Will not so graceless be to be ingrate.
HORTENSIO Sir, you say well, and well you do conceive;
   And since you do profess to be a suitor,   265
   You must, as we do, gratify this gentleman
   To whom we all rest generally beholding.
TRANIO Sir, I shall not be slack; in sign whereof,
   Please ye we may contrive this afternoon

---

260 feat] *Rowe;* seeke F

---

242 **prove a jade** i.e. soon tire. A 'jade' is a worn-out horse (see 76–7 n.) whose debility would soon be revealed by 'giving it its head'.

249 **let…by** pass her over, forget about her.

250–1 **Hercules…twelve** Hercules or Alcides, the descendant of Alcaeus in classical mythology, undertook twelve mighty tasks or 'labours'. Gremio is implying that Petruchio has taken on an even greater task.

253 **hearken for** lie in wait for, seek to win (*OED* sv 7).

259 **stead** help, be of use to.

260 **do this *feat** All modern editors follow Rowe's emendation of F's 'seeke' to 'feat', which corrects a presumed compositorial misreading of 'f'

as long 's' and 't' as 'k': both easy enough errors.

262–3 Tranio seems to be imitating affected upper-class speech here and begins to sound like Polonius; see *Ham.* 2.2.97–104.

262 **whose hap** the man whose luck.

263 **ingrate** ungrateful.

264 **conceive** understand (the situation).

266 **gratify** reward, compensate. Hortensio continues his plan to get money out of his rivals for his friend Petruchio; see 176 and 208–9.

269 **contrive** pass, while away (*OED* sv v^2). This is Shakespeare's only use of the verb in this obsolete sense and it is the latest example recorded by the *OED*, so perhaps it should be seen as part of Tranio's affectation (see 262–3 and n.).

And quaff carouses to our mistress' health,   270
And do as adversaries do in law,
Strive mightily, but eat and drink as friends.

GRUMIO ⎫
          ⎬ O excellent motion! Fellows, let's be gone.
BIONDELLO ⎭

HORTENSIO The motion's good indeed, and be it so.
Petruchio, I shall be your *ben venuto*.   275

Exeunt

[2.1] *Enter* KATHERINA *and* BIANCA [*with her hands tied*].

BIANCA Good sister, wrong me not, nor wrong yourself
To make a bondmaid and a slave of me.
That I disdain. But for these other gauds –
Unbind my hands, I'll pull them off myself,
Yea, all my raiment, to my petticoat,   5
Or what you will command me will I do,
So well I know my duty to my elders.

KATHERINA Of all thy suitors here I charge thee tell
Whom thou lov'st best. See thou dissemble not.

BIANCA Believe me, sister, of all the men alive   10
I never yet beheld that special face
Which I could fancy more than any other.

KATHERINA Minion, thou liest! Is't not Hortensio?

BIANCA If you affect him, sister, here I swear
I'll plead for you myself but you shall have him.   15

KATHERINA O then, belike, you fancy riches more:
You will have Gremio to keep you fair.

Act 2, Scene 1   2.1] *Pope; no act or scene division in* F   0 SD *with...tied*] *Capell subst.; not in* F   3 gauds] *Theobald;*
goods F, *Oliver*   8 thee] F2; *not in* F

270 quaff carouses drink toasts.

273 motion proposal (with perhaps a pun on the other sense of 'motion' – 'movement' – since it is followed by 'let's be gone').

275 *ben venuto* welcome, i.e. 'I'll pay for you.' See 1.1.25 n. on the Italian phrases in this play.

Act 2, Scene 1

1–36 Katherina's violence towards Bianca firmly establishes her shrewish character. Shakespeare rarely depicts women fighting or even quarrelling, but compare *MND* 3.2.282–344.

8 *I...tell Most editors accept F2's addition of 'thee' here. The metrically superfluous 'the' in 10 may have been a marginal correction of 8 misplaced by the compositor.

12 fancy seriously affect, love. The word could be more forceful than it is today; compare 4.2.2 below and *Tro.* 5.2.165–6: 'Never did young man fancy / With so eternal and so fix'd a soul'.

13 Minion Spoilt darling.

14 affect love.

15 i.e. I'll plead for you myself if you will not have him otherwise. See Abbott 126.

17 fair fine, well-dressed.

BIANCA Is it for him you do envy me so?
  Nay then, you jest, and now I well perceive
  You have but jested with me all this while.   20
  I prithee, sister Kate, untie my hands.
      [Katherina] strikes her.
KATHERINA If that be jest, then all the rest was so.

      Enter BAPTISTA.

BAPTISTA Why, how now, dame! Whence grows this insolence?
  Bianca, stand aside. Poor girl, she weeps.
      [He unties her hands.]
  Go, ply thy needle; meddle not with her.   25
  For shame, thou hilding of a devilish spirit!
  Why dost thou wrong her that did ne'er wrong thee?
  When did she cross thee with a bitter word?
KATHERINA Her silence flouts me, and I'll be revenged.
      Flies after Bianca.
BAPTISTA What, in my sight? Bianca, get thee in.   30
          Exit [Bianca]
KATHERINA What, will you not suffer me? Nay, now I see
  She is your treasure, she must have a husband.
  I must dance barefoot on her wedding day
  And, for your love to her, lead apes in hell.
  Talk not to me! I will go sit and weep   35
  Till I can find occasion of revenge.   *[Exit]*
BAPTISTA Was ever gentleman thus grieved as I?
  But who comes here?

Enter GREMIO, LUCENTIO *in the habit of a mean man [disguised as Cambio],* PETRUCHIO *with* [HORTENSIO *disguised as Litio,*] TRANIO *[disguised as Lucentio,] with his boy* [BIONDELLO] *bearing a lute and books.*

21 SD *Katherina...her*] F has / Strikes her / in margin beside 22 24 SD *He...hands*] Kittredge; not in F 30 SD *Bianca*] Rowe; not in F 36 SD *Exit*] Rowe; not in F 38 SD.1–3 *disguised as Cambio...*HORTENSIO *disguised as Litio...disguised as Lucentio...*BIONDELLO] Rowe subst.; not in F

18 **envy** hate.
26 **hilding** worthless creature, good-for-nothing.
29 **flouts** mocks, disdains.
31 **suffer me** i.e. let me have my own way.
33 **dance...day** Behaviour traditionally expected of an older, unmarried sister.
34 **lead...hell** Also traditionally expected of old maids. Compare *Ado* 2.1.41, and *The London Prodigal* 1.2.28–9: ''Tis an old proverb, and you know it well, / That women dying maids lead apes

in hell.' These references underline the familiar, folkloristic nature of Katherina's position.
38 SD.1 **mean man** Thus F, perhaps following Lucentio's own phrase at 1.1.196. 'Mean' = poor, lower-class.
38 SD.2 *•HORTENSIO The omission of Hortensio from F's stage direction can be seen in relation to several other problems and inconsistencies about his role; see Textual Analysis, pp. 161–4 below.

GREMIO Good morrow, neighbour Baptista.

BAPTISTA Good morrow, neighbour Gremio. God save you, gentlemen.   40

PETRUCHIO And you, good sir. Pray have you not a daughter
Called Katherina, fair and virtuous?

BAPTISTA I have a daughter, sir, called Katherina.

GREMIO You are too blunt; go to it orderly.

PETRUCHIO You wrong me, Signor Gremio. Give me leave.   45
[*To Baptista*] I am a gentleman of Verona, sir,
That hearing of her beauty and her wit,
Her affability and bashful modesty,
Her wondrous qualities and mild behaviour,
Am bold to show myself a forward guest   50
Within your house, to make mine eye the witness
Of that report which I so oft have heard.
And for an entrance to my entertainment,
I do present you with a man of mine,
[*Presents Hortensio.*]
Cunning in music and the mathematics,   55
To instruct her fully in those sciences,
Whereof I know she is not ignorant.
Accept of him, or else you do me wrong.
His name is Litio, born in Mantua.

BAPTISTA Y'are welcome, sir, and he for your good sake,   60
But for my daughter Katherine, this I know:
She is not for your turn, the more my grief.

PETRUCHIO I see you do not mean to part with her,
Or else you like not of my company.

BAPTISTA Mistake me not; I speak but as I find.   65
Whence are you, sir? What may I call your name?

PETRUCHIO Petruchio is my name, Antonio's son,
A man well known throughout all Italy.

41–2 And...virtuous] *As verse, Capell; as prose,* F   54 SD *Presents Hortensio*] *Rowe subst.; not in* F   59 Litio] F,
Riverside, Morris, Oliver; Licio F2, *Rowe, Bond, NS, Hibbard*

44 **orderly** in a properly conducted manner. The contrast between an orderly 'performance' and an exaggerated one has been drawn at Induction 1.63–97 and it is to be an important aspect of Petruchio's impact on the other characters. See also p. 37 above for the thematic significance of this motif.

50 **forward** eager, with sense of over-eager, presumptuous, as at 72 below.

53 **entrance...entertainment** entrance-fee for my reception. The metaphor continues to stress the idea of a 'performance'.

55 **Cunning** Skilful, as at 79 below.

56 **sciences** branches of knowledge or skill. See 1.1.93 and n.

59 **Litio** See note on this name in List of Characters, p. 45 above.

62 **She...turn** She will not suit your requirements. Baptista assumes from Petruchio's speech (46–52) that he is ignorant of Katherina's true character.

BAPTISTA I know him well. You are welcome for his sake.

GREMIO Saving your tale, Petruchio, I pray   70
   Let us that are poor petitioners speak too.
   Backare! You are marvellous forward.

PETRUCHIO O pardon me, Signor Gremio, I would fain be doing.

GREMIO I doubt it not, sir, but you will curse your wooing.
   [*To Baptista*] Neighbour, this is a gift very grateful, I am sure of   75
   it. To express the like kindness, myself, that have been more kindly
   beholding to you than any, freely give unto you this young scholar
   [*Presents Lucentio.*] that hath been long studying at Rheims, as
   cunning in Greek, Latin and other languages as the other in music
   and mathematics. His name is Cambio. Pray accept his service.   80

BAPTISTA A thousand thanks, Signor Gremio. Welcome, good Cambio.
   [*To Tranio*] But, gentle sir, methinks you walk like a stranger. May
   I be so bold to know the cause of your coming?

TRANIO Pardon me, sir, the boldness is mine own
   That, being a stranger in this city here,   85
   Do make myself a suitor to your daughter,
   Unto Bianca, fair and virtuous.
   Nor is your firm resolve unknown to me
   In the preferment of the eldest sister.
   This liberty is all that I request   90
   That, upon knowledge of my parentage,
   I may have welcome 'mongst the rest that woo,
   And free access and favour as the rest,
   And toward the education of your daughters
   I here bestow a simple instrument   95
   And this small packet of Greek and Latin books.
   [*Biondello steps forward with the lute and books.*]

70–2 Saving...forward] *As verse, divided thus, Stockdale; after* let *and* too, *Capell; as prose,* F, *Oliver*   74–5 wooing.
Neighbour, this] *Theobald;* wooing neighbors: this F*;* wooing, neighbours. This *Rowe*   75–83 Neighbour...coming]
As prose, Pope; as verse, divided after guift, expresse, beene, any, hath, cunning, Languages, Mathematickes, service,
Gremio, *sir, stranger,* F   77 unto you] *Capell;* unto F   78 SD *Presents Lucentio*] *Rowe subst.; not in* F   82 SD *To
Tranio*] *Rowe; not in* F   96 SD *Biondello...books*] *Capell subst.; not in* F

69 I...well Again, the social world of Italy seems
very compact; see 1.2.97 n.

70–83 The lineation is puzzling in F, which prints
70–2 as prose and 75–83 as verse. See Textual
Analysis, p. 155 below.

70 Saving With no offence to.

72 Backare! Stand back. A proverbial piece of
mock-Latin.

73 doing Perhaps including the meaning 'having
sexual intercourse'.

75 grateful pleasing, welcome.

76–7 myself...any Presumably Gremio means

that Baptista has favoured his suit to Bianca; there
is no mention of any other sort of obligation.

77 unto *you this F omits 'you' but Capell's
emendation is clearly necessary.

80 Cambio The name, aptly, means 'exchange'
in Italian.

82 walk...stranger are standing apart, i.e. are
not one of this group.

87 fair and virtuous Petruchio applied this
conventional tag to Katherina at 42 above.

91 upon...of when you know about.

      If you accept them, then their worth is great.

BAPTISTA Lucentio is your name. Of whence, I pray?

TRANIO Of Pisa, sir, son to Vincentio.

BAPTISTA A mighty man of Pisa. By report   100
    I know him well. You are very welcome, sir.
    [*To Hortensio*] Take you the lute, [*To Lucentio*] and you the
        set of books;
    You shall go see your pupils presently.
    Holla, within!

                Enter a SERVANT.

             Sirrah, lead these gentlemen
    To my daughters, and tell them both   105
    These are their tutors. Bid them use them well.
               [*Exeunt Servant, Hortensio, Lucentio*]
    We will go walk a little in the orchard
    And then to dinner. You are passing welcome,
    And so I pray you all to think yourselves.

PETRUCHIO Signor Baptista, my business asketh haste,   110
    And every day I cannot come to woo.
    You knew my father well, and in him me,
    Left solely heir to all his lands and goods,
    Which I have bettered rather than decreased.
    Then tell me, if I get your daughter's love,   115
    What dowry shall I have with her to wife?

BAPTISTA After my death, the one half of my lands,

100–1 Pisa. By report / I] *Rowe subst.*; *Pisa* by report, / I F   102 SD *To Hortensio...To Lucentio*] *Theobald; not in* F
105 my daughters] F; my two daughters F2   106 SD *Exeunt...Lucentio*] *Theobald; not in* F; *Capell adds* / Biondello
following

---

98 **Lucentio...name** It is not clear how
Baptista knows this. Theobald inserted a stage
direction *They greet privately* after 97, and others
have assumed that Baptista reads an inscription in
one of the books. In the Royal Shakespeare
Company's modern-dress production at Stratford
in 1978 Tranio presented a visiting card.

100–1 **Pisa. By report / I** F reads '*Pisa* by
report, / I'. It is clear from the Merchant's
successful impersonation of Vincentio in 4.4 and 5.1
that Baptista does not know Vincentio personally,
so most editors accept Rowe's emended
punctuation.

103 **presently** immediately.

105 F2 inserts 'two' before 'daughters' in an
attempt to fill up a proper pentameter line, but more
than this must be missing.

108 **passing** surpassingly, extremely.

111 'I cannot come every day to woo' was the
refrain of a sixteenth-century ballad on 'The
Wooing of John and Joan'. See Baskervill, *The
Elizabethan Jig*, pp. 193–4.

116–23 Petruchio and Baptista assume the
conventional arrangement whereby the father had
to part with capital and/or land to his daughter's
husband whereas she would qualify only for an
allowance from her husband's estate if she were
widowed, the substance of the estate passing to his
heirs, lineal or collateral. See 330–87 below for a
longer discussion of dowries by Baptista, Tranio
and Gremio.

And in possession twenty thousand crowns.

PETRUCHIO And for that dowry I'll assure her of
Her widowhood, be it that she survive me,   120
In all my lands and leases whatsoever.
Let specialties be therefore drawn between us,
That covenants may be kept on either hand.

BAPTISTA Ay, when the special thing is well obtained,
That is, her love, for that is all in all.   125

PETRUCHIO Why, that is nothing, for I tell you, father,
I am as peremptory as she proud-minded,
And where two raging fires meet together
They do consume the thing that feeds their fury.
Though little fire grows great with little wind,   130
Yet extreme gusts will blow out fire and all.
So I to her, and so she yields to me,
For I am rough and woo not like a babe.

BAPTISTA Well mayst thou woo, and happy be thy speed!
But be thou armed for some unhappy words.   135

PETRUCHIO Ay, to the proof, as mountains are for winds,
That shakes not though they blow perpetually.

Enter Hortensio with his head broke.

BAPTISTA How now, my friend! Why dost thou look so pale?

HORTENSIO For fear, I promise you, if I look pale.

BAPTISTA What, will my daughter prove a good musician?   140

HORTENSIO I think she'll sooner prove a soldier!
Iron may hold with her, but never lutes.

137 shakes] F, *Hibbard, Morris, Oliver*; shake F2, *Bond, NS, Riverside*

---

118 **in possession** i.e. immediately.

118 **twenty...crowns** Maynard Mack argues, in 'Rescuing Shakespeare', *International Shakespeare Association Occasional Papers* 1 (1979), 19, that this would have been an extraordinarily high figure and is probably a joke against Katherina.

119–20 **assure...widowhood** guarantee her her widow's rights. See 116–23 n. above.

122 **specialties** special contracts.

123 **covenants** financial undertakings or indentures.

125 **her love** Baptista's stress on this contrasts sharply with his attitude to Bianca in 331–3 below, and shows that Katherina's unconventional behaviour has at least gained her this important point.

126 **father** father-in-law. Petruchio's use of the term indicates how confident he is of success.

132 **So...her** So I behave to her.

136 **to...proof** so as to be invulnerable (picking up 'armed' from 135). Armour of proof is that which has been tested and proved to withstand attack.

137 **shakes** F2 corrects to 'shake', but a third-person plural in 's' is common in Shakespeare: see Abbott 333.

137 SD **broke** injured, bleeding.

139 **promise** assure.

141 **prove a soldier** (1) make a good soldier, (2) put a soldier to the test (compare 'proof' in 136).

142 **hold...her** stand up to her handling.

142 **lutes** Following on from 'hold with' there is a quibble here on 'lute' meaning a kind of mud used as a glue or cement.

BAPTISTA Why then, thou canst not break her to the lute?
HORTENSIO Why no, for she hath broke the lute to me.
    I did but tell her she mistook her frets   145
    And bowed her hand to teach her fingering,
    When, with a most impatient devilish spirit,
    'Frets, call you these?' quoth she, 'I'll fume with them!'
    And with that word she struck me on the head,
    And through the instrument my pate made way,   150
    And there I stood amazèd for a while,
    As on a pillory, looking through the lute,
    While she did call me rascal fiddler
    And twangling Jack, with twenty such vile terms,
    As had she studied to misuse me so.   155
PETRUCHIO Now, by the world, it is a lusty wench!
    I love her ten times more than e'er I did.
    O how I long to have some chat with her.
BAPTISTA [*To Hortensio*]
    Well, go with me, and be not so discomfited.
    Proceed in practice with my younger daughter;   160
    She's apt to learn and thankful for good turns.
    Signor Petruchio, will you go with us,
    Or shall I send my daughter Kate to you?
PETRUCHIO I pray you do. I'll attend her here –
                           [*Exeunt all but Petruchio*]
    And woo her with some spirit when she comes!   165
    Say that she rail, why then I'll tell her plain
    She sings as sweetly as a nightingale.
    Say that she frown, I'll say she looks as clear
    As morning roses newly washed with dew.

157 e'er] *Rowe*; ere F   159 SD *To Hortensio*] *Gentleman; not in* F   164 SD *Exeunt...Petruchio*] F *subst. after 163*

143 break...lute teach her to play the lute. The implied analogy of a horse being broken to the bit is the first of many 'taming' metaphors.

144 broke...me broken the lute on me.

145 frets Ridges on the lute to regulate fingering. Katherina quibbles on 'frets' meaning 'vexations'.

148 fume be in a rage (as in 'to fret and fume').

152 As...pillory i.e. with my head in a wooden collar.

155 studied planned, rehearsed.

155 misuse ill-treat, abuse, either physically or verbally – the latter seems upmost here.

156 lusty spirited. It is appropriate that

Petruchio is attracted by outrageous, 'forward' behaviour not unlike his own.

158 chat familiar conversation.

164 attend wait for.

165–76 Petruchio encourages us to appreciate his 'performance' by telling us what to expect, as at 4.1.159–82. His relationship with the audience is somewhat similar to that of the Bastard in *John* (a sympathetic character) but it is more often Shakespearean villains – Richard III, Iago, Edmund – who reveal their plans to manipulate others in this way. See p. 8 above.

168 clear serene.

Say she be mute and will not speak a word,   170
Then I'll commend her volubility
And say she uttereth piercing eloquence.
If she do bid me pack, I'll give her thanks
As though she bid me stay by her a week.
If she deny to wed, I'll crave the day   175
When I shall ask the banns, and when be married.

Enter Katherina.

But here she comes, and now, Petruchio, speak.
Good morrow, Kate, for that's your name, I hear.
KATHERINA Well have you heard, but something hard of hearing –
They call me Katherine that do talk of me.   180
PETRUCHIO You lie, in faith, for you are called plain Kate,
And bonny Kate, and sometimes Kate the curst.
But Kate, the prettiest Kate in Christendom,
Kate of Kate-Hall, my super-dainty Kate –
For dainties are all Kates – and therefore, Kate,   185
Take this of me, Kate of my consolation:
Hearing thy mildness praised in every town,
Thy virtues spoke of and thy beauty sounded –
Yet not so deeply as to thee belongs –
Myself am moved to woo thee for my wife.   190
KATHERINA 'Moved' – in good time! Let him that moved you hither
Remove you hence. I knew you at the first
You were a movable.
PETRUCHIO   Why, what's a movable?

---

176 SD *Enter Katherina*] *Follows 177 in* F   182 bonny] F4; bony F

---

173 **pack** be gone.

179 **heard...hard** Both words were pronounced 'hard', providing a homonymic pun. See Kökeritz, *Pronunciation*, p. 112.

182 *bonny F reads 'bony' here, which is accepted by Kökeritz as another homonymic pun (*Pronunciation*, p. 96), but F4's correction to 'bonny' seems attractive in the light of 'my bonny Kate' at 3.2.216 and the fact that Shakespeare never uses 'bony' elsewhere. (Ferando in *A Shrew* refers to 'bonnie *Kate*' in the equivalent of this scene (v) if further support is needed.)

184 **Kate-Hall** Perhaps a topical reference as other editors suggest, though the allusion is obscure. More probably an ironic or mock heroic form of address; compare the celebration of the 'red

herring of Red Herrings' Hall' at the end of Nashe's *Lenten Stuff* (1598), and Cocledemoy's salutation of the courtesan Franceschina as 'Frank o' Frank Hall' in Marston's *The Dutch Courtesan* (1604) 4.3.1.

185 **dainties...Kates** delicacies or 'dainties' are called 'cates'.

188 **sounded** (1) proclaimed, (2) plumbed or measured. The latter – a nautical metaphor – leads to 'deeply' in 189.

190–2 **moved...Remove** See 1.2.69 for the identical word-play. Petruchio 'feeds' Katherina several good lines during this exchange and seems to relish her performance as much as his own.

193 **movable** (1) portable item of furniture, (2) inconsistent or changeable person.

KATHERINA A joint stool.

PETRUCHIO   Thou hast hit it. Come sit on me.

KATHERINA Asses are made to bear, and so are you.   195

PETRUCHIO Women are made to bear, and so are you.

KATHERINA No such jade as you, if me you mean.

PETRUCHIO Alas, good Kate, I will not burden thee,

   For, knowing thee to be but young and light –

KATHERINA Too light for such a swain as you to catch,   200

   And yet as heavy as my weight should be.

PETRUCHIO 'Should be'! Should – buzz!

KATHERINA   Well tane, and like a buzzard.

PETRUCHIO O slow-winged turtle, shall a buzzard take thee?

KATHERINA Ay, for a turtle, as he takes a buzzard.

PETRUCHIO Come, come, you wasp! I'faith you are too angry.   205

KATHERINA If I be waspish, best beware my sting.

PETRUCHIO My remedy is then to pluck it out.

KATHERINA Ay, if the fool could find it where it lies.

194 joint] *Capell;* joyn'd F

194 joint stool Wooden stool made by a joiner. The insult was proverbial: compare *Lear* 3.6.52: 'Cry you mercy, I took you for a joint stool.'

195 bear i.e. bear loads.

196 bear i.e. bear children.

197 jade worn-out horse. Katherina implies that Petruchio is either too old for her or insufficiently virile.

198 burden (1) lie heavy on (in the act of sexual intercourse and hence 'make pregnant'), (2) make accusations against (*OED* sv v 2). T. R. Waldo and T. W. Herbert point out that the musical sense (refrain or drone bass) is also relevant in the light of other musical quibbles on 'light', 'heavy', 'catch', 'buzz', etc. in this passage: 'Musical terms in *The Taming of the Shrew*: evidence of single authorship', *SQ* 10 (1959), 185–99.

199 light (1) slender, (2) promiscuous. For the latter implication, see 283 n.

200 swain bumpkin.

201 as heavy...be The metaphor is now one from money: Katherina denies that she is 'light' in the way that clipped or counterfeit coins are.

202 'Should...buzz This seems a little feeble (as Katherina says): Petruchio puns on 'bee', hence 'buzz' which also means 'rumour' or 'scandal'; he implies that he has heard stories of Kate's promiscuity. Waldo and Herbert (see 198 n.) point out that the singer of a drone bass part is said to 'buzz the burden', thus continuing the musical quibbles.

202 tane taken, caught in flight (a term from falconry).

202 buzzard A kind of hawk that cannot be trained, hence a foolish or unobservant person who will only hit on things by chance. Tilley lists 'He is a blind buzzard' as proverbial (B792). Through the musical metaphor Katherina implies that Petruchio is droning the bass to her melody, but in reply he accepts this in a more favourable sense: that he should become the basic music or foundation of her life.

203 turtle turtle-dove (often a symbol of faithful love, as in Shakespeare's poem *The Phoenix and the Turtle* (1601)).

203 take (1) capture (with sexual reference), (2) mistake.

204 Ay...buzzard Obscure. The editors of NS suggest 'the fool will take me for a faithful wife, as the turtle-dove swallows the cockchafer' (2.1.208 n.). 'Cockchafer' or 'buzzing insect' is yet another possible meaning for 'buzzard' and one which is supported by the subsequent references to wasps. At this point in *A Shrew* Ferando's servant Sander (= Grumio) understandably expresses impatience with his master's handling of this conversation, which he has overheard but not understood: '...and you talke of Woodcocks with her, and I cannot tell you what' (scene v, 65–6). (Grumio calls Gremio a 'woodcock' in *The Shrew* 1.2.154.)

PETRUCHIO Who knows not where a wasp does wear his sting?
     In his tail.
KATHERINA   In his tongue.
PETRUCHIO   Whose tongue?   210
KATHERINA Yours, if you talk of tales, and so farewell.
                    [*She turns to go.*]
PETRUCHIO What, with my tongue in your tail? Nay, come again.
     Good Kate, I am a gentleman –
KATHERINA   That I'll try.
                    She strikes him.
PETRUCHIO I swear I'll cuff you if you strike again.
                    [*He holds her.*]
KATHERINA So may you lose your arms.   215
     If you strike me, you are no gentleman,
     And if no gentleman, why then no arms.
PETRUCHIO A herald, Kate? O put me in thy books.
KATHERINA What is your crest – a coxcomb?
PETRUCHIO A combless cock, so Kate will be my hen.   220
KATHERINA No cock of mine; you crow too like a craven.
PETRUCHIO Nay, come, Kate, come; you must not look so sour.
KATHERINA It is my fashion when I see a crab.
PETRUCHIO Why, here's no crab, and therefore look not sour.
KATHERINA There is, there is.   225
PETRUCHIO Then show it me.
KATHERINA   Had I a glass I would.
PETRUCHIO What, you mean my face?
KATHERINA   Well aimed of such a young
     one.

209–10 Who...tail] *As verse, Rowe; as prose,* F   211 tales] F; *tails* Q   211 SD *She...go*] *Eds.; not in* F
212–13 What...gentleman] *Eds.; as two lines in* F *divided after* tail   214 SD *He...her*] *Eds.; not in* F   215 lose] *Rowe;*
loose F

211 **tales** rumours (referring back to 202), with
a quibble on 'tails' meaning 'genital organs'. See
TGV 2.3.46–9 for the identical pun.
     213 **try** make trial of.
     215 **lose...arms** (1) relax your grip, (2) forfeit
your coat of arms (the mark of a gentleman).
     218 **A herald...?** i.e. are you skilled in
heraldry...?
     218 **put...books** (1) register me as a gentleman,
(2) accept me into your favour. For the second
meaning, compare the comment on Benedick made
to Beatrice in *Ado* 1.1.78–9: 'I see, lady, the
gentleman is not in your books.'

219 **crest** (1) heraldic device, (2) tuft of feathers
on a bird's head.
     219 **coxcomb** fool's cap (resembling the crest of
a cock).
     220 **combless** i.e. peaceable, with a sense of
'sexually gratified' depending on the usage of 'cock'
for 'penis'.
     221 **craven** unsuccessful (cowardly) fighting
cock.
     223 **crab** crab-apple, which is sour, hence an
ill-tempered or fractious person.
     227 **Well...one** A good guess for such a novice.
(Sarcastic.) The metaphor is from archery.

PETRUCHIO Now, by Saint George, I am too young for you.

KATHERINA Yet you are withered.

PETRUCHIO   'Tis with cares.

KATHERINA   I care not.

PETRUCHIO Nay, hear you, Kate – in sooth you scape not so.   230

KATHERINA I chafe you if I tarry. Let me go.

PETRUCHIO Nay, not a whit. I find you passing gentle.
   'Twas told me you were rough and coy and sullen,
   And now I find report a very liar,
   For thou art pleasant, gamesome, passing courteous,   235
   But slow in speech, yet sweet as springtime flowers.
   Thou canst not frown, thou canst not look askance,
   Nor bite the lip as angry wenches will,
   Nor hast thou pleasure to be cross in talk,
   But thou with mildness entertain'st thy wooers,   240
   With gentle conference, soft and affable.
      [He lets her go.]
   Why does the world report that Kate doth limp?
   O sland'rous world! Kate like the hazel twig
   Is straight and slender, and as brown in hue
   As hazel-nuts and sweeter than the kernels.   245
   O let me see thee walk. Thou dost not halt.

KATHERINA Go, fool, and whom thou keep'st command.

PETRUCHIO Did ever Dian so become a grove
   As Kate this chamber with her princely gait?
   O be thou Dian, and let her be Kate,   250
   And then let Kate be chaste and Dian sportful!

KATHERINA Where did you study all this goodly speech?

PETRUCHIO It is extempore, from my mother-wit.

---

237 askance] *Rowe* (a scance); a sconce F 241 SD *He...go*] *Eds.; not in* F

229 withered (See 'crab' in 223.) Shakespeare elaborates this 'withered apple' insult in *2H4* 2.4.1–9.

232 passing surpassing, extremely.

233 coy disdainful.

234 a very an absolute.

235 gamesome playful, with perhaps a secondary meaning 'full of sexual sport or provocation'.

244 brown...hue dark-complexioned. This was not usually a compliment to an Elizabethan woman: compare Berowne's unflattering description of Rosaline as 'a whitely wanton with a velvet brow' (*LLL* 3.1.196) and references to the Dark Lady as 'a woman coloured ill' in the *Sonnets*. Nevertheless 'nutbrown' was sometimes seen as a sort of happy medium, as in George Gascoigne's sonnet written

c. 1570 in praise of 'Mistress E.P.' (J. W. Cunliffe (ed.), *Complete Works*, 2 vols., 1907, I, 332), which finishes '"Twixt faire and foule therfore, 'twixt great and small, / A lovely nutbrowne face is best of all.' Petruchio is anyway trying to baffle Katherina with a mixture of compliments and insults.

246 halt limp. (Petruchio behaves as if he is buying a horse.)

247 whom...command i.e. order your servants about (not me).

248 Dian Diana, goddess in Roman mythology of hunting and chastity.

251 sportful i.e. amorous.

252 Where...speech Katherina's sarcastic enquiry reminds us that Petruchio's speech is indeed a calculated performance.

KATHERINA A witty mother! Witless else her son.

PETRUCHIO Am I not wise?

KATHERINA   Yes, keep you warm.   255

PETRUCHIO Marry, so I mean, sweet Katherine, in thy bed.
      And therefore, setting all this chat aside,
      Thus in plain terms: your father hath consented
      That you shall be my wife, your dowry 'greed on,
      And will you, nill you, I will marry you.   260
      Now Kate, I am a husband for your turn,
      For, by this light whereby I see thy beauty –
      Thy beauty that doth make me like thee well –
      Thou must be married to no man but me,
      For I am he am born to tame you, Kate,   265
      And bring you from a wild Kate to a Kate
      Conformable as other household Kates.

            Enter Baptista, Gremio and Tranio.

      Here comes your father. Never make denial –
      I must and will have Katherine to my wife.

BAPTISTA
      Now, Signor Petruchio, how speed you with my daughter?   270

PETRUCHIO How but well, sir? How but well?
      It were impossible I should speed amiss.

BAPTISTA Why, how now, daughter Katherine, in your dumps?

KATHERINA Call you me 'daughter'? Now I promise you
      You have showed a tender fatherly regard   275
      To wish me wed to one half lunatic,
      A mad-cap ruffian and a swearing Jack
      That thinks with oaths to face the matter out.

267 SD *Enter...Tranio*] *Follows 264 in* F

253 **mother-wit** natural intelligence.

254 **A...son** She must be witty, for her son has no wit of his own. (Katherina takes 'mother-wit' in a literal sense.)

255 **Yes...warm** Yes, you have (just enough) wits to keep you warm. 'He is wise enough that can keep himself warm' was proverbial (Tilley K10). Shakespeare uses the saying again in *Ado* 1.1.68.

256 **in thy bed** The shock-effect of this climax is very like that of the comparably outrageous wooing scene in *R3* where Richard tells Anne that the one place other than hell that he is fit for is 'your bedchamber' (1.2.111).

260 **will you, nill you** whether you are willing or not.

261 **for your turn** just right for you (with, perhaps, an ironic reference back to Baptista's comment at 62). The phrase also continues the sexual *doubles entendres*: compare *Ant.* 2.5.58–9: 'He's bound unto Octavia... / For the best turn i'th'bed.'

266 **wild Kate** A pun on 'wildcat'.

267 **Conformable** Compliant, submissive.

267 SD This anticipatory entry is placed after 264 in F.

270 **speed** progress, get on.

273 **in...dumps** low-spirited, out of temper.

277 **Jack** ill-bred fellow.

278 **face...out** get his way by brazen effrontery.

PETRUCHIO Father, 'tis thus: yourself and all the world
        That talked of her have talked amiss of her.   280
        If she be curst, it is for policy,
        For she's not froward, but modest as the dove;
        She is not hot, but temperate as the morn;
        For patience she will prove a second Grissel,
        And Roman Lucrece for her chastity.   285
        And, to conclude, we have 'greed so well together
        That upon Sunday is the wedding day.
KATHERINA I'll see thee hanged on Sunday first!
GREMIO Hark, Petruchio, she says she'll see thee hanged first.
TRANIO Is this your speeding? Nay then, goodnight our part.   290
PETRUCHIO Be patient, gentlemen. I choose her for myself.
        If she and I be pleased, what's that to you?
        'Tis bargained 'twixt us twain, being alone,
        That she shall still be curst in company.
        I tell you, 'tis incredible to believe   295
        How much she loves me – O the kindest Kate!
        She hung about my neck, and kiss on kiss
        She vied so fast, protesting oath on oath,
        That in a twink she won me to her love.
        O you are novices! 'Tis a world to see   300
        How tame, when men and women are alone,
        A meacock wretch can make the curstest shrew.
        Give me thy hand, Kate. I will unto Venice,

281 for policy as a deliberate tactic.

282 froward perverse, wilful.

283 hot (1) hot-tempered, choleric, (2) sexually eager, unchaste. The latter meaning seems to relate to the preceding exchange in which Katherina has displayed considerable skill in sexual innuendo and provocation; Petruchio is probably not making a serious question of her virginity, though he is not the only Shakespearean hero to assume that a woman with spirit must be unchaste: compare Berowne's description of Rosaline as 'one that will do the deed / Though Argus were her eunuch and her guard', *LLL* 3.1.198–9.

284 Grissel Famous model of wifely patience and obedience, an anti-type of the shrew. Shakespeare probably knew Chaucer's version of her story in *The Clerk's Tale.*

285 Lucrece Equally famous model of wifely chastity who killed herself after being raped by Tarquin. William Painter included the story in his *Palace of Pleasure* (1566), one of the most successful Elizabethan collections of *novelle*, and Shakespeare published his poem *The Rape of Lucrece* on the same theme in 1594.

286 'greed agreed.

290 speeding progress, success.

290 goodnight...part (1) we can say goodbye to our hopes too, (2) that's the end of our promise to contribute to the expenses of Petruchio's courtship (?).

293–4 Petruchio deprives Katherina of her principal weapon, leaving her, in most productions, speechless with rage.

298 vied redoubled. A term used for raising the stakes in card games. See 'out-vied' at 374 below, and see pp. 36–7 above for a general discussion of the play's references to games and sports.

300 'Tis a world It's a treat.

302 meacock meek, timid.

To buy apparel 'gainst the wedding day.

Provide the feast, father, and bid the guests.   305

I will be sure my Katherine shall be fine.

BAPTISTA I know not what to say, but give me your hands.

God send you joy, Petruchio! 'tis a match.

GREMIO ⎱
TRANIO ⎰ Amen say we. We will be witnesses.

PETRUCHIO Father, and wife, and gentlemen, adieu.   310

I will to Venice – Sunday comes apace.

We will have rings, and things, and fine array,

And kiss me, Kate, 'We will be married a' Sunday.'

Exeunt Petruchio and Katherina [separately]

GREMIO Was ever match clapped up so suddenly?

BAPTISTA Faith, gentlemen, now I play a merchant's part,   315

And venture madly on a desperate mart.

TRANIO 'Twas a commodity lay fretting by you.

'Twill bring you gain, or perish on the seas.

BAPTISTA The gain I seek is quiet in the match.

GREMIO No doubt but he hath got a quiet catch!   320

But now, Baptista, to your younger daughter:

Now is the day we long have lookèd for;

I am your neighbour and was suitor first.

TRANIO And I am one that love Bianca more

Than words can witness, or your thoughts can guess.   325

GREMIO Youngling, thou canst not love so dear as I.

TRANIO Greybeard, thy love doth freeze.

GREMIO   But thine doth fry.

---

313 SD *separately*] *Theobald subst.; not in* F   319 in] *Rowe³; me* F

---

307 **give...hands** This action, performed as here before witnesses, formed a 'pre-contract' more binding than a modern engagement.

313 **'We...Sunday'** The refrain of several ballads, one of which ('I mun be married a Sunday') is sung by Ralph Roister Doister in 3.3 of Nicholas Udall's play of that name, written *c.* 1550.

314 **clapped up** fixed up in a hurry – a bargain quickly struck by clapping hands. Shakespeare uses the expression in romantic contexts in *H5* 5.2.129–30 and *WT* 1.2.103–4, but here it serves also to introduce a strain of mercantile metaphors in the following conversation which modulates into outright bidding from 330 onwards.

316 **venture...mart** speculate wildly in a market where there is no certainty of profit.

317 **commodity** (1) piece of goods or merchandise, (2) woman seen as sexual convenience, prostitute. See Partridge, *Bawdy*.

317 **fretting** (1) decaying, wearing out, (2) chafing with vexation.

319 **in...match* F reads 'me the match', a clear use of minim error emended by Rowe. There is an identical mistake at 4.2.71.

326 **dear** (1) affectionately, (2) with as much wealth to back you up. Portia uses the same pun in *MV* 3.2.313: 'Since you are dear bought, I will love you dear.'

Skipper, stand back! 'Tis age that nourisheth.
TRANIO But youth in ladies' eyes that flourisheth.
BAPTISTA Content you, gentlemen; I will compound this strife.   330
'Tis deeds must win the prize, and he of both
That can assure my daughter greatest dower
Shall have my Bianca's love.
Say, Signor Gremio, what can you assure her?
GREMIO First, as you know, my house within the city   335
Is richly furnishèd with plate and gold,
Basins and ewers to lave her dainty hands;
My hangings all of Tyrian tapestry;
In ivory coffers I have stuffed my crowns,
In cypress chests my arras counterpoints,   340
Costly apparel, tents and canopies,
Fine linen, Turkey cushions bossed with pearl,
Valance of Venice gold in needlework,
Pewter and brass, and all things that belongs
To house or housekeeping. Then at my farm   345
I have a hundred milch-kine to the pail,
Six score fat oxen standing in my stalls,
And all things answerable to this portion.
Myself am struck in years I must confess,
And if I die tomorrow this is hers,   350
If whilst I live she will be only mine.
TRANIO That 'only' came well in. Sir, list to me:
I am my father's heir and only son.
If I may have your daughter to my wife,

---

343 Valance] *Pope;* Vallens F

---

328 Skipper Playboy, irresponsible youth. Compare Henry's reference to Richard II as 'the skipping king', *1H4* 3.2.60. There may also be a nautical or 'fishy' flavour to the imagery here, with the references to 'seas' (318), 'catch' (320) and even 'fry' (327); 'skipper' could mean a common seaman as well as a captain.

330 compound settle, resolve.

331 he of both As in 1.1, two men are competing for Bianca, but Tranio ('Lucentio') has replaced Hortensio. It is odd that both Baptista and Gremio seem to forget about Hortensio at this point and hereafter. Admittedly, he can hardly take part here since he is disguised as Litio and is supposedly teaching Bianca to play the lute at this very moment. For a general discussion of 'loose ends' in the plot relating to Hortensio, see Textual Analysis, pp. 161–4 below.

337 lave wash.

338 Tyrian Purple. So called after a dye originally made at Tyre.

340 arras counterpoints counterpanes of Arras tapestry. The phrase occurs in similar lists of luxurious furnishings in both *A Shrew* and the anonymous play *A Knack to Know a Knave* (*c.* 1592); see p. 3 above.

341 tents bed-testers or hangings.

342 bossed embroidered.

343 Valance Fringes on a bed canopy.

346–7 These lines are also paralleled in *A Knack to Know a Knave;* see 340 n. and p. 3 above.

346 milch-kine...pail cows whose milk is sold for human consumption rather than kept for their calves.

348 answerable...portion in proportion for an estate on this scale (with, perhaps, a pun on 'wedding-portion').

349 struck advanced.

I'll leave her houses three or four as good   355
Within rich Pisa walls as any one
Old Signor Gremio has in Padua,
Besides two thousand ducats by the year
Of fruitful land, all which shall be her jointure.
What, have I pinched you, Signor Gremio?   360
GREMIO Two thousand ducats by the year of land?
[*Aside*] My land amounts not to so much in all! –
That she shall have, besides an argosy
That now is lying in Marsellis' road. –
What, have I choked you with an argosy?   365
TRANIO Gremio, 'tis known my father hath no less
Than three great argosies, besides two galliasses
And twelve tight galleys. These I will assure her,
And twice as much whate'er thou off'rest next.
GREMIO Nay, I have offered all. I have no more,   370
And she can have no more than all I have.
If you like me, she shall have me and mine.
TRANIO Why, then the maid is mine from all the world
By your firm promise. Gremio is out-vied.
BAPTISTA I must confess your offer is the best,   375
And, let your father make her the assurance,
She is your own; else, you must pardon me.
If you should die before him, where's her dower?
TRANIO That's but a cavil. He is old, I young.
GREMIO And may not young men die as well as old?   380
BAPTISTA Well, gentlemen, I am thus resolved.
On Sunday next you know

---

362 SD *Aside*] *Neilson; not in* F   362 not] F; *but Theobald*   364 Marsellis'] *Riverside;* Marcellus F, *Oliver;* Marsellis
F2; Marsellies *Rowe;* Marseilles's *Pope;* Marseilles' *Bond, NS, Hibbard;* Marseilles *Morris*

---

358 ducats Venetian gold coins.

359 Of In, from. Tranio is specifying the amount of rent or income yielded annually by the land.

359 jointure settlement to provide for her widowhood; see 116–23 n.

360 pinched put pressure on. (Compare 'choked' in 365.) Here, the physical action is only metaphorical, unlike the contest of Petruchio and Katherina.

363 argosy Largest type of merchant ship, originally one from Ragusa, whence the name.

364 Marsellis' road The safe anchorage outside Marseilles harbour. 'Marsellis' is from F2; F has 'Marcellus' here, which may be Shakespeare's

spelling since of the two other occurrences of the name (both in *AWW*) one is given in F as 'Marcellus' (4.4.9) and the other as 'Marcellae' (4.5.80), an easy misreading for '-us'. Clearly it was trisyllabic.

367 galliasses Heavy, low-built cargo vessels, larger than galleys.

368 tight sound, water-tight.

369 This line serves to remind us that Tranio is making it all up anyway and so is bound to win.

374 out-vied out-bidden, a metaphor from card-playing; see 298 n. This train of images continues through 'gamester' in 389 to 'I have faced it with a card of ten' in 394.

My daughter Katherine is to be married.
Now, on the Sunday following shall Bianca
Be bride to you, if you make this assurance.   385
If not, to Signor Gremio.
And so I take my leave, and thank you both.
GREMIO Adieu, good neighbour.

                                                        Exit Baptista
                              Now I fear thee not.
Sirrah, young gamester, your father were a fool
To give thee all and in his waning age   390
Set foot under thy table. Tut, a toy!
An old Italian fox is not so kind, my boy.   *Exit*
TRANIO A vengeance on your crafty withered hide!
Yet I have faced it with a card of ten.
'Tis in my head to do my master good: 395
I see no reason but supposed Lucentio
Must get a father called supposed Vincentio.
And that's a wonder – fathers commonly
Do get their children, but in this case of wooing
A child shall get a sire, if I fail not of my cunning.   *Exit* 400

3.[1] *Enter* LUCENTIO [*as Cambio*], HORTENSIO [*as Litio*] *and* BIANCA.

LUCENTIO Fiddler, forbear! You grow too forward, sir.
Have you so soon forgot the entertainment
Her sister Katherine welcomed you withal?
HORTENSIO But, wrangling pedant, this is

---

388 SD *Exit Baptista*] *Follows* 387 *in* F   Act 3, Scene 1   3.1] *Rowe; Actus Tertia* F   0 SD *as Cambio...as Litio*]
Kittredge; both disguised / Irving; not in F   4 But...is] F; She is a shrew, but, wrangling pedant, this is *Theobald;* But,
wrangling pedant, know this lady is *Hanmer;* But, wrangling pedant, this Urania is *conj. Tillyard*

391 Set...table i.e. live on your charity.
391 toy joke, piece of nonsense.
392 'An old fox cannot be taken by a snare' was
proverbial (Tilley F647). Presumably an Italian fox
would be even more cunning (Machiavellian?) than
an English one.
394 faced...ten bluffed my way through the
situation even though I held only a low-valued card.
'To outface with a card of ten' was proverbial
(Tilley C75). The expression apparently derives
from the game called Primero; see A. S. C. Ross
and D. G. Rees, 'Face it out with a card of ten',
N&Q 211 (1966), 403–7.
396–7 supposed...supposed false, substitute.
The repetition of the word seems a deliberate
pointer to the fact that Shakespeare took the plot

concerning the courtship of Bianca from George
Gascoigne's play *Supposes* written in 1566 and
published in 1575 with a Prologue explaining the
term 'suppose' and marginal notes pointing out
the various 'supposes' of the plot. See 5.1.92 and
n., and pp. 9–17 above for a general discussion of
Shakespeare's sources.
399 get beget.
399 case Tranio may be punning on 'case'
meaning (1) 'disguise' and (2) 'vagina' here, as in
4.2.45 and 4.4.6.

Act 3, Scene 1
4 But...is There seems to be something missing
from this line: see collation for various editorial
conjectures.

The patroness of heavenly harmony.   5
Then give me leave to have prerogative,
And when in music we have spent an hour,
Your lecture shall have leisure for as much.

LUCENTIO Preposterous ass, that never read so far
To know the cause why music was ordained!   10
Was it not to refresh the mind of man
After his studies or his usual pain?
Then give me leave to read philosophy
And, while I pause, serve in your harmony.

HORTENSIO Sirrah! I will not bear these braves of thine!   15

BIANCA Why, gentlemen, you do me double wrong
To strive for that which resteth in my choice.
I am no breeching scholar in the schools:
I'll not be tied to hours nor 'pointed times
But learn my lessons as I please myself.   20
And, to cut off all strife, here sit we down.
Take you your instrument; play you the whiles;
His lecture will be done ere you have tuned.

HORTENSIO You'll leave his lecture when I am in tune?

LUCENTIO That will be never. Tune your instrument.   25

BIANCA Where left we last?

LUCENTIO Here, madam. [*He reads.*]
Hic ibat Simois, hic est Sigeia tellus,
Hic steterat Priami regia celsa senis.

BIANCA Conster them.   30

LUCENTIO *Hic ibat* – as I told you before; *Simois* – I am Lucentio; *hic
est* – son unto Vincentio of Pisa; *Sigeia tellus* – disguised thus to get
your love. *Hic steterat* – and that Lucentio that comes a-wooing;

---

27 SD *He reads*] *Capell subst.; not in* F   28–9 *Hic…senis*] *As verse, Theobald; as prose,* F   28 *Sigeia*] F2; *sigeria* F
(throughout)

6 **prerogative** precedence, priority.
8 **lecture** lesson.
9 **Preposterous** Used literally to mean that Hortensio puts first things which should come later. The argument over what is 'orderly' continues a theme from 2.1 (see 44 n.).
12 **usual pain** regular labours.
14 **serve in** A contemptuous phrase; 'Lucentio speaks of music as if it were some after-dinner trifle' (NS 3.1.14 n.). Compare the opening of 5.2 with the banquet and Lucentio's line 'At last, though long, our jarring notes agree.' For a general discussion of music in the play, see Appendix 3, pp. 186–8 below.

15 **braves** insults.
18 **breeching** (1) in breeches (i.e. young), (2) liable to be whipped.
20 **learn…myself** The 'mild' Bianca echoes her sister here ('What, shall I be appointed hours…?', 1.1.103).
28–9 *Hic…senis* 'Here ran the [river] Simois; here is the Sigeian land [Troy]; here stood the lofty palace of old Priam' (Ovid, *Heroides* 1, 33–4). (The context is a letter written by Penelope to Ulysses.)
30 **Conster** Construe, translate.

Priami – is my man Tranio; *regia* – bearing my port; *celsa senis* –
that we might beguile the old pantaloon.   35
HORTENSIO Madam, my instrument's in tune.
BIANCA Let's hear. [*He plays.*] O fie! The treble jars.
LUCENTIO Spit in the hole, man, and tune again.
BIANCA Now let me see if I can conster it. *Hic ibat Simois* – I know
you not; *hic est Sigeia tellus* – I trust you not; *Hic steterat*   40
Priami – take heed he hear us not; *regia* – presume not; *celsa*
senis – despair not.
HORTENSIO Madam, 'tis now in tune.
                          [*He plays again.*]
LUCENTIO   All but the bass.
HORTENSIO The bass is right; 'tis the base knave that jars.
       [*Aside*] How fiery and forward our pedant is!   45
       Now, for my life, the knave doth court my love.
       Pedascule, I'll watch you better yet.
BIANCA In time I may believe, yet I mistrust.
LUCENTIO Mistrust it not, for sure Aeacides
       Was Ajax, called so from his grandfather.   50
BIANCA I must believe my master, else, I promise you,
       I should be arguing still upon that doubt.
       But let it rest. Now, Litio, to you.
       Good master, take it not unkindly, pray,
       That I have been thus pleasant with you both.   55

---

37 SD *He plays*] Capell; *not in* F   43 SD *He...again*] *Eds.; not in* F   45–55 *How...both*] *Assigned as in* Pope[2]; F
gives 45–8 to Lucentio, 49–50 to Bianca and 51–5 to Hortensio   45 SD *Aside*] *Capell subst.; not in* F   54 master] F; *masters*
Rowe[3]

34 **port** style, status.

35 **pantaloon** Gremio. See 1.1.45 SD n. As in
2.1.331 ff., Gremio is thought of as the only rival
to Lucentio/Tranio, though Lucentio met Hortensio
and heard him speak of his love in 1.1. See Textual
Analysis, pp. 161–4 below.

38 **Spit...again** A contemptuously appropriate
version of the proverb 'Spit in your hands and take
better hold' (Tilley H120–1).

39–42 Bianca's skill at 'holding off' here seems
rather ominous in terms of other Shakespearean
heroines, linking her with Cressida who knows all
about such techniques (*Tro.* 1.2.282–95) rather than
with the more sympathetic characters who plunge
straight into their love-affairs and only later reflect,
like Juliet, 'I should have been more strange' (*Rom.*
2.2.102).

45–55 F allots 45–8 to Lucentio, 49–50 to Bianca

and 51–5 to Hortensio, perhaps because the copyist
or compositor was confused by the forms *Luc.*, *Lit.*
and *Bia.* in the manuscript. See Textual Analysis,
p. 157 below.

47 **Pedascule** Little pedant (a nonce-word). The
fact that Hortensio is set up as a comic pedant in
these scenes (2.1, 3.1, 4.2) makes it unlikely that
Shakespeare would have repeated the joke by
making the false Vincentio a pedant too. See 4.2.71
SD n.

49 **Aeacides** Lucentio continues *Heroides* 1 (see
28–9 n.) at 35 which begins *Illic Aeacides*. As he
says, 'Aeacides' means 'descendant of Aeacus' – in
this case, Ajax.

54 **master** Thus F. Many editors emend to
'masters', after Rowe, but this does not seem
textually or dramatically necessary.

55 **pleasant** teasing, witty (as in 1.2.44).

HORTENSIO [*To Lucentio*]
     You may go walk, and give me leave awhile.
     My lessons make no music in three parts.
LUCENTIO Are you so formal, sir? Well, I must wait –
     [*Aside*] And watch withal, for, but I be deceived,
     Our fine musician groweth amorous.   60
HORTENSIO Madam, before you touch the instrument
     To learn the order of my fingering,
     I must begin with rudiments of art,
     To teach you gamut in a briefer sort,
     More pleasant, pithy and effectual   65
     Than hath been taught by any of my trade;
     And there it is in writing, fairly drawn.
BIANCA Why, I am past my gamut long ago.
HORTENSIO Yet read the gamut of Hortensio.
BIANCA [*Reads*]
     '*Gamut* I am, the ground of all accord: 70
     A re, to plead Hortensio's passion;
     B mi, Bianca, take him for thy lord;
     C fa ut, that loves with all affection;
     D sol re, one clef, two notes have I;
     E la mi, show pity or I die.'   75
     Call you this 'gamut'? Tut, I like it not!
     Old fashions please me best. I am not so nice
     To change true rules for odd inventions.

                    Enter a SERVANT.

56 SD *To Lucentio*] *Gentleman; not in* F   59 SD *Aside*] *Johnson; not in* F   64 gamut] *Rowe;* gamoth F *(gamouth at*
68, 69, 70, 76)   70 SD *Reads*] *Pope; not in* F   71 *A re*] Q; *Are* F   72 *B mi*] *Pope; Beeme* F   73 *C fa ut*] Q: *C favt* F
75 *E la*] *Johnson; Ela* F   78 change] F2; *charge* F   78 odd] *Theobald;* old F; *new Pope*   78 SD SERVANT] *Rowe;*
Messenger F

57 three parts Hortensio refers to the common
practice of composing songs out of three harmonising
melodies. In contemporary song books the three
parts would be displayed on a single page so that
all the singers could gather around the same book;
perhaps Hortensio means that Lucentio is standing
close enough to himself and Bianca for this purpose,
i.e. too close.

64 gamut The musical scale as systematised by
Guido d'Arezzo *c*. 1024 and called after 'Gamma
ut', its first note.

65 effectual effective.

71–5 *A re*, *B mi*, etc. are the names of the
subsequent notes in the gamut. It can be argued that
Hortensio (unlike Lucentio in his patently absurd
'translation' from Ovid at 31–5 above) finds clever
applications or double meanings for the terms: see
Appendix 3, pp. 186–8 below.

77 nice whimsical, capricious.

78 odd F has 'old', presumably repeated from 77.
Theobald's emendation is generally accepted.

SERVANT Mistress, your father prays you leave your books,
And help to dress your sister's chamber up.   80
You know tomorrow is the wedding-day.
BIANCA Farewell, sweet masters both, I must be gone.
                                        [*Exeunt Bianca and Servant*]
LUCENTIO Faith, mistress, then I have no cause to stay.   [*Exit*]
HORTENSIO But I have cause to pry into this pedant:
Methinks he looks as though he were in love.   85
Yet if thy thoughts, Bianca, be so humble
To cast thy wand'ring eyes on every stale,
Seize thee that list! If once I find thee ranging
Hortensio will be quit with thee by changing.   *Exit*

[3.2] *Enter* BAPTISTA, GREMIO, TRANIO [*disguised as Lucentio*],
KATHERINA, BIANCA, [LUCENTIO *disguised as Cambio,*] *other*
GUESTS *and* ATTENDANTS.

BAPTISTA [*To Tranio*] Signor Lucentio, this is the 'pointed day
That Katherine and Petruchio should be married,
And yet we hear not of our son-in-law.
What will be said? What mockery will it be
To want the bridegroom when the priest attends   5
To speak the ceremonial rites of marriage!
What says Lucentio to this shame of ours?
KATHERINA No shame but mine. I must, forsooth, be forced
To give my hand, opposed against my heart,

---

79 SH SERVANT] *Rowe; Nicke* F   82 SD *Exeunt...Servant*] *Capell; not in* F   83 SD *Exit*] *Rowe; not in* F   Act 3,
Scene 2 3.2] *Pope; no scene division in* F   0 SD.1–2 *disguised as Lucentio...disguised as Cambio*] *Kittredge; not in* F
0 SD.2 LUCENTIO] *Rowe; not in* F   1 SD *To Tranio*] *Capell; not in* F

---

79 SH *SERVANT F has 'Nicke', presumed by
Steevens to be Nicholas Tooley who appears in the
list of the principal actors of the King's Men at the
beginning of the First Folio. See Textual Analysis,
pp. 156–8 below, for a general discussion of actors'
names in this text.

82 SD *Exeunt...Servant* There are no *exit*
directions in F until the end of the scene, but Bianca
must leave before the following speeches. Moreover
she has to re-enter (decked as a bridesmaid in most
productions) seven lines later.

87 **stale** decoy, lure (a term from falconry).

88 **Seize...list** Let him who wants catch you.

88 **ranging** (1) straying (of a hawk), (2) being
inconstant.

89 **quit with** (1) requited, (2) rid of.

89 **changing** i.e. finding another love too. It is
ironic that a disguised man should talk of
'changing'.

Act 3, Scene 2

0 SD.2 *LUCENTIO Lucentio is clearly needed
at 118 so most editors and producers follow Rowe
and bring him on at this point, but the lack of an
entry for him in F may relate to larger textual
problems in this scene. See 3.2.117–18 n.

1–7 It is significant that Baptista addresses
'Lucentio' and ignores Gremio, showing (as at the
end of this scene) how confident he is that
'Lucentio' will marry Bianca.

5 **want** lack.

Unto a mad-brain rudesby, full of spleen,   10
Who wooed in haste and means to wed at leisure.
I told you, I, he was a frantic fool,
Hiding his bitter jests in blunt behaviour.
And to be noted for a merry man,
He'll woo a thousand, 'point the day of marriage,   15
Make feast, invite friends, and proclaim the banns,
Yet never means to wed where he hath wooed.
Now must the world point at poor Katherine
And say, 'Lo, there is mad Petruchio's wife
If it would please him come and marry her!'   20
TRANIO Patience, good Katherine, and Baptista too.
Upon my life, Petruchio means but well,
Whatever fortune stays him from his word.
Though he be blunt, I know him passing wise;
Though he be merry, yet withal he's honest.   25
KATHERINA Would Katherine had never seen him though!
                Exit weeping [followed by Bianca and others]
BAPTISTA Go, girl. I cannot blame thee now to weep,
For such an injury would vex a very saint,
Much more a shrew of thy impatient humour.

                Enter BIONDELLO.

BIONDELLO Master, master, news! And such old news as you never   30
    heard of!

___

16 Make...friends] *Dyce;* Make friends, invite *F, Oliver;* Make friends, invite, yes *F2*   26 SD *followed...others] Capell subst.; not in* F   28 a very saint] F, *Bond, Riverside, Oliver;* a saint *F2, NS, Hibbard, Morris*   29 thy] *F2; not in* F
30 news! And such old news] *Collier;* newes, and such newes *F, Oliver;* old news, and such news *Rowe*

___

10 **rudesby** insolent, unmannerly fellow.
10 **spleen** caprice, changeable temper. 'Spleen' was originally a physiological term: see Induction 1.133 n.
11 Katherina plays bitterly on the familiar proverb 'to marry in haste and repent at leisure' (Tilley H196).
14 **to...for** to get a reputation as.
16 ***Make...friends** Dyce's emendation follows the analogy of 2.1.305, 'Provide the feast, father, and bid the guests', and this improvement of F's sense and metre has been generally accepted by modern editors.
21–5 Tranio's intimacy with Petruchio in this scene – he is familiar with his eccentric way of dressing at 64 and even offers to lend him some better clothes at 103 – seems surprising. It is possible that the lines were originally written for

Hortensio, Petruchio's 'best belovèd and approvèd friend' (1.2.3): see Textual Analysis, pp. 161–4 below.
22 **means but well** intends nothing but good.
23 **fortune...word** accident prevents him from keeping his word.
25 **merry** humorous, facetious.
28 **a very saint** Many editors follow F2 and omit 'very'.
29 **of *thy impatient** F2's addition of 'thy' improves F's sense and metre.
30 **such *old news** Baptista's response makes Rowe's emendation necessary. (See Textual Analysis, pp. 158–9 below, for a discussion of these short-word omissions.) 'Old' could mean 'rare' or 'strange' in this context, or, more likely, it is a reference to Petruchio's clothes and equipment as described below.

BAPTISTA Is it new and old too? How may that be?

BIONDELLO Why, is it not news to hear of Petruchio's coming?

BAPTISTA Is he come?

BIONDELLO Why no, sir.   35

BAPTISTA What then?

BIONDELLO He is coming.

BAPTISTA When will he be here?

BIONDELLO When he stands where I am and sees you there.

TRANIO But say, what to thine old news?   40

BIONDELLO Why, Petruchio is coming in a new hat and an old jerkin;
    a pair of old breeches thrice turned; a pair of boots that have been
    candle-cases, one buckled, another laced; an old rusty sword tane
    out of the town armoury, with a broken hilt and chapeless; with
    two broken points; his horse hipped – with an old mothy saddle   45
    and stirrups of no kindred – besides, possessed with the glanders
    and like to mose in the chine; troubled with the lampass, infected
    with the fashions, full of windgalls, sped with spavins, rayed with
    the yellows, past cure of the fives, stark spoiled with the staggers,
    begnawn with the bots, swayed in the back and shoulder-shotten,   50

33 hear] Q; heard F   50 swayed] *Hanmer*; Waid F; weighed *Oliver*

41–62 As Hibbard points out, this description of
Petruchio and his horse, Gremio's account of the
wedding at 148–72 below, and Petruchio's abuse of
the Tailor in 4.3 are all 'bravura pieces, conscious
displays of the rhetorical arts of grotesque
description, farcical narrative and inventive vitupe-
ration' and Shakespeare's achievement in this line
can be compared with the linguistic virtuosity of his
contemporary Thomas Nashe; see Hibbard, pp. 8–9,
and G. R. Hibbard, *The Making of Shakespeare's
Dramatic Poetry*, 1981, pp. 95–7.
    41 jerkin short jacket.
    42 turned i.e. turned inside out to get more wear
out of them.
    43 candle-cases i.e. worn out and used for
storing candles.
    44 chapeless without a sheath.
    45 points Tagged laces used to fasten hose to
doublet.
    45 his horse An old and wretched horse is
an important feature of folktale versions of the
Shrew story; see p. 12 above. Most of the diseases
mentioned here are discussed by Gervase Markham
in *A Discource of Horsmanshippe* (1593).
    45 hipped lame in the hips.
    46 of no kindred not matching.
    46 glanders Disease causing swelling of the jaw
and discharge from nostrils.

47 mose...chine Probably an error (attributable
either to Biondello or to some transmitter of the
text) for 'mourn of the chine', meaning to suffer
from the final stages of glanders.
    47–8 lampass...fashions Further diseases
affecting the animal's mouth. Clearly Biondello
includes all the horse-diseases he can think of for
the sake of comic exaggeration.
    48 windgalls Tumours on the fetlocks.
    48 sped...spavins ruined by swellings on the
leg-joints.
    48–9 rayed...yellows discoloured with jaun-
dice.
    49 fives Swelling of glands below the ears.
    49 stark spoiled quite destroyed.
    49 staggers Disease causing giddiness and loss
of balance.
    50 begnawn...bots eaten by intestinal worms.
    50 *swayed F reads 'Waid', which has not been
satisfactorily explained, though the meaning might
be 'weighed', i.e. overloaded to the point of
permanent damage or distortion. Hanmer's emendation to 'swayed' (meaning 'strained', hence
'sagging' or 'crooked') is supported by several
contemporary examples: see *OED* Swayed *ppl a* 1
and Sway-backed.
    50 shoulder-shotten with a dislocated shoulder.

near-legged before, and with a half-cheeked bit and a headstall of
sheep's leather, which, being restrained to keep him from stumbling,
hath been often burst and now repaired with knots; one girth six
times pieced, and a woman's crupper of velour, which hath two
letters for her name fairly set down in studs, and here and there   55
pieced with packthread.

BAPTISTA Who comes with him?

BIONDELLO O sir, his lackey, for all the world caparisoned like the
horse, with a linen stock on one leg and a kersey boot-hose on the
other, gartered with a red and blue list; an old hat and the humour   60
of forty fancies pricked in't for a feather; a monster, a very monster
in apparel, and not like a Christian footboy or a gentleman's lackey.

TRANIO 'Tis some odd humour pricks him to this fashion,
    Yet oftentimes he goes but mean-apparelled.

BAPTISTA I am glad he's come, howsoe'er he comes.   65

BIONDELLO Why, sir, he comes not.

BAPTISTA Didst thou not say he comes?

BIONDELLO Who? That Petruchio came?

BAPTISTA Ay, that Petruchio came.

BIONDELLO No, sir, I say his horse comes with him on his back.   70

BAPTISTA Why, that's all one.

BIONDELLO Nay, by Saint Jamy,

---

51 half-cheeked] *Hanmer;* halfe-chekt F, *Oliver*   53 now repaired] F, *Bond, Riverside, Oliver;* new-repaired *NS, conj.
Walker, Hibbard, Morris*   72–6 Nay...many] *As five lines of verse, Collier; as prose,* F; *as two lines of verse divided after*
penny, *Rowe*[3]

---

51 **near-legged before** knock-kneed at the front.
51 **half-cheeked** having the 'cheeks' or side-
pieces broken or wrongly adjusted.
51 **headstall** Part of bridle or halter that goes
round the head.
52 **sheep's leather** i.e. not the more usual (and
stronger) pigskin or cowhide.
52 **restrained** drawn up tight.
53 **girth** Saddle-strap going under the horse's
belly.
54 **pieced** patched, mended.
54 **woman's...velour** The crupper is the strap
passing under the horse's tail to hold the saddle
steady. A woman's crupper might be covered with
velour (a fabric like velvet) and studded with her
initials.
56 **pieced...packthread** mended with string.
58 **caparisoned** fitted out.
59 **stock** stocking.
59 **kersey** Woollen cloth.
59 **boot-hose** Overstocking usually worn with
riding-boots.

60 **list** strip of cloth.
60–1 **humour...fancies** The exact meaning is
obscure; some excessively elaborate decoration is
implied.
61 **for** instead of.
63 **odd...pricks** strange whim that incites.
70 **his horse comes** Biondello indulges in the
kind of quibbling Grumio has employed in his
deliberate mistaking of Petruchio (1.2.6–40) and is
to use again with Curtis (4.1.73–9). It is a common
feature of the clowns in the early comedies (see, for
example, *TGV* 1.1, 2.5, etc.), though other
characters often find it irritating or tedious, as
when Lorenzo comments on Launcelot Gobbo's
witticisms in this vein 'How every fool can play
upon the word' (*MV* 3.5.43).
71 **all one** the same thing.
72–6 This jingle (which is printed as prose in F)
has not been traced. It is generally assumed to be
from some lost ballad or riddle. In this context it
rather oddly anticipates a fragment of the
conversation between Grumio and Curtis in the

I hold you a penny,
A horse and a man
Is more than one,   75
And yet not many.

Enter PETRUCHIO *and* GRUMIO.

PETRUCHIO Come, where be these gallants? Who's at home?
BAPTISTA You are welcome, sir.
PETRUCHIO   And yet I come not well.
BAPTISTA And yet you halt not.
TRANIO   Not so well apparelled
As I wish you were.   80
PETRUCHIO Were it better, I should rush in thus.
But where is Kate? Where is my lovely bride?
How does my father? Gentles, methinks you frown,
And wherefore gaze this goodly company
As if they saw some wondrous monument,   85
Some comet or unusual prodigy?
BAPTISTA Why, sir, you know this is your wedding-day.
First were we sad, fearing you would not come,
Now sadder that you come so unprovided.
Fie, doff this habit, shame to your estate,   90
An eye-sore to our solemn festival.
TRANIO And tell us what occasion of import

79–80 Not...were] *Capell; as one line in* F   81 Were it better] F, *Bond, Riverside;* Why, were it better *Hanmer;* Tut!
were it better *Capell;* Were it not better *NS, conj. Keightley, Hibbard, Morris, Oliver*

following scene – 'What's that to thee? / Why, a
horse' – where again the question of number is
important. See 4.1.49–52 and n.
  73 hold bet.
  76 SD In *A Shrew* (which has no equivalent of
Biondello's description) the stage direction reads
*Enter Ferando baselie attired, and a red cap on his
head* and later Sander describes the clothes to his
fellow-servants – 'when they should / Go to church
to be maried he puts on an olde / Jerkin and a paire
of canvas breeches downe to the / Small of his legge
and a red cap on his head' (scene ix, 10–13).
Moreover Ferando explains his attire to the
assembled company thus: 'Shees such a shrew, if
we should once fal out, / Sheele pul my costlie sutes
over mine eares' (scene vii, 30–1). See illustration
5 (p. 23 above) for Douglas Fairbanks's appearance
in this scene in the 1929 film.
  78 come not well Perhaps Petruchio is

acknowledging the impropriety of his outfit. Or
perhaps he is challenging the sincerity of Baptista's
welcome, which is presumably delivered somewhat
coldly.
  79 halt (1) limp, i.e. your lateness is not excused
by ill-health or infirmity, (2) hesitate, i.e. your entry
is abrupt and unceremonious.
  81 Were it better i.e. even if I were better
dressed. Some editors find F's reading strained and
emend, mainly to 'Were it not better'; see collation.
  85 monument portent, something that gives a
warning.
  86 prodigy omen.
  89 unprovided unprepared, lacking the right
clothes.
  90 habit outfit.
  90 estate status, position.
  92 occasion of import important business or
circumstance.

Hath all so long detained you from your wife
And sent you hither so unlike yourself.

PETRUCHIO Tedious it were to tell, and harsh to hear.   95
Sufficeth I am come to keep my word
Though in some part enforcèd to digress,
Which at more leisure I will so excuse
As you shall well be satisfied with all.
But where is Kate? I stay too long from her.   100
The morning wears, 'tis time we were at church.

TRANIO See not your bride in these unreverent robes;
Go to my chamber, put on clothes of mine.

PETRUCHIO Not I, believe me; thus I'll visit her.

BAPTISTA But thus, I trust, you will not marry her.   105

PETRUCHIO Good sooth, even thus. Therefore ha' done with words;
To me she's married, not unto my clothes.
Could I repair what she will wear in me
As I can change these poor accoutrements,
'Twere well for Kate and better for myself.   110
But what a fool am I to chat with you
When I should bid good morrow to my bride
And seal the title with a lovely kiss!

Exit [with Grumio]

TRANIO He hath some meaning in his mad attire.
We will persuade him, be it possible,   115
To put on better ere he go to church.

---

113 SD *with Grumio*] *Capell subst.; not in* F

94 **unlike yourself** Tranio, who reassured Baptista at 64 that Petruchio 'oftentimes...goes but mean-apparelled', seems anxious to point out that this is not, nevertheless, his normal or proper style.

96 **Sufficeth** It is enough that.

97 **digress** i.e. from my promise (or my route).

101 **wears** is passing.

102–3 Again, Tranio seems surprisingly intimate with Petruchio; see 21–5 n. and Textual Analysis, pp. 161–4 below.

106 **Good sooth** Yes indeed. A common but rather mild oath firmly rejected by Hotspur at *1H4* 3.1.253–6: 'Swear me, Kate, like a lady as thou art, / A good mouth-filling oath, and leave "in sooth", / And such protest of pepper-gingerbread, / To velvet-guards and Sunday-citizens.' Petruchio, who is otherwise rather like Hotspur in his impulsiveness, haste and impatience with convention, has already used 'in sooth' at 2.1.230; it may, in both instances, be part of a deliberate or teasing appearance of mildness.

107–10 This emphasis on clothes and personal decoration as a kind of moral symbolism begins with Bianca's offer, under compulsion, to pull off her 'other gawds' at 2.1.3–4 and runs through the play to the point where Katherina tramples her cap underfoot at 5.2.122. Petruchio moralises on the topic again at 4.3.163–74. See also p. 34 above.

108 **wear** possess and wear out (with sexual implication, and perhaps a glance at the strains of the taming process).

113 **seal...title** A return to the legal and mercantile metaphors of 2.1.314 ff.

113 **lovely** loving.

BAPTISTA I'll after him and see the event of this.

> *Exit [with Gremio, Biondello and Attendants]*

TRANIO *[To Lucentio]* But, sir, to love concerneth us to add
>   Her father's liking, which to bring to pass,
>   As I before imparted to your worship,   120
>   I am to get a man – whate'er he be
>   It skills not much, we'll fit him to our turn –
>   And he shall be Vincentio of Pisa
>   And make assurance here in Padua
>   Of greater sums than I have promisèd.   125
>   So shall you quietly enjoy your hope
>   And marry sweet Bianca with consent.

LUCENTIO Were it not that my fellow schoolmaster
>   Doth watch Bianca's steps so narrowly,
>   'Twere good, methinks, to steal our marriage,   130
>   Which once performed, let all the world say no,
>   I'll keep mine own despite of all the world.

TRANIO That by degrees we mean to look into
>   And watch our vantage in this business.
>   We'll overreach the greybeard Gremio,   135
>   The narrow-prying father Minola,
>   The quaint musician, amorous Litio,

---

117 SD *with...Attendants*] Capell subst.; *not in* F   118 SD *To Lucentio*] Eds.; *not in* F   118 But, sir, to love] *Knight, Hibbard, Morris, Oliver;* But sir, Love F, *Riverside;* But sir, our love *Pope;* But to her love *Capell, Bond, NS* 120 As I before] *Pope;* As before F, *Oliver;* As before I F2

---

117 **event** outcome.

117–18 The transition here is very awkward; Tranio has just agreed with Baptista to try to persuade Petruchio to change his clothes but he fails to follow the other characters off. Moreover, at 118 he seems to be in the middle of a conversation with Lucentio (who has been silent throughout the scene and is indeed omitted from F's stage direction: see 3.2.0 SD n.), which is difficult to manage if he is talking to Baptista at 116. This awkwardness might be resolved by omitting Tranio and Lucentio from this scene altogether, giving Tranio's lines before 118 to Hortensio, to whom they seem more appropriate anyway (see 21–5 n.), and beginning a new scene with *Enter* TRANIO *and* LUCENTIO at 118.

NS conjectures that a whole scene may be missing here since the conversation between Tranio and Lucentio allows a mere twenty lines of stage time for Petruchio to find Katherina, take her to church and get through the marriage ceremony. If we look at *A Shrew* we find at precisely this point a comic scene between Polidor's servant (Biondello)

and Sander (Grumio); see Appendix 1, pp. 178–80 below, for a text of this scene and a discussion of whether it can be seen as a reported version of a Shakespearean original.

118 ***But...love*** F's 'But sir, Love' does not make much sense. The omission of small words is common in this forme (see Textual Analysis, pp. 158–9 below), so Knight's emendation seems acceptable. Capell's suggested reading 'But to her love' is less likely, combining an omission and a misreading.

118 **concerneth us** it is necessary or important for us.

120 **As *I* before** Pope's emendation seems metrically preferable.

122 **skills** matters.

130 **steal...marriage** elope.

134 **watch...vantage** look out for our best opportunities.

136 **narrow-prying** closely prying, suspicious or watchful.

137 **quaint** cunning, ingenious.

All for my master's sake, Lucentio.

Enter Gremio.

Signor Gremio! Came you from the church?
GREMIO As willingly as e'er I came from school.   140
TRANIO And is the bride and bridegroom coming home?
GREMIO A bridegroom, say you? 'Tis a groom indeed –
A grumbling groom, and that the girl shall find.
TRANIO Curster than she? Why, 'tis impossible.
GREMIO Why, he's a devil, a devil, a very fiend!   145
TRANIO Why, she's a devil, a devil, the devil's dam!
GREMIO Tut, she's a lamb, a dove, a fool, to him.
I'll tell you, Sir Lucentio: when the priest
Should ask if Katherine should be his wife,
'Ay, by gogs-wouns!' quoth he, and swore so loud   150
That, all-amazed, the priest let fall the book,
And as he stooped again to take it up,
This mad-brained bridegroom took him such a cuff
That down fell priest and book, and book and priest!
'Now take them up', quoth he, 'if any list.'   155
TRANIO What said the wench when he rose again?
GREMIO Trembled and shook, for why he stamped and swore
As if the vicar meant to cozen him.
But after many ceremonies done
He calls for wine. 'A health', quoth he, as if   160
He had been aboard, carousing to his mates
After a storm; quaffed off the muscadel
And threw the sops all in the sexton's face,

---

143 grumbling] F2; grumlling F   156 rose] F, *Bond, Riverside, Oliver;* rose up F2, *Hibbard, Morris;* arose *Reed, NS*
157–73 Trembled…play] *As verse,* F2; *as prose,* F

142 **groom** rough (lower-class) fellow.

143 **grumbling** bad-tempered. F's 'grumlling' may be an obsolete or dialect form, or perhaps a spelling reflecting pronunciation.

147 **fool** harmless, innocent.

147 **to** compared with.

148–9 **when…ask** at the point in the service when the priest must ask.

150 **gogs-wouns** God's wounds (a common oath and quite a strong one; see 106 n.).

155 **list** pleases to.

156 **What…wench** How did the wench behave, react.

156 **rose** Thus F. Some editors follow F2's 'rose up' or Reed's 'arose'.

157–73 **Trembled…play** Printed as prose in F but corrected to verse in F2; see Textual Analysis, p. 155 below.

157 **for why** wherefore, because; see Abbott 75.

158 **cozen** cheat.

161 **aboard** on board ship. As at 1.2.194–200, we have an image of Petruchio as a man of adventure and travel, ill at ease in this cautious, conventional society.

162 **muscadel** Sweet white wine, traditional at weddings.

163 **sops** pieces of cake soaked in wine.

Having no other reason
But that his beard grew thin and hungerly   165
And seemed to ask him sops as he was drinking.
This done, he took the bride about the neck
And kissed her lips with such a clamorous smack
That at the parting all the church did echo.
And I, seeing this, came thence for very shame,   170
And after me, I know, the rout is coming.
Such a mad marriage never was before!
                        Music plays.
Hark, hark! I hear the minstrels play.

Enter Petruchio, Katherina, Bianca, Hortensio [as Litio], Baptista,
              [Grumio and others].

PETRUCHIO Gentlemen and friends, I thank you for your pains.
          I know you think to dine with me today   175
          And have prepared great store of wedding cheer,
          But so it is, my haste doth call me hence,
          And therefore here I mean to take my leave.
BAPTISTA Is't possible you will away tonight?
PETRUCHIO I must away today, before night come.   180
          Make it no wonder; if you knew my business,
          You would entreat me rather go than stay.
          And, honest company, I thank you all
          That have beheld me give away myself
          To this most patient, sweet and virtuous wife.   185
          Dine with my father, drink a health to me,
          For I must hence, and farewell to you all.
TRANIO Let us entreat you stay till after dinner.
PETRUCHIO It may not be.
GREMIO   Let me entreat you.
PETRUCHIO It cannot be.
KATHERINA   Let me entreat you.   190
PETRUCHIO I am content.
KATHERINA   Are you content to stay?

---

172 SD *Music plays*] *Follows 173 in* F   173 SD.1 *as Litio*] *Pelican; not in* F   173 SD.2 *Grumio...others*] *Capell subst.;*
not in F   189 SH GREMIO] F2 (*Gre.*); *Gra.* F

165 **hungerly** as if ill-fed.   176 **cheer** food and drink.
166 **ask him sops** ask him for the sops.   181 **Make...wonder** Don't be amazed at it.
171 **rout** crowd (of guests).

PETRUCHIO I am content you shall entreat me stay –
  But yet not stay, entreat me how you can.
KATHERINA Now, if you love me, stay.
PETRUCHIO   Grumio, my horse!
GRUMIO Ay, sir, they be ready – the oats have eaten the horses.   195
KATHERINA Nay then,
  Do what thou canst, I will not go today!
  No, nor tomorrow – not till I please myself.
  The door is open, sir, there lies your way;
  You may be jogging whiles your boots are green.   200
  For me, I'll not be gone till I please myself.
  'Tis like you'll prove a jolly surly groom
  That take it on you at the first so roundly.
PETRUCHIO O Kate, content thee; prithee be not angry.
KATHERINA I will be angry. What hast thou to do?   205
  – Father, be quiet. He shall stay my leisure.
GREMIO Ay, marry, sir, now it begins to work.
KATHERINA Gentlemen, forward to the bridal dinner.
  I see a woman may be made a fool
  If she had not a spirit to resist.   210
PETRUCHIO They shall go forward, Kate, at thy command.
  Obey the bride, you that attend on her.
  Go to the feast, revel and domineer,
  Carouse full measure to her maidenhead,
  Be mad and merry – or go hang yourselves.   215
  But for my bonny Kate, she must with me.
  Nay, look not big, nor stamp, nor stare, nor fret;
  I will be master of what is mine own.

194 horse horses. Possible as a plural in Shakespeare's time.

195 oats...horses Either a deliberate slip of the tongue (motivated by the 'preposterous' situation) or an ironic reference to the fact that these broken-down horses have been incapable of eating a normal feed.

200 You...green Be off while your boots are fresh. A proverbial expression for hastening the departure of an unwelcome guest (Tilley B536).

202 jolly bold, overbearing.

203 take ..roundly assume your authority in such a peremptory way at the very beginning.

205 What...do? What right have you to interfere?

206 Father, be quiet Baptista has not spoken, but perhaps he is about to. Alternatively, Katherina may mean 'don't be perturbed'. Father and daughter are, unusually, on the same side in this scene, both wanting a 'proper' wedding.

206 stay...leisure wait until I am ready.

207 work seethe, rage. The metaphor is from liquor fermenting or the sea becoming stormy (see *OED* Work *v* B 32 and 34).

213 domineer feast luxuriously.

217 look not big don't look angry or threatening. Katherina is presumably the one who is looking angry but Petruchio pretends it is the rest of the company who are threatening to deprive him of his lawful property.

She is my goods, my chattels; she is my house,
My household-stuff, my field, my barn,   220
My horse, my ox, my ass, my anything,
And here she stands. Touch her whoever dare,
I'll bring mine action on the proudest he
That stops my way in Padua. Grumio,
Draw forth thy weapon – We are beset with thieves!   225
Rescue thy mistress, if thou be a man.
– Fear not, sweet wench, they shall not touch thee, Kate;
I'll buckler thee against a million!

> *Exeunt Petruchio, Katherina [and Grumio]*

BAPTISTA Nay, let them go – a couple of quiet ones!
GREMIO Went they not quickly, I should die with laughing.   230
TRANIO Of all mad matches never was the like.
LUCENTIO Mistress, what's your opinion of your sister?
BIANCA That being mad herself, she's madly mated.
GREMIO I warrant him, Petruchio is Kated.
BAPTISTA

Neighbours and friends, though bride and bridegroom wants   235
For to supply the places at the table,
You know there wants no junkets at the feast.
[*To Tranio*] Lucentio, you shall supply the bridegroom's
place,
And let Bianca take her sister's room.
TRANIO Shall sweet Bianca practise how to bride it?   240
BAPTISTA She shall, Lucentio. Come, gentlemen, let's go.

> *Exeunt*

---

228 SD *Exeunt...Grumio*] Capell *subst.; Exeunt P. Ka.* F   238 SD *To Tranio*] *This edn; not in* F

219–21 She is...my anything Petruchio recalls the Tenth Commandment, implicitly accusing the assembled company of coveting his wife. His insistence on property and legal rights is perhaps a parody of Paduan mercantile attitudes, as his 'defence' of Katherina is a parody of chivalry.

223 action on lawsuit against.

228 buckler shield.

228 SD Grumio may have been omitted from F's SD here because of a miscalculation about space.

234 Kated afflicted with 'the Kate' (as if it were a disease). Compare Beatrice's remark in *Ado*

1.1.88–9, 'God help the noble Claudio! If he have caught the Benedick...'

235–41 Three marriage-feasts are arranged in the course of the play: this one lacks the bride and groom, the one set up for 'Lucentio' (Tranio) and Bianca in 4.4 is interrupted in 5.1 by the arrival of the true Vincentio, and it is not until 5.2 that the ritual is properly observed (see 5.2.184 n.).

235–6 wants...supply are not here to fill.

237 there...junkets there is no lack of delicacies.

[4.1] *Enter* GRUMIO.

GRUMIO Fie, fie on all tired jades, on all mad masters, and all foul ways!
Was ever man so beaten? Was ever man so rayed? Was ever man
so weary? I am sent before to make a fire, and they are coming after
to warm them. Now were not I a little pot and soon hot, my very
lips might freeze to my teeth, my tongue to the roof of my mouth,   5
my heart in my belly, ere I should come by a fire to thaw me. But
I with blowing the fire shall warm myself, for, considering the
weather, a taller man than I will take cold. Holla, ho! Curtis!

Enter CURTIS.

CURTIS Who is that calls so coldly?

GRUMIO A piece of ice. If thou doubt it, thou mayst slide from my   10
shoulder to my heel with no greater a run but my head and my
neck. A fire, good Curtis.

CURTIS Is my master and his wife coming, Grumio?

GRUMIO O ay, Curtis, ay, and therefore fire, fire! Cast on no water.

CURTIS Is she so hot a shrew as she's reported?   15

GRUMIO She was, good Curtis, before this frost. But thou know'st
winter tames man, woman and beast; for it hath tamed my old
master, and my new mistress, and myself, fellow Curtis.

Act 4, Scene 1 4.1] *Pope; no act or scene division in* F   18 myself] F; thyself *Hanmer, conj. Warburton*

Act 4, Scene 1

4.1 This scene is set in Petruchio's country house which is, as we learn at 4.3.181–4, about four or five hours' riding distance from Padua. The change of location is not strictly necessary for the taming plot but the journey home after the wedding which is described here is an important feature of folktale versions of the story. It is also typical of Shakespeare to use a special location for a metamorphosis.

o SD No act or scene division in F.

1 jades worn-out horses.

1 foul ways dirty roads.

2 rayed soiled, bespattered (with mud).

3 sent before There is a hint of religious parody here: Grumio compares himself with John the Baptist who was 'sent before' Christ.

4 little...hot 'A little pot is soon hot' was proverbial for a small person who gets angry quickly (Tilley P497). From this reference and those at 8 and 19–20 below it is clear that the original actor of Grumio's role was a small man.

7–8 considering the weather The cold and

mud indicate that it is winter here, which is appropriate for Petruchio's plan to subject his wife to physical discomfort and deprivation, though it seemed to be summer in Padua when Baptista invited his guests to 'walk a little in the orchard' before dinner at 2.1.107. See also 16–17 n.

8 taller bolder, more capable (with a glance at the literal meaning, too).

9 coldly (1) like one numbed with cold, (2) mildly, without passion or choler (ironic).

11 run run up, running start.

14 fire...water Grumio alludes ironically to the round 'Scotland's burning' which has the refrain 'Fire, fire! Cast on water.' Curtis takes Grumio's 'fire!' as a warning about Katherina's temper.

15 hot angry, violent.

16 before...frost (1) before this cold journey, (2) before she encountered Petruchio (see 17 n.).

17 winter...beast A reference to the proverb 'Age (or winter) and wedlock tame both man and beast' (Tilley A64).

18 fellow Curtis This phrase implies that Curtis, along with Grumio, takes the place of the beast in the preceding analogy.

CURTIS Away, you three-inch fool, I am no beast!

GRUMIO Am I but three inches? Why, thy horn is a foot, and so long   20
am I at the least. But wilt thou make a fire, or shall I complain on
thee to our mistress, whose hand – she being now at hand – thou
shalt soon feel, to thy cold comfort, for being slow in thy hot office.

CURTIS I prithee, good Grumio, tell me, how goes the world?

GRUMIO A cold world, Curtis, in every office but thine, and therefore,   25
fire. Do thy duty, and have thy duty, for my master and mistress
are almost frozen to death.

CURTIS There's fire ready, and therefore, good Grumio, the news.

GRUMIO Why, 'Jack boy, ho boy!' and as much news as wilt thou.

CURTIS Come, you are so full of cony-catching.   30

GRUMIO Why, therefore fire, for I have caught extreme cold. Where's
the cook? Is supper ready, the house trimmed, rushes strewed,
cobwebs swept, the servingmen in their new fustian, their white
stockings, and every officer his wedding garment on? Be the Jacks
fair within, the Jills fair without, the carpets laid, and everything   35
in order?

CURTIS All ready, and therefore, I pray thee, news.

GRUMIO First know my horse is tired, my master and mistress fallen
out.

CURTIS How?   40

GRUMIO Out of their saddles into the dirt, and thereby hangs a tale.

CURTIS Let's ha't, good Grumio.

GRUMIO Lend thine ear.

CURTIS Here.

---

19 SH CURTIS] Q (*Cur.*); *Gru.* F   33 their white] F3; the white F, *Oliver*

19 SH *CURTIS F gives Grumio three speeches
running here, but this middle one must belong to
Curtis.

19 three-inch fool Another reference to
Grumio's size.

20 horn (1) cuckold's horn, (2) penis. Grumio
implies that he is 'big enough' ('so long am I') to
have cuckolded Curtis.

26 have thy duty have (earn) your reward.

29 Jack...boy An allusion to another round
(compare 14 above) called 'The devil is dead' which
begins 'Jack boy, ho boy, News.' See Baskervill,
Elizabethan Jig, p. 68.

30 cony-catching trickery. The literal reference
is to rabbit-hunting but the term was applied to
swindling and thievery in general, especially after
the publication of Robert Greene's popular *Art of
Cony-catching* in 1592.

32 rushes strewed i.e. on the floor.

33 fustian Coarse cloth used for working-
clothes.

34 officer official, servant.

34–5 Jacks...Jills (1) leather drinking-vessels
and metal drinking-vessels, (2) male and female
servants – with a suggestion of rustic stereotypes, as
in the use of the names in *LLL* 5.2.875 and *MND*
3.2.461.

35 carpets Probably used in its now obsolete
sense of 'tablecloths', both from its position in the
list and from the fact that the floors have been
referred to above ('rushes strewed').

37 All ready This is contradicted at 103–9 below.
Perhaps we are to assume that Curtis is so eager to
hear the news that he just brushes aside Grumio's
questions.

42 ha't have it.

43–8 Compare the knockabout comedy and the
play on 'here' / 'ear' at 1.2.5–10.

GRUMIO There.   45

[*He boxes Curtis's ear.*]

CURTIS This 'tis to feel a tale, not to hear a tale.

GRUMIO And therefore 'tis called a sensible tale; and this cuff was but
to knock at your ear and beseech listening. Now I begin. *Imprimis*
we came down a foul hill, my master riding behind my mistress.

CURTIS Both of one horse?   50

GRUMIO What's that to thee?

CURTIS Why, a horse.

GRUMIO Tell thou the tale. But hadst thou not crossed me, thou
shouldst have heard how her horse fell, and she under her horse;
thou shouldst have heard in how miry a place, how she was   55
bemoiled, how he left her with the horse upon her, how he beat
me because her horse stumbled, how she waded through the dirt
to pluck him off me, how he swore, how she prayed that never
prayed before, how I cried, how the horses ran away, how her bridle
was burst, how I lost my crupper – with many things of worthy   60
memory which now shall die in oblivion, and thou return un-
experienced to thy grave.

CURTIS By this reckoning he is more shrew than she.

GRUMIO Ay, and that thou and the proudest of you all shall find when
he comes home. But what talk I of this? Call forth Nathaniel,   65

---

45 SD He...ear] *Rowe subst.; not in* F   48 *Imprimis*] *Rowe;* Inprimis F

46 **feel** experience.

47 **sensible** (1) rational, (2) capable of being felt.

48 *Imprimis* First (Latin). Grumio parodies the
form of official documents or bills (compare
4.3.130).

50 **of** on.

50 **one horse** J. H. Brunvand notes this brief
allusion as evidence of Shakespeare's knowledge of
the oral tradition behind the taming plot ('Comparative Study', p. 297). See 3.2.72–6 n. and
discussion of sources, p. 12 above.

53 **crossed** challenged, interrupted.

56 **bemoiled** covered with mud.

56–7 **he beat...stumbled** Another element in
the oral tradition.

58–9 **she...before** As Steevens pointed out, this
line appears in a totally different context in the old
King Leir play: the supporters of Leir take an oath
to reinstate him in his kingdom and the comic
character Lord Mumford joins in, saying 'Let me
pray to, that never pray'd before' (2349). Here, it
is perhaps part of the association of Katherina with
the devil – another folklore motif.

60 **crupper** See 3.2.54 n.

60 **of worthy** worthy of. Grumio continues his

parody of 'officialese': here the reference is perhaps
to a funeral speech.

63 **shrew** bad-tempered. Used of either sex,
though more often of women. This exchange (63–5)
implies that the servants have not seen this side of
Petruchio before, and reminds the audience that he
is putting on a performance.

65 **what** why (what for).

65–6 **Nathaniel...Sugarsop** Some of these
names are used again in F's speech headings at 80–8
(*Nat., Phil., Ios., Nick*), Nathaniel and Philip re-
appear in Petruchio's summons at 93 (along with
the previously unmentioned Gregory), and Nathaniel and Walter are mentioned in Grumio's
explanation at 103–9 (along with Gregory and the
additional newcomers Gabriel, Peter, Adam and
Rafe). If we include Grumio and Curtis this makes
a total of thirteen servants, far more than are ever
likely to have appeared on stage. Textual corruption
is possible (see NS 4.1.121–7 n.) but it is just as
likely that the general intention was to suggest that
the house is full of servants and to have as many of
them as possible milling about on stage at the
climactic moments of this scene.

Joseph, Nicholas, Philip, Walter, Sugarsop and the rest. Let their
heads be slickly combed, their blue coats brushed, and their garters
of an indifferent knit. Let them curtsy with their left legs, and not
presume to touch a hair of my master's horse-tail till they kiss their
hands. Are they all ready?   70
CURTIS They are.
GRUMIO Call them forth.
CURTIS Do you hear, ho? You must meet my master to countenance
      my mistress.
GRUMIO Why, she hath a face of her own.   75
CURTIS Who knows not that?
GRUMIO Thou, it seems, that calls for company to countenance her.
CURTIS I call them forth to credit her.
GRUMIO Why, she comes to borrow nothing of them.

Enter four or five SERVINGMEN.

NATHANIEL Welcome home, Grumio.   80
PHILIP How now, Grumio.
JOSEPH What, Grumio.
NICHOLAS Fellow Grumio.
NATHANIEL How now, old lad.
GRUMIO Welcome you; how now you; what you; fellow you; and thus   85
      much for greeting. Now, my spruce companions, is all ready, and
      all things neat?
NATHANIEL All things is ready. How near is our master?
GRUMIO E'en at hand, alighted by this. And therefore be not – Cock's
      passion, silence! I hear my master.   90

Enter PETRUCHIO *and* KATHERINA.

PETRUCHIO Where be these knaves? What, no man at door
          To hold my stirrup, nor to take my horse?
          Where is Nathaniel, Gregory, Philip?
ALL SERVINGMEN Here! Here sir, here sir!

79 SD *Enter...*SERVINGMEN] *Follows 78 in* F   **89** SH GRUMIO] *Rowe; Gre.* F

67 blue The usual colour for servants' clothing;
see 1.1.198 n.
68   indifferent Either 'matching' or
'unobtrusive'.
68 curtsy A gesture of respect used by both
sexes.
68 left legs To kneel with the left leg was
thought to be more submissive.

73 countenance pay your respects to. Grumio
pretends to take it literally as 'provide a face for'.
78 credit her do her honour. Again Grumio
quibbles.
79 SD *four or five* See 65–6 n. and Textual
Analysis, p. 156 below.
89 Cock's God's.
92 hold my stirrup i.e. help me dismount.

PETRUCHIO 'Here sir, here sir, here sir, here sir'!   95
          You logger-headed and unpolished grooms!
          What, no attendance? No regard? No duty?
          Where is the foolish knave I sent before?
GRUMIO Here sir, as foolish as I was before.
PETRUCHIO You peasant swain! You whoreson malthorse drudge!   100
          Did I not bid thee meet me in the park
          And bring along these rascal knaves with thee?
GRUMIO Nathaniel's coat, sir, was not fully made,
          And Gabriel's pumps were all unpinked i'th'heel.
          There was no link to colour Peter's hat   105
          And Walter's dagger was not come from sheathing.
          There were none fine but Adam, Rafe and Gregory;
          The rest were ragged, old and beggarly.
          Yet, as they are, here are they come to meet you.
PETRUCHIO Go, rascals, go, and fetch my supper in.   110

                                        Exeunt Servingmen

          [*Sings*] Where is the life that late I led?
          Where are those –
          Sit down, Kate, and welcome. Food, food, food, food!

                    Enter Servants with supper.

          Why, when, I say? Nay, good sweet Kate, be merry.
          Off with my boots, you rogues, you villains! When?   115
          [*Sings*] It was the friar of orders grey
          As he forth walkèd on his way –

---

110 SD *Exeunt Servingmen*] *Capell subst.; Ex. Ser.* F   111 SD *Sings*] *Theobald; not in* F   112 Where...those] *As part of the song, Theobald;* F *prints* Where...soud *as two verse lines divided after* Kate   113 Food, food] *NS, Hibbard, Morris;* Soud, soud F, *Bond, Riverside, Oliver*   116 SD *Sings*] *Rowe; not in* F (*but* F *prints 116–17 in italics*)

---

96 logger-headed blockheaded, stupid.

100 whoreson Literally 'son of a whore'; actually 'bastard', a general insult.

100 malthorse drudge horse used for grinding malted barley in a mill, hence 'slow', 'heavy'.

103–9 For the servants' names, see 65–6 n. For their unreadiness, see 37 n.; it is also of course possible that Grumio is in league with Petruchio here and is inventing inadequacies where none exists.

104 all unpinked entirely lacking their proper decoration. (To 'pink' leather was to punch small holes in it.)

105 link blacking made from burnt torches.

106 sheathing having its scabbard fitted or repaired.

111–12 Where...those A popular song now

lost, but reinvented by Cole Porter for *Kiss Me Kate*, the Broadway musical version of *The Taming of the Shrew*, first performed in 1948. The original song presumably also lamented the newly-married man's loss of freedom.

113 *Food, food F has 'Soud, soud', etc. here, which some editors retain though it can only be explained as 'a unique form of exclamation'. The emendation to 'Food', first suggested by the editors of NS, gives better sense and is convincing because of the easy confusion of 'f' and long 's' in Secretary hand.

114 when An exclamation of impatience (*OED* sv 1 1b).

116–17 It was...way Another fragment of a lost song.

Out, you rogue! You pluck my foot awry.
Take that!

[He strikes the Servant.]

And mend the plucking off the other.
Be merry, Kate. Some water here! What ho!   120

Enter one with water.

Where's my spaniel Troilus? Sirrah, get you hence
And bid my cousin Ferdinand come hither –

[Exit a Servant]

One, Kate, that you must kiss and be acquainted with.
Where are my slippers? Shall I have some water?
Come, Kate, and wash, and welcome heartily.   125
You whoreson villain! Will you let it fall?

[He strikes the Servant.]

KATHERINA Patience, I pray you. 'Twas a fault unwilling.
PETRUCHIO A whoreson, beetle-headed, flap-eared knave!
Come, Kate, sit down, I know you have a stomach.
Will you give thanks, sweet Kate, or else shall I?   130
What's this? Mutton?
FIRST SERVINGMAN   Ay.
PETRUCHIO   Who brought it?
PETER   I.
PETRUCHIO 'Tis burnt, and so is all the meat.
What dogs are these! Where is the rascal cook?
How durst you villains bring it from the dresser
And serve it thus to me that love it not?   135

---

119 SD *He...Servant*] *Rowe; not in* F   119 off] *Rowe; of* F   122 SD *Exit...Servant*] *Capell; not in* F
126 *He...Servant*] *Capell subst.; not in* F   131 SH PETER] F; *Ser.* F2

121 **spaniel Troilus** In folktale versions of the taming plot, the husband often intimidates his wife by punishing his dog for some supposed fault, as Petruchio strikes the servant here and as he has beaten Grumio because Katherina's horse stumbled; see Brunvand, 'Comparative Study', p. 299. Troilus, the name of the great tragic lover of the medieval Troy legends, is ironically given to a spaniel. In some productions a dog does appear on stage to add to the general confusion in this scene.

122 **cousin Ferdinand** Another loose end in the plot; see Textual Analysis, pp. 161–4 below. The editors of NS conjecture that Hortensio appears (4.3.35 SD) in what was originally Ferdinand's place (see NS 4.1.141 n.).

126 **it** Presumably the basin of water. Perhaps Petruchio should knock it out of the servant's hands himself.

127 Katherina's attitude here (and on the journey as described at 57–9 above) is quite different from what we have seen before.

127 **unwilling** not deliberate.

128 **beetle-headed** thick-headed, stupid. A beetle was a wooden mallet.

129 **stomach** (1) appetite, (2) proud spirit or temper (as at 5.2.176).

130 **give thanks** say grace.

134 **dresser** sideboard, serving-table.

There, take it to you, trenchers, cups and all!
[*He throws the food and dishes at them.*]
You heedless joltheads and unmannered slaves!
What, do you grumble? I'll be with you straight.

[*Exeunt Servants*]

KATHERINA I pray you, husband, be not so disquiet.
The meat was well, if you were so contented.   140
PETRUCHIO I tell thee, Kate, 'twas burnt and dried away,
And I expressly am forbid to touch it,
For it engenders choler, planteth anger;
And better 'twere that both of us did fast,
Since, of ourselves, ourselves are choleric,   145
Than feed it with such over-roasted flesh.
Be patient. Tomorrow't shall be mended,
And for this night we'll fast for company.
Come, I will bring thee to thy bridal chamber.

Exeunt

Enter Servants severally.

NATHANIEL Peter, didst ever see the like?   150
PETER He kills her in her own humour.

Enter Curtis.

GRUMIO Where is he?
CURTIS In her chamber,
Making a sermon of continency to her,
And rails and swears and rates, that she, poor soul,   155

---

136 SD *He...them*] Rowe subst.; *not in* F   138 SD *Exeunt Servants*] Dyce; *not in* F   151 SD *Enter Curtis*] *Follows 152*
in F   154–58 Making...hither] *As verse,* Pope; *as prose,* F

136 **trenchers** wooden plates.
137 **joltheads** fools.
138 **be...straight** be after you (to punish you) at once.
140 **if...contented** if you had been pleased to acknowledge it as such.
141 **dried away** dried up.
143 **choler** anger, or, more technically, the bile humour which was thought to cause anger in the Elizabethan psycho-physiological theory of humours. Compare *Err.* 2.2.56–63 where the same idea occurs. Sir Thomas Elyot in *The Castel of Helthe* (1541) agrees with this general notion of correspondences but he lists 'hot wynes, peppers, garlycke, onyons and salte' as being 'noyfull to them whych be choleryke' (fol. 17ᵛ). See also 4.3.17–31 below.

148 **for company** together. Many directors ignore this statement and have Petruchio eat his supper when he returns alone at 158. *A Shrew* has at this point the stage direction *Manent servingmen and eate up all the meate.*
151 **in...humour** i.e. by outdoing her in anger and arbitrary bad temper. See 143 n. above.
154 **continency** restraint, self-control. The specifically sexual reference here neatly counters the commonplace innuendo of 'in her chamber'. It is important that the marriage is not actually consummated until after the last scene of the play; see 5.2.184 n.
155 **rates** scolds.

Knows not which way to stand, to look, to speak,
And sits as one new-risen from a dream.
Away, away, for he is coming hither.

[*Exeunt*]

Enter Petruchio.

PETRUCHIO Thus have I politicly begun my reign,
And 'tis my hope to end successfully.   160
My falcon now is sharp and passing empty,
And till she stoop she must not be full-gorged,
For then she never looks upon her lure.
Another way I have to man my haggard,
To make her come and know her keeper's call,   165
That is, to watch her, as we watch these kites
That bate and beat and will not be obedient.
She ate no meat today, nor none shall eat;
Last night she slept not, nor tonight she shall not.
As with the meat, some undeservèd fault   170
I'll find about the making of the bed,
And here I'll fling the pillow, there the bolster,
This way the coverlet, another way the sheets.
Ay, and amid this hurly I intend
That all is done in reverend care of her.   175
And, in conclusion, she shall watch all night,
And if she chance to nod I'll rail and brawl
And with the clamour keep her still awake.

158 SD *Exeunt*] Pope; *not in* F

157 **new-risen…dream** This description of
Katherina is one of a number of parallels between
her situation here and that of Christopher Sly in
Induction 2. The 'sermon of continency' is another
link. See pp. 35 and 40 above.
159–82 Again Petruchio tells the audience how he
intends to proceed; see 2.1.165–76 n. A garbled
version of this speech in *A Shrew* provides good
evidence for the theory that that play is, in part at
least, a memorially reconstructed version of *The
Shrew*; see Textual Analysis, pp. 168–71 below.
159 **politicly** calculatedly.
161 **falcon** The taming of Katherina is again
likened to the taming of a wild creature; see 2.1.143
n. For a contemporary account of the training of
falcons see George Turberville's *Booke of Falconrie*
(1575). It is worth noting that the purpose of
training a falcon is not to break the bird's spirit.

161 **sharp** hungry.
162 **stoop** (1) flies to the lure, (2) submits to my
will.
163 **lure** Device used in training hawks: when
they return to the lure they are rewarded with food.
164 **man my haggard** tame my wild hawk.
166 **watch her** keep her awake.
166 **kites** There may be a pun on 'Kate' here.
167 **bate and beat** flap and flutter wildly away
from the lure.
169 **Last night** No night has passed since the
wedding: perhaps Petruchio supposes that Katherina would have been too excited to sleep the night
before. Or perhaps strict consistency has been
subordinated to dramatic effect.
170–8 Again it is clear that Petruchio will himself
suffer the deprivations he imposes on Katherina.
174 **intend** (will) claim, pretend.

This is a way to kill a wife with kindness,
And thus I'll curb her mad and headstrong humour.   180
He that knows better how to tame a shrew,
Now let him speak – 'tis charity to show.   *Exit*

[4.2] *Enter* TRANIO [*disguised as Lucentio*] *and* HORTENSIO [*disguised as Litio*].

TRANIO Is't possible, friend Litio, that mistress Bianca
                    Doth fancy any other but Lucentio?
                    I tell you, sir, she bears me fair in hand.
HORTENSIO Sir, to satisfy you in what I have said,
                    Stand by, and mark the manner of his teaching.   5
                    [*They stand aside.*]

                    Enter BIANCA [*and* LUCENTIO *disguised as Cambio*].

LUCENTIO Now, mistress, profit you in what you read?
BIANCA What, master, read you? First resolve me that.

Act 4, Scene 2   4.2] *Steevens; no scene division in* F   0 SD *disguised as Lucentio...disguised as Litio*] *Kittredge; not*
in F   1–5 Is't...teaching] *As verse,* F; *as prose, Oliver*   4 SH HORTENSIO] F2; *Luc.* F   5 SD.1 *They...aside*] *Theobald*
subst.; not in F   5 SD.2 *and* LUCENTIO] *Rowe; not in* F   5 SD.2 *disguised as Cambio*] *Kittredge; not in* F   6 SH LUCENTIO]
F2; *Hor.* F   7 you? First] *Theobald; you first* F

179 kill...kindness An ironic allusion to the
proverbial 'To kill with kindness' (Tilley K51),
meaning to harm someone through misguided
indulgence.

181–2 shrew ...show A true rhyme on the 'o'
sound; compare the final couplet of the play. Many
such rhymes are found in the earlier shrew play,
Tom Tyler and His Wife.

Act 4, Scene 2

0 SD No act or scene division in F.

2 fancy seriously affect, love. See 2.1.12 and n.

3 bears...hand is deceiving me beautifully.
Tranio's claim that Bianca is deceiving him is ironic
but it allows him to manipulate Hortensio.

4–8 F's incorrect allocation of lines here was
corrected in F2. The confusion may have arisen (as
at 3.1.45–55) because the copyist or compositor
tried to clarify forms given in the manuscript as *Luc.*
and *Lit.* (for *Lucentio* and *Litio*). See Textual
Analysis, p. 157 below.

4 satisfy convince, furnish with proof. We must
assume that Hortensio has just told Tranio what he
observed of the relationship between Bianca and

'Cambio' (Lucentio) at the end of 3.1, and has
brought him to eavesdrop so that he can see for
himself. This 'overheard courtship' scene might be
compared with that in *TGV* (4.2) and the one in
Tro. (5.2).

5 Stand...mark A clear case of a stage direction
being given within the dialogue, as in 27. See
p. 31 above for a general discussion of *The Shrew*'s
use of stage audiences.

5 SD F has simply *Enter Bianca* here, perhaps
because the copyist was led by his own misreading
of the speech heading at 4 (which he gives as *Luc.*)
to assume that Lucentio was already on stage. The
instruction to 'stand by' suggests Bianca and
Lucentio enter the main stage while Hortensio and
Tranio move to one side of it.

6 mistress Used both as a polite form of address
and to imply that Bianca is the object of Lucentio's
love.

7 master Literally 'schoolmaster', but Bianca
also plays on the (hypothetical) sense of the word
as the male equivalent of 'mistress'. This word-play
continues in 9–10.

7 resolve answer.

LUCENTIO I read that I profess, *The Art to Love*.

BIANCA And may you prove, sir, master of your art.

LUCENTIO While you, sweet dear, prove mistress of my heart.   10

[*They court.*]

HORTENSIO Quick proceeders, marry! Now tell me, I pray,

You that durst swear that your mistress Bianca

Loved none in the world so well as Lucentio.

TRANIO O despiteful love, unconstant womankind!

I tell thee, Litio, this is wonderful.   15

HORTENSIO Mistake no more – I am not Litio,

Nor a musician as I seem to be,

But one that scorn to live in this disguise

For such a one as leaves a gentleman

And makes a god of such a cullion.   20

Know, sir, that I am called Hortensio.

TRANIO Signor Hortensio, I have often heard

Of your entire affection to Bianca,

And since mine eyes are witness of her lightness,

I will with you, if you be so contented,   25

Forswear Bianca and her love for ever.

HORTENSIO See how they kiss and court! Signor Lucentio,

Here is my hand, and here I firmly vow

Never to woo her more, but do forswear her

---

8 SH LUCENTIO] F2; *Hor.* F   10 SD *They court*] *Capell subst.; They retire backward | Theobald; not in* F
11–13 Quick...Lucentio] *As verse,* F; *as prose,* F3, *Oliver*   13 none] *Rowe;* me F

---

8 **profess** avow, practise.

8 ***The Art to Love*** i.e. Ovid's *Ars Amatoria*, a witty poem which presents love as a science and which was notorious in Elizabethan England. See also Induction 2.45 n. and 1.1.33 n.

11 **proceeders** Hortensio picks up the academic vocabulary of 9 and puns on the expression 'to proceed Master of Arts', meaning to progress from B.A. to M.A. within the university system.

13 **Loved *none** Most modern editors follow Rowe's emendation of F's 'me' to 'none'. It is possible, however, that something has been omitted here since Hortensio's 'tell me...' seems incomplete.

14 **despiteful** cruel.

15 **wonderful** amazing.

20 **cullion** low fellow (literally, 'testicle'). Hortensio, who is comically unaware of the implications of his own disguise, seems as much offended by what he takes to be the low social class of Bianca's new favourite as he is by the betrayal itself.

22 **I...heard** It is inconsistent that Tranio has only 'heard of' Hortensio's suit here when he had direct knowledge of it from Hortensio himself in 1.2 and seemed totally ignorant of it in 2.1. See 2.1.331 n. and 3.1.35 n., and Textual Analysis pp. 161–4 below.

23 **entire** complete, utter.

24 **lightness** inconstancy, lack of seriousness. See 2.1.199 n.

25–6 **I will...ever** Tranio has worked out how to turn what could have been a disastrous exposure of Lucentio into a trick to get rid of Hortensio. He continues with his own pretended suit later, of course.

26 **Forswear Bianca** The formality of the oaths which follow is comical, especially as Tranio's 'unfeignèd oath' is totally sincere! Shakespeare gets considerable mileage out of the swearing and forswearing of lovers in his early comedies, as in *TGV* 2.6 and *LLL* 4.3, and it is not surprising that a sincere lover like Juliet (in the balcony scene, *Rom.* 2.2) has a deep distrust of oaths.

As one unworthy all the former favours   30
That I have fondly flattered her withal.

TRANIO And here I take the like unfeignèd oath
Never to marry with her though she would entreat.
Fie on her! See how beastly she doth court him.

HORTENSIO Would all the world but he had quite forsworn!   35
For me, that I may surely keep mine oath,
I will be married to a wealthy widow
Ere three days pass, which hath as long loved me
As I have loved this proud disdainful haggard.
And so farewell, Signor Lucentio.   40
Kindness in women, not their beauteous looks,
Shall win my love; and so I take my leave,
In resolution as I swore before.   [*Exit*]
    [*Tranio joins Lucentio and Bianca.*]

TRANIO Mistress Bianca, bless you with such grace
As 'longeth to a lover's blessèd case!   45
Nay, I have tane you napping, gentle love,
And have forsworn you with Hortensio.

BIANCA Tranio, you jest – but have you both forsworn me?

TRANIO Mistress, we have.

LUCENTIO   Then we are rid of Litio.

TRANIO I'faith, he'll have a lusty widow now   50
That shall be wooed and wedded in a day.

31 her] F3; them F   43 SD.1 *Exit*] *Rowe; not in* F   43 SD.2 *Tranio…Bianca*] *Capell subst.; Lucentio and Bianca come forward | Theobald; not in* F

31 fondly foolishly, with credulity caused by misplaced affection.

34 beastly like an animal (i.e. unashamedly). Tranio lays it on with a trowel.

35 Would…forsworn Hortensio wishes that Lucentio (whom he takes to be the poor low-born Cambio) were Bianca's only lover. He perhaps assumes that she will actually marry Gremio.

37 a wealthy widow This character is introduced very abruptly in order to round off the Hortensio plot and provide three women (the traditional number in the folklore versions) for the final scene. See also 50 n.

39 haggard wild hawk. See 4.1.161–7 and n.

41 Kindness Natural, kind feeling, i.e. constant affection.

44–7 From his mode of address here ('Mistress Bianca', 'gentle love'), it is possible that Tranio is claiming Lucentio's rights, producing a moment of confusion for characters and audience. He might even embrace Bianca as he speaks, elated as he is with his ingenious tricking of Hortensio.

45 'longeth to belongs to, is appropriate for.

45 case Perhaps Tranio is punning on 'case' meaning (1) 'disguise' and (2) 'vagina' here, as at 2.1.399 and 4.4.6.

46 tane you napping caught you unawares, i.e. seen you courting.

48 Tranio…jest Either Bianca is embarrassed by Tranio's attitude to her in 44–7 (see note above) or she is at first unwilling to believe what he says. The 'but' in this line suggests that Tranio's 'jest' is something different from what he actually reports.

50 lusty widow Presumably the widow is thought to be 'lusty' in the sense of 'full of sexual desire' since she is ready to be courted and married in such a short time, but there was a more general association of widows with sexual appetite or promiscuity, as in Jonson's Dame Pliant (*Alchemist*) and, perhaps, in the puzzling jocularity about 'widow Dido' in *Temp.* 2.1.77–83.

BIANCA God give him joy!

TRANIO Ay, and he'll tame her.

BIANCA He says so, Tranio?

TRANIO Faith, he is gone unto the taming-school.

BIANCA The taming-school? What, is there such a place? 55

TRANIO Ay, mistress, and Petruchio is the master,

That teacheth tricks eleven and twenty long

To tame a shrew and charm her chattering tongue.

Enter BIONDELLO.

BIONDELLO O master, master, I have watched so long

That I am dog-weary, but at last I spied 60

An ancient angel coming down the hill

Will serve the turn.

TRANIO What is he, Biondello?

BIONDELLO Master, a marcantant, or a pedant,

I know not what, but formal in apparel,

In gait and countenance surely like a father. 65

LUCENTIO And what of him, Tranio?

TRANIO If he be credulous and trust my tale,

---

63 marcantant] F, *Bond, Hibbard, Riverside, Oliver;* Mercatante *Capell, NS, Morris*

---

53 He says so Again Bianca's reply is problematic. Is she perhaps being sarcastic? Riverside cuts this particular knot by adding a question mark where F has none. It is notable that this remark, together with the rest of the dialogue from 53 to 56, is reproduced with unusual precision in *A Shrew*, scene x.

54 he...taming-school Hortensio has not revealed any such intention here (unlike Polidor in *A Shrew*, scene viii), though he is next seen at Petruchio's house in 4.3 where he comments on the taming process. Two problems of consistency arise: (1) How does Tranio know where Hortensio is going? (2) When does he in fact woo the widow? For a general discussion of the inconsistencies relating to the role of Hortensio, see Textual Analysis, pp. 161–4 below. The notion of a 'taming-school' (where husbands learn how to tame their wives) testifies to the strongly exemplary nature of the folklore originals of this story (and implies that the sympathetic scholar or playgoer is likely to be male).

57 eleven and twenty Probably another allusion to the card-game 'thirty-one' mentioned by Grumio at 1.2.30–1. In that case 'two and thirty' was 'a pip out' (meaning slightly too much or too many) whereas here the meaning is that tricks 'eleven and twenty long' are exactly right.

61 ancient angel An angel was a gold coin, hence this phrase seems to mean 'an old man of good class' (and therefore appropriate). Hibbard suggests that he is also seen as an angel who comes in response to a prayer. Or Biondello may simply see him as an innocent old man whose goodness can be exploited.

62 serve the turn suffice for our purposes.

62 What What kind of man.

63 marcantant merchant. This is the only use of the word recorded in *OED*, but there seems little doubt that it is Biondello's version of the Italian *mercatante*. See 1.1.25 n. for further discussion of Shakespeare's use of Italian words and phrases in this play.

66 Lucentio still seems unsure of the plot, though Tranio explained it to him at 3.2.118 ff. In general, Lucentio's role as the somewhat slow master to whom everything has to be explained by his witty servants (see, for example, 4.4.80–93) is taken over from Roman comedy. It is of course a very convenient device for the audience, who may also be having trouble following this complicated plot.

67 trust believe.

I'll make him glad to seem Vincentio
And give assurance to Baptista Minola
As if he were the right Vincentio.   70
Take in your love, and then let me alone.

                    [*Exeunt Lucentio and Bianca*]

                    Enter a MERCHANT.

MERCHANT God save you, sir.
TRANIO   And you, sir. You are welcome.
          Travel you farre on or are you at the farthest?
MERCHANT Sir, at the farthest for a week or two,
          But then up farther, and as far as Rome,   75
          And so to Tripoli, if God lend me life.
TRANIO What countryman, I pray?
MERCHANT   Of Mantua.
TRANIO Of Mantua, sir? Marry, God forbid!
          And come to Padua careless of your life?
MERCHANT My life, sir? How, I pray? For that goes hard.   80
TRANIO 'Tis death for anyone in Mantua
          To come to Padua. Know you not the cause?

---

71 Take] F2; *Par.* Take F   71 in] *Theobald; me* F   71 SD.1 *Exeunt...Bianca] Rowe; not in* F
71 SD.2 MERCHANT] *This edn, conj. Hosley; Pedant* F *(throughout)*   73 farre] F; far *Rowe and most edns;* farrer *Hibbard*

---

71 F has a mysterious and unnecessary speech heading *Par.* attached to this line, which W. W. Greg suggested might be the name of the actor about to play the Merchant (or Pedant – see 71 SD n. below), which was written in the margin and then mistakenly included in the text (Greg, p. 214). This suggestion is supported and refined by Karl P. Wentersdorf, 'Actors' names in Shakespearean texts', *Theatre Studies* 23 (1976–7), 18–30. Alternatively, *Par.* might relate to the confusion about the man's profession: the copyist wrote *Mar.*, tried correcting it to *Ped.* but found it too messy, cancelled the resulting *Par.* and wrote *Ped.* below it; see Textual Analysis, pp. 157–8 below.

71 Take *in F reads 'Take me', emended by Theobald.

71 SD.2 *MERCHANT F reads *Pedant* here and in all subsequent stage directions and speech headings, but as Richard Hosley pointed out, it is clear from what he says below about his 'bills of money' (89–90) that he is in fact a merchant, like the corresponding characters in Ariosto's *Suppositi*, Gascoigne's *Supposes*, and *A Shrew* (Hosley, 'Sources and analogues', pp. 289–308). His anxiety that he may have met Baptista before (4.4.2–5) is further confirmation. What seems to have happened

is that whoever copied the text and attempted to tidy it up chose the wrong profession out of the two possibilities offered by Biondello – 'a marcantant or a pedant' (63) – probably influenced by the unfamiliarity of the word 'marcantant'.

73 farre on 'Farre' is an obsolete comparative (= 'farther'). Compare 'Farre then Deucalion off', *WT* 4.4.431. In this instance the final 'e' should probably be pronounced.

75–6 This itinerary confirms that the character is a merchant, not a pedant. Tripoli is probably the trading city on the North African coast south of Sicily, not the Syrian one (see E. H. Sugden, *A Topographical Dictionary to the Works of Shakespeare and his Fellow Dramatists*, 1925).

80 goes hard is a serious matter.

81–2 'Tis death...Padua This piece of plot from Gascoigne's *Supposes* (2.1) is also used by Shakespeare in *Err.* 1.1. It is not meant to present a realistic picture of the hazards of trade in sixteenth-century Italy, though it contributes its mite to the general image of a violent and lawless country which is so widespread in the Elizabethan and Jacobean drama (see Praz, 'Shakespeare's Italy').

Your ships are stayed at Venice, and the Duke,
For private quarrel 'twixt your Duke and him,
Hath published and proclaimed it openly. 85
'Tis marvel – but that you are but newly come,
You might have heard it else proclaimed about.
MERCHANT Alas, sir, it is worse for me than so.
For I have bills for money by exchange
From Florence, and must here deliver them. 90
TRANIO Well, sir, to do you courtesy,
This will I do, and this I will advise you –
First tell me, have you ever been at Pisa?
MERCHANT Ay, sir, in Pisa have I often been,
Pisa renownèd for grave citizens. 95
TRANIO Among them know you one Vincentio?
MERCHANT I know him not, but I have heard of him,
A merchant of incomparable wealth.
TRANIO He is my father, sir, and sooth to say,
In count'nance somewhat doth resemble you. 100
BIONDELLO [*Aside*] As much as an apple doth an oyster, and all one!
TRANIO To save your life in this extremity,
This favour will I do you for his sake –
And think it not the worst of all your fortunes
That you are like to Sir Vincentio – 105
His name and credit shall you undertake,

---

86 but that you are but newly] F, *Rowe, Bond, Riverside, Morris, Oliver;* but that you're but newly *Pope;* but that you are newly *Collier, NS, Hibbard*   101 SD *Aside*] *Rowe;* not in F

---

83 **Your ships** This must be a general reference to 'ships under your flag' rather than a specific one to ships owned by this particular merchant. Like Padua, Mantua may also be thought of as a port. See 1.1.42 n.

83 **stayed** detained.

84 **For...quarrel** Because of a private quarrel.

86 **but...but newly** Some editors (e.g. NS, Hibbard) omit the second 'but' here, supposing it to be an erroneous repetition, but the line could make sense as it stands with the first 'but' meaning 'except that' while the second is an intensive meaning 'only'. The real problem is the lack of the expected consequence to ''Tis marvel' (viz., 'that you've not heard of it').

88 **than so** than it might appear from what you say.

89–90 **bills...Florence** i.e. bills or promissory notes from Florence to exchange here for cash.

95 **Pisa...citizens** A curious repetition of 1.1.10. See note on that line.

97 **I know him** Conveniently for the needs of the plot, this is an exception to the otherwise compact social world of the play – see 1.2.97 n.

100 **count'nance** Printed thus in F, presumably to signify the pronunciation as in the case of 'court'sy' in 111 below. In both cases the medial elision produces a regular line.

101 **apple...oyster** 'As like as an apple is to an oyster' was proverbial (Tilley A291). It is of course ironic.

101 **all one** just the same.

105 **Sir Vincentio** Compare 'Sir Lucentio', 3.2.148.

106 **credit** status, position. The financial sense (used by Shakespeare in *MV* 1.1.180) may also be present, since an 'assurance' is to be given, as in 117.

106 **undertake** put on, adopt.

And in my house you shall be friendly lodged.
Look that you take upon you as you should –
You understand me, sir? So shall you stay
Till you have done your business in the city.   110
If this be court'sy, sir, accept of it.
MERCHANT O sir, I do, and will repute you ever
    The patron of my life and liberty.
TRANIO Then go with me to make the matter good.
    This, by the way, I let you understand: 115
    My father is here looked for every day
    To pass assurance of a dower in marriage
    'Twixt me and one Baptista's daughter here.
    In all these circumstances I'll instruct you.
    Go with me to clothe you as becomes you.   120

                                        Exeunt

4.[3] *Enter* KATHERINA *and* GRUMIO.

GRUMIO No, no, forsooth, I dare not for my life!
KATHERINA The more my wrong, the more his spite appears.
    What, did he marry me to famish me?
    Beggars that come unto my father's door
    Upon entreaty have a present alms;   5

---

120 me to] F, *Bond, Riverside, Morris, Oliver;* me sir to F2, *Rowe, NS, Hibbard*   Act 4, Scene 3   4.3] *Steevens;*
Actus Quartus. Scena Prima. F

107 **friendly** Used adverbially, as above at 1.1.129–30, 'it shall be so far forth friendly maintained'.

108 **take upon you** play your role.

112 **repute you** esteem you, think of you.

113 **patron** protector, champion. (Shakespeare may have had in mind the Roman meaning referring to one who quite literally set free his slave.)

114 **make...good** carry out the plan.

115 **by the way** as we go along.

115 **let you understand** cause you to understand, inform you. For this use of 'let' compare *Ham.* 4.6.11–12.

116 **looked for** A pun, since he (or any man who can play Vincentio) has been 'watched for', and Tranio's 'father' is 'expected'.

117 **pass assurance** make a settlement, guarantee.

120 The printers of F2 apparently found this line metrically deficient and added a 'sir' ('Go with me, sir,...'). Some modern editors (e.g. NS, Hibbard)

follow, but it is not strictly necessary if 'Go' is stressed. See Textual Analysis, pp. 158–9 below.

120 **to clothe...you** This has generally been taken to mean that the character must change his 'pedant's' costume for that of a merchant (see, for example, the note on this line in Bond), but it is just as likely that he needs to improve his style of dress rather than change it, since Vincentio is 'a merchant of incomparable wealth' (98 above) and the present character is presumably not quite in that class. The question of whether his disguise will 'become' him raises the whole issue of the moral symbolism of clothing again – see 3.2.107–10 n.

Act 4, Scene 3

0 SD F's *Actus Quartus, Scena Prima* here is the first formal act or scene division since *Actus Tertia* at the beginning of 3.1.

2 **The...wrong** The more wrong done to me.

3 **famish** starve.

5 **present** immediate, as at 14 below.

If not, elsewhere they meet with charity.
But I, who never knew how to entreat,
Nor never needed that I should entreat,
Am starved for meat, giddy for lack of sleep,
With oaths kept waking, and with brawling fed.   10
And that which spites me more than all these wants,
He does it under name of perfect love,
As who should say, if I should sleep or eat
'Twere deadly sickness or else present death.
I prithee go and get me some repast –   15
I care not what, so it be wholesome food.
GRUMIO What say you to a neat's foot?
KATHERINA 'Tis passing good. I prithee let me have it.
GRUMIO I fear it is too choleric a meat.
How say you to a fat tripe finely broiled?   20
KATHERINA I like it well. Good Grumio, fetch it me.
GRUMIO I cannot tell, I fear 'tis choleric.
What say you to a piece of beef and mustard?
KATHERINA A dish that I do love to feed upon.
GRUMIO Ay, but the mustard is too hot a little.   25
KATHERINA Why then, the beef, and let the mustard rest.
GRUMIO Nay then, I will not. You shall have the mustard,
Or else you get no beef of Grumio.
KATHERINA Then both, or one, or anything thou wilt.
GRUMIO Why then, the mustard without the beef.   30
KATHERINA Go, get thee gone, thou false deluding slave
                    Beats him.
That feed'st me with the very name of meat.
Sorrow on thee and all the pack of you
That triumph thus upon my misery!
Go, get thee gone, I say.   35

Enter PETRUCHIO *and* HORTENSIO *with meat.*

7 Compare Grumio's 'she prayed that never prayed before', 4.1.58–9.
9 **meat** food (in general).
11 **spites** irritates, vexes.
12 **name** pretence.
13 **As...say** As if to say.
16 **so** so long as.
17 **neat's** calf's or ox's.
18 **passing** extremely.
19 Grumio's reply shows that he is acting in collusion with Petruchio: he uses the same argument as his master; see 4.1.143 n.

32 **very name** i.e. only the name.
35 There is no exit for Grumio in F; presumably Petruchio's entry saves him from Katherina but he does not speak again until 117. Perhaps he is busily attending Petruchio and preparing to act on his instructions (e.g. at 44).
35 SD The stage direction in *A Shrew* at this point reads *Enter Ferando with a peece of meate uppon his daggers point and Polidor with him.* Possibly the author is drawing on the Bajazeth sequence in *1 Tamburlaine* 4.4 for this cruder and more sensational version.

PETRUCHIO How fares my Kate? What, sweeting, all amort?
HORTENSIO Mistress, what cheer?
KATHERINA   Faith, as cold as can be.
PETRUCHIO Pluck up thy spirits; look cheerfully upon me.
        Here, love, thou seest how diligent I am
        To dress thy meat myself, and bring it thee.   40
        I am sure, sweet Kate, this kindness merits thanks.
        What, not a word? Nay then, thou lov'st it not,
        And all my pains is sorted to no proof.
        Here, take away this dish.
KATHERINA   I pray you, let it stand.
PETRUCHIO The poorest service is repaid with thanks,   45
        And so shall mine before you touch the meat.
KATHERINA I thank you, sir.
HORTENSIO Signor Petruchio, fie, you are to blame.
        Come, Mistress Kate, I'll bear you company.
PETRUCHIO [*Aside*] Eat it up all, Hortensio, if thou lov'st me –   50
        [*To Katherina*] Much good do it unto thy gentle heart.
        Kate, eat apace. And now, my honey love,
        Will we return unto thy father's house
        And revel it as bravely as the best,
        With silken coats and caps, and golden rings,   55
        With ruffs and cuffs and farthingales and things,
        With scarves and fans and double change of brav'ry,
        With amber bracelets, beads and all this knav'ry.
        What, hast thou dined? The tailor stays thy leisure,
        To deck thy body with his ruffling treasure.   60

                        Enter TAILOR.

        Come, tailor, let us see these ornaments.

48 to blame] Q; too blame F   50 SD *Aside*] *Theobald; not in* F   51 SD *To Katherina*] *Collier; not in* F

36 **amort** lifeless, depressed.
37 **what cheer?** how are you? (Compare Sly's
use of 'cheer' in Induction 2.97.)
37 **cold** According to the theory of humours (see
4.1.143 n.), Katherina has lost her 'hot' choler and
become phlegmatic or even melancholy.
43 **all...proof** all my labour has been in vain.
46 **before** Thus F. One might read 'be 'fore'.
47 Katherina's expression of gratitude is as unlike
her former character as her expressions of entreaty,
but much depends on the tone here.
48 **to blame** in the wrong.
50–9 Hortensio does presumably eat all the food

while Petruchio is talking. There is a somewhat
comparable episode in John Heywood's *Merry Play
between John John the Husband, Tyb his Wife and Sir
John the Priest* (1533) where Tyb and Sir John eat
a whole pie without allowing the husband any.
54 **bravely** showily, splendidly dressed.
56 **farthingales** hooped skirts.
57 **brav'ry** finery.
58 **knav'ry** trickery, nonsense. See 163–76 and
n.
59 **stays** awaits.
60 **ruffling** ornate (elaborately ruffled).

Lay forth the gown.

Enter HABERDASHER.

What news with you, sir?
HABERDASHER Here is the cap your worship did bespeak.
PETRUCHIO Why, this was moulded on a porringer –
    A velvet dish! Fie, fie, 'tis lewd and filthy. 65
    Why, 'tis a cockle or a walnut-shell,
    A knack, a toy, a trick, a baby's cap.
    Away with it! Come, let me have a bigger.
KATHERINA I'll have no bigger. This doth fit the time,
    And gentlewomen wear such caps as these. 70
PETRUCHIO When you are gentle you shall have one too,
    And not till then.
HORTENSIO [*Aside*]   That will not be in haste.
KATHERINA Why, sir, I trust I may have leave to speak,
    And speak I will. I am no child, no babe.
    Your betters have endured me say my mind, 75
    And if you cannot, best you stop your ears.
    My tongue will tell the anger of my heart,
    Or else my heart concealing it will break,
    And, rather than it shall, I will be free
    Even to the uttermost, as I please, in words. 80
PETRUCHIO Why, thou say'st true – it is a paltry cap.
    A custard-coffin, a bauble, a silken pie!
    I love thee well in that thou lik'st it not.
KATHERINA Love me or love me not, I like the cap,
    And it I will have, or I will have none. 85

62 SD *Enter* HABERDASHER] *Follows 61 in* F   63 SH HABERDASHER] *Rowe; Fel.* F   72 SD *Aside*] *Hanmer; not in* F
81 is a paltry] Q; is paltrie F

63 SH •HABERDASHER Although F has *Enter Haberdasher* after 61, the speech heading here is *Fel.*, presumably an abbreviation of *Fellow*. There is some awkwardness about the abrupt switch cᶠ address from the Tailor to the Haberdasher, and F gives no exit for the latter. Possibly we can infer from this a decision at some point to conflate the two roles for the sake of economy in casting; see Textual Analysis, p. 158 below. If *A Shrew*, which is more than usually close to the text of *The Shrew* here, preserves the original staging it is clear that the Haberdasher leaves before the Tailor enters, since Ferando ends his criticisms of the cap with a firm 'sirra begon with it' (scene xiii, 15).
    63 bespeak order.
    64 porringer porridge basin. The hat must be

a small one in the Italian style; see illustration 6 (p. 33 above).
    65 lewd vile.
    66 cockle cockle-shell.
    69 doth...time is the current fashion.
    71 The fact that a version of this line appears slightly out of context and without the cue ('gentlewoman' in 70) in *A Shrew* (scene xi, 43) is an important part of the evidence for believing in the memorial reconstruction theory; see Textual Analysis, pp. 168–71 below.
    82 custard-coffin Pastry case for custard.
    85–6 none...gown This is part of Petruchio's deliberate misunderstanding of Katherina, and serves to bring in the Tailor.

PETRUCHIO Thy gown? Why, ay. Come, tailor, let us see't.

                                                 [*Exit Haberdasher*]

    O mercy God! What masking stuff is here?

    What's this – a sleeve? 'Tis like a demi-cannon.

    What, up and down carved like an apple-tart?

    Here's snip and nip and cut and slish and slash, 90

    Like to a censer in a barber's shop.

    Why, what a devil's name, tailor, call'st thou this?

HORTENSIO [*Aside*] I see she's like to have neither cap nor gown.

TAILOR You bid me make it orderly and well,

    According to the fashion and the time. 95

PETRUCHIO Marry, and did. But if you be remembered,

    I did not bid you mar it to the time.

    Go, hop me over every kennel home,

    For you shall hop without my custom, sir.

    I'll none of it. Hence, make your best of it. 100

KATHERINA I never saw a better-fashioned gown,

    More quaint, more pleasing, nor more commendable.

    Belike you mean to make a puppet of me.

PETRUCHIO Why, true, he means to make a puppet of thee.

TAILOR She says your worship means to make a puppet of her. 105

PETRUCHIO O monstrous arrogance! Thou liest, thou thread, thou

    thimble,

    Thou yard, three-quarters, half-yard, quarter, nail!

    Thou flea, thou nit, thou winter-cricket thou!

---

86 gown?] *Rowe;* gowne, F   86 SD *Exit Haberdasher*] *Cam.; not in* F   88 like a demi-cannon] Q*;* like demi cannon F
91 censer] *Rowe*[3]*;* Censor F   93 SD *Aside*] *Theobald; not in* F   105 She says...her] *As verse, Pope; as prose,* F
106 O monstrous...thimble] *As one line, Capell; as two lines divided after* arrogance, F

87 masking stuff Extravagant or gaudy clothes more suitable for the stage.

88 demi-cannon large cannon. See illustration 6 (p. 33 above).

89 up...apple-tart slit open all over like the pastry crust of an apple-tart. Such 'slashing' of fabrics to show a different colour underneath was fashionable; see illustration 6 (p. 33 above). Perhaps Petruchio's comparisons ('porringer' (64), 'custard-coffin' (82), 'apple-tart') deliberately tantalise Katherina with thoughts of food.

91 censer Incense-burner with holes in the top. The use of such objects in barbers' shops is not supported by any other contemporary reference, but it was presumably important to sweeten the air in them since they were used for minor surgery as well as hairdressing.

96 Marry...did Yes, indeed I did.

97 mar...time ruin it for ever, or ruin it by following the fashion (with a pun on 'marry').

98 hop me Literally 'hop for me', an archaic dative like 'knock me' at 1.2.8.

98 kennel gutter.

102 quaint ingeniously designed.

103 puppet doll, plaything.

106–13 As Johnson commented, 'The tailor's trade, having an appearance of effeminacy, has always been, among the rugged English, liable to sarcasms and contempt.' Compare the unflattering reference in *Lear* 2.2.54–60, but see also the surprising dignity granted to Francis Feeble, the woman's tailor, in *2H4* 3.2.147–62 and 234–40.

107 nail One-sixteenth of a yard.

108 nit Egg of a louse.

Braved in mine own house with a skein of thread?
Away, thou rag, thou quantity, thou remnant!   110
Or I shall so bemete thee with thy yard
As thou shalt think on prating whilst thou liv'st.
I tell thee, I, that thou hast marred her gown.

TAILOR Your worship is deceived. The gown is made
Just as my master had direction.   115
Grumio gave order how it should be done.

GRUMIO I gave him no order; I gave him the stuff.

TAILOR But how did you desire it should be made?

GRUMIO Marry, sir, with needle and thread.

TAILOR But did you not request to have it cut?   120

GRUMIO Thou hast faced many things.

TAILOR I have.

GRUMIO Face not me. Thou hast braved many men; brave not me. I
will neither be faced nor braved. I say unto thee, I bid thy master
cut out the gown, but I did not bid him cut it to pieces. *Ergo*, thou   125
liest.

TAILOR Why, here is the note of the fashion to testify.

PETRUCHIO Read it.

GRUMIO The note lies in's throat if he say I said so.

TAILOR [*Reads*] '*Imprimis*, a loose-bodied gown –'   130

GRUMIO Master, if ever I said 'loose-bodied gown', sew me in the skirts
of it and beat me to death with a bottom of brown thread. I said
'a gown'.

PETRUCHIO Proceed.

TAILOR 'With a small compassed cape.'   135

GRUMIO I confess the cape.

130 SD *Reads*] Capell; *not in* F

109 **Braved...with** Defied...by. See also 123
and n.
110 **quantity** quantity of cloth. Petruchio
presumably means a small quantity ('remnant')
though this word more often indicates a 'fair or
considerable amount' (*OED* sv II 8b).
111 **bemete** Literally 'measure'; used here to
imply 'beat'.
111 **yard** tailor's measuring-stick.
112 **As...on** So that you will think carefully
before.
117 **stuff** material.
121 **faced** (1) trimmed, (2) outfaced.
123 **braved** (1) provided with finery, (2) defied.
The same pun may be intended in 109 above. See
also 5.1.95 n.
125 *Ergo* Therefore (Latin). A comic 'trial'

follows with both Grumio and the Tailor using legal
terms.
127 **note** written order.
129 **lies...throat** lies utterly.
129 **he** it. The note is personified as a witness.
130 *Imprimis* First (Latin).
130 **loose-bodied** loose-fitting. See illustration 6
(p. 33 above). Grumio pretends to understand it
as meaning 'suitable for a loose woman', i.e. a
prostitute. His distortion of what the Tailor says
here is the same trick as Petruchio's deliberate
misunderstanding of Katherina at 86 and 104 above.
Grumio turns it back on Petruchio at 152.
132 **bottom** spool, bobbin. (With obscene
reference as well.)
135 **compassed** of circular cut. See illustration 6
(p. 33 above).

TAILOR 'With a trunk sleeve.'

GRUMIO I confess two sleeves.

TAILOR 'The sleeves curiously cut.'

PETRUCHIO Ay, there's the villainy.   140

GRUMIO Error i'th'bill, sir, error i'th'bill! I commanded the sleeves
should be cut out and sewed up again – and that I'll prove upon
thee, though thy little finger be armed in a thimble.

TAILOR This is true that I say, and I had thee in place where thou
should'st know it.   145

GRUMIO I am for thee straight. Take thou the bill, give me thy mete-yard
and spare not me.

HORTENSIO God-a-mercy, Grumio, then he shall have no odds.

PETRUCHIO Well, sir, in brief, the gown is not for me.

GRUMIO You are i'th'right sir, 'tis for my mistress.   150

PETRUCHIO Go, take it up unto thy master's use.

GRUMIO Villain, not for thy life! Take up my mistress' gown for thy
master's use?

PETRUCHIO Why, sir, what's your conceit in that?

GRUMIO O sir, the conceit is deeper than you think for.   155
Take up my mistress' gown to his master's use?
O fie, fie, fie!

PETRUCHIO [*Aside*] Hortensio, say thou wilt see the tailor paid.
[*To Tailor*] Go, take it hence; be gone and say no more.

HORTENSIO [*Aside*] Tailor, I'll pay thee for thy gown tomorrow,   160
Take no unkindness of his hasty words.
Away I say, commend me to thy master.

Exit Tailor

PETRUCHIO Well, come, my Kate, we will unto your father's

155–7 O...fie] *As verse*, F; *as prose, Oliver*   158 SD *Aside*] *Rowe; not in* F   159 SD *To Tailor*] *Irving; not in* F
160 SD *Aside*] *Capell; not in* F

137 **trunk** full.
139 **curiously** carefully, elaborately.
141 **bill** Presumably the 'note' or order of 127.
142–3 **prove upon thee** prove by fighting you.
144 **and...where** if I had you in a suitable
place. The Tailor presumably means a proper court
of law but Grumio takes him to mean a place
suitable for fighting.
146 **for thee straight** ready to fight you at once.
148 **odds** advantage. With perhaps a pun on
'odds' meaning 'cause for quarrel', i.e. the Tailor
will be at such a disadvantage that he will give up
his cause.
151 **unto...use** Petruchio means 'for your
master to do what he can with it' but Grumio

pretends he means 'for your master to use
Katherina (sexually)'.
154 **conceit** meaning, implication.
155 **deeper** more serious, more devious (with
sexual reference).
158–62 Again we are reminded that Petruchio's
behaviour is calculated. This kindness to a minor
character is a likeable characteristic on his (and
Shakespeare's) part and can be contrasted with the
way the fate of such characters is usually completely
ignored once they have served the plot in Roman
comedy.
163–76 Petruchio repeats his view that fine
clothes are not important; see 3.2.107–10 n.

Even in these honest mean habiliments.
Our purses shall be proud, our garments poor,   165
For 'tis the mind that makes the body rich,
And as the sun breaks through the darkest clouds,
So honour peereth in the meanest habit.
What, is the jay more precious than the lark
Because his feathers are more beautiful?   170
Or is the adder better than the eel
Because his painted skin contents the eye?
O no, good Kate; neither art thou the worse
For this poor furniture and mean array.
If thou account'st it shame, lay it on me,   175
And therefore frolic! We will hence forthwith
To feast and sport us at thy father's house.
[*To Grumio*] Go call my men, and let us straight to him,
And bring our horses unto Long-lane end,
There will we mount, and thither walk on foot.   180
Let's see, I think 'tis now some seven o'clock,
And well we may come there by dinner-time.

KATHERINA I dare assure you, sir, 'tis almost two,
And 'twill be supper-time ere you come there.

PETRUCHIO It shall be seven ere I go to horse.   185
Look what I speak, or do, or think to do,
You are still crossing it. Sirs, let't alone.
I will not go today, and, ere I do,
It shall be what o'clock I say it is.

HORTENSIO [*Aside*] Why so this gallant will command the sun.   190

[*Exeunt*]

---

169 What, is] *Pope subst.;* What is F   175 account'st] *Rowe;* accountedst F   178 SD *To Grumio*] *Irving; not in* F
190 SD *Aside*] *Irving; not in* F   190 SD *Exeunt*] *Rowe; not in* F

164 **mean habiliments** poor or ordinary clothes.

167–8 The simile is a favourite with Shakespeare (compare *1H4* 1.2.197–215), as is the thought, which becomes an important theme in the Romances.

168 **peereth** can be seen peeping through.

168 **habit** outfit.

169 **What, is** Like most editors, I read 'What' as an exclamation, but F has no comma here, and it is conceivable that 'What' could be used to mean something like 'In what way', 'To what extent', as in *Venus and Adonis* 207: 'What were thy lips the worse for one poor kiss?' (*OED* sv *adv* 20b).

172 **painted** colourfully patterned.

174 **furniture** equipment, dress.

175 **lay it on** blame.

176 **frolic** be merry.

182 **dinner-time** i.e. about midday. It is apparently a four or five hour ride from Petruchio's house to Padua.

184 **supper-time** i.e. about 7 p.m.

186 **Look what** Whatever.

187 **crossing** opposing, contradicting.

190 Perhaps Hortensio has in mind the story of Phaëton, who came to grief when he stole the chariot of the sun, but Petruchio continues to 'command the sun' in another sense in 4.5.1–25.

[4.4] *Enter* TRANIO [*disguised as Lucentio*] *and the* MERCHANT, *booted and bare headed, dressed like Vincentio.*

TRANIO Sir, this is the house. Please it you that I call?
MERCHANT Ay, what else? And, but I be deceived,
　　　Signor Baptista may remember me
　　　Near twenty years ago in Genoa
　　　Where we were lodgers at the Pegasus.　　　　　　　　　5
TRANIO 'Tis well. And hold your own, in any case,
　　　With such austerity as 'longeth to a father.
MERCHANT I warrant you.

Enter BIONDELLO.

　　　　　　　But, sir, here comes your boy;
　　　'Twere good he were schooled.
TRANIO Fear you not him. Sirrah Biondello,　　　　　　　10
　　　Now do your duty throughly, I advise you:
　　　Imagine 'twere the right Vincentio.
BIONDELLO Tut, fear not me.
TRANIO But hast thou done thy errand to Baptista?
BIONDELLO I told him that your father was at Venice,　　　15
　　　And that you looked for him this day in Padua.
TRANIO Th'art a tall fellow; hold thee that to drink.
　　　　　　[*He gives him money.*]

Enter BAPTISTA *and* LUCENTIO [*disguised as Cambio*].

　　　Here comes Baptista. Set your countenance, sir.

Act 4, Scene 4 4.4] *Steevens; no scene division in* F　　0 SD.1 *disguised...Lucentio*] *Kittredge; not in* F
0 SD.1–2 *booted...bare headed*] *Transposed from 18 where the entry is mistakenly repeated in* F　1 Sir] *Theobald;* Sirs F
5 Where...Pegasus] *Ascribed to Pedant (Merchant) by Theobald, to Tranio by* F　7 'longeth] *Hanmer;* longeth F
8 SD *Enter* BIONDELLO] *Follows* 7 *in* F　17 SD.1 *He...money*] *Kittredge; not in* F　17 SD.2 *Enter...Cambio*] *Follows*
18 *in* F　17 SD.2 *disguised...Cambio*] *Kittredge; not in* F

Act 4, Scene 4
　0 SD No act or scene division in F.
　0 SD.1–2 **booted and bare headed** This unusual description is given in F when the Merchant's entry is mistakenly repeated at 17 below; see Textual Analysis, p. 157 below. 'Booted' presumably implies that he is dressed like a traveller, and 'bare headed' that he has taken off his hat out of respect for Baptista, to whom he is about to be introduced.
　2 **but I be** unless I am.
　5 **Pegasus** Winged horse of classical mythology. A common name for inns in Shakespeare's London. (Compare references to the Centaur in *Err.* 2.2.)

6 **hold your own** keep up your role.
6 **case** circumstance (with, perhaps, a pun on 'case' meaning 'disguise' as at 2.1.399 and 4.2.45).
8 **warrant** promise.
9 **schooled** instructed (in the deception).
12 **right** real.
17 **tall** capable (with, perhaps, an ironic glance at the literal meaning, since Biondello is clearly a boy and not very large).
17 **hold...drink** take this (tip) to buy yourself a drink. Tranio presumably enjoys being able to patronise his fellow-servant.
18 **Set your countenance** Assume an appropriate expression.

Signor Baptista, you are happily met.
Sir, this is the gentleman I told you of. 20
I pray you stand good father to me now:
Give me Bianca for my patrimony.

MERCHANT Soft, son.
Sir, by your leave, having come to Padua
To gather in some debts, my son Lucentio 25
Made me acquainted with a weighty cause
Of love between your daughter and himself.
And – for the good report I hear of you,
And for the love he beareth to your daughter,
And she to him – to stay him not too long, 30
I am content, in a good father's care,
To have him matched. And if you please to like
No worse than I, upon some agreement
Me shall you find ready and willing
With one consent to have her so bestowed, 35
For curious I cannot be with you,
Signor Baptista, of whom I hear so well.

BAPTISTA Sir, pardon me in what I have to say.
Your plainness and your shortness please me well.
Right true it is your son Lucentio here 40
Doth love my daughter, and she loveth him –
Or both dissemble deeply their affections –
And therefore, if you say no more than this,
That like a father you will deal with him,
And pass my daughter a sufficient dower, 45
The match is made and all is done:
Your son shall have my daughter with consent.

TRANIO I thank you, sir. Where, then, do you know best

23–4 Soft...Padua] *As two lines, Hanmer; as one line,* F　34 ready and willing] F; *most ready and most willing,* F2,
Rowe　48 know best] F; *trow is best Hanmer; trow best conj. Johnson*

20–2 These lines could be addressed to Baptista,
with 21–2 meaning 'Fulfil your promise to be my
father-in-law and give me Bianca now that my
father is here to confirm my inheritance', or they
could be addressed to the Merchant, with the
meaning 'Be a good father and invest my
inheritance in the purchase of Bianca.' The latter
is more likely, since the Merchant speaks next and
even picks up the cue at 31.
　21 **stand** show yourself as.
　23 **Soft** Gently, just a moment.
　26 **weighty cause** serious question.

28 **for** because of.
　30 **to stay...long** not to keep him waiting too
long.
　32 **to like** to be satisfied (i.e. with this match).
　33–4 These lines are metrically awkward in F and
the emendation to 'most ready and most willing' in
F2 does not really solve the problem.
　36 **curious** over-particular (i.e. fussy about the
details of the financial settlement).
　42 The audience can share Tranio's appreciation
of the irony of this line.
　45 **pass** settle upon.

We be affied and such assurance tane
As shall with either part's agreement stand?   50
BAPTISTA Not in my house, Lucentio, for you know
Pitchers have ears, and I have many servants.
Besides, old Gremio is heark'ning still,
And happily we might be interrupted.
TRANIO Then at my lodging, and it like you.   55
There doth my father lie, and there this night
We'll pass the business privately and well.
Send for your daughter by your servant here.
  [*He indicates Lucentio and winks at him.*]
My boy shall fetch the scrivener presently.
The worst is this, that at so slender warning   60
You are like to have a thin and slender pittance.
BAPTISTA It likes me well. Cambio, hie you home,
And bid Bianca make her ready straight,
And, if you will, tell what hath happenèd:
Lucentio's father is arrived in Padua,   65
And how she's like to be Lucentio's wife.
                              [*Exit Lucentio*]
BIONDELLO I pray the gods she may, with all my heart!
TRANIO Dally not with the gods, but get thee gone.
                              Exit Biondello

---

55 like you] F; like you, sir F2   58 SD He...him] *Eds.; not in* F; *at 67, Irving*   62–3 It...straight] *Steevens; divided after* well *in* F   64 happenèd] *Capell subst.;* hapned F   66 SD *Exit Lucentio*] NS; *not in* F   67 I...heart] *Ascribed to Biondello by* F, *to Lucentio by Rowe and many later edns*   68 SD *Exit Biondello*] *Follows 67 in* F   68–9] *Between these 2 lines* F *has* / *Enter Peter*

49 **affied** formally betrothed.
50 As shall confirm the agreements on both sides.
52 **Pitchers have ears** 'Small pitchers have wide ears' was proverbial (Tilley P363). The literal reference is to the 'ears' or handles of water-jugs.
53 **heark'ning** lying in wait (as at 1.2.253).
54 **happily** perhaps.
55 **and...you** if it please you.
56 **lie** stay (with a pun on 'lie' meaning 'deceive').
58 SD No SD in F here, but this is indicated by what Biondello says at 75.
59 **scrivener** notary (to draw up the agreements).
59 **presently** at once.
61 **thin...pittance** meagre (unceremonious) meal.
66 SD *Exit Lucentio...* 68 SD *Exit Biondello* F has an exit for Biondello after 68 followed by *Enter Lucentio and Biondello* after 72, implying that Lucentio has also gone off. It is possible that

Lucentio and Biondello just move downstage at this point, concealing themselves from Baptista, since Biondello describes himself as being 'left here behind' to explain things to Lucentio at 77. If they do leave the stage we should begin a new scene at 73, as in Pope, Hanmer and Warburton.
68 **Dally...gods** Either (1) Don't speak lightly of the gods, or (2) Don't waste time talking about the gods.
68 Following this line F has *Enter Peter*, a stage direction which is difficult to explain. Most editors presume that Peter is one of 'Lucentio's' servants who enters to tell his master that the meal is ready for him and Baptista. It is true that they leave the stage in order to go to 'Lucentio's' lodging for this purpose and that 'Lucentio' begins to welcome Baptista as they go off, but they have only just decided upon this course of action (48–61) and it seems unlikely that the servant has anticipated them. There is no reason why this Peter should be identified with Petruchio's servant Peter who has a

– Signor Baptista, shall I lead the way?

Welcome. One mess is like to be your cheer.   70

Come sir, we will better it in Pisa.

BAPTISTA I follow you.

Exeunt

Enter Lucentio [disguised as Cambio] and Biondello.

BIONDELLO Cambio!

LUCENTIO What say'st thou, Biondello?

BIONDELLO You saw my master wink and laugh upon you?   75

LUCENTIO Biondello, what of that?

BIONDELLO Faith, nothing – but 'has left me here behind to expound
the meaning or moral of his signs and tokens.

LUCENTIO I pray thee, moralise them.

BIONDELLO Then thus: Baptista is safe, talking with the deceiving   80
father of a deceitful son.

LUCENTIO And what of him?

BIONDELLO His daughter is to be brought by you to the supper.

LUCENTIO And then?

BIONDELLO The old priest at Saint Luke's church is at your command   85
at all hours.

LUCENTIO And what of all this?

BIONDELLO I cannot tell, except they are busied about a counterfeit
assurance. Take you assurance of her *cum privilegio ad imprimendum
solum*. To the church! Take the priest, clerk and some sufficient   90
honest witnesses.

If this be not that you look for, I have no more to say,

But bid Bianca farewell for ever and a day.

LUCENTIO Hear'st thou, Biondello?

---

77 'has] *Hanmer subst.;* has F   88 except] F2; expect F   90 church! Take] *Rann subst.;* Church take F
92–3 If...day] *As verse,* F; *as prose, Warburton, Oliver*

---

very small part in 4.1, and the suggestion that Peter
is the name of an actor rather than a character goes
no further to solve the problem of who he is or why
he should appear at all. It is possible that there is
a link between this anomaly and the awkwardness
about the exits at 66 and 68 (see 66 n.).

70 One...cheer A single dish is likely to
constitute your whole entertainment.

75 my master i.e. Tranio. Perhaps Biondello is
deliberately teasing and confusing Lucentio here;
he keeps using 'schoolmasterly' language such as
'expound' (77), '*cum privilegio...solum*' (89–90)
and 'appendix' (99). See also 103 n.

77 'has he has.

79 moralise interpret.

80–93 Again the servant explains the plot to the
master; compare 4.2.66 ff. and *TGV* 2.1.135 ff.

89 Take...assurance Make sure (with a pun on
'assurance' meaning 'legal settlement').

89–90 cum...solum with the exclusive right to
print, a phrase used for licensing books but here
with 'print' in the sense of fathering a child
(printing a likeness).

90 Take the priest It seems from this and from
98, where the priest is described as 'ready to come',
that the wedding is to take place somewhere other
than St Luke's church but we never learn where.

92 that...for what you are longing for.

94 Lucentio is still confused and perhaps
exasperated.

BIONDELLO I cannot tarry. I knew a wench married in an afternoon   95
  as she went to the garden for parsley to stuff a rabbit. And so may
  you, sir; and so adieu, sir. My master hath appointed me to go to
  Saint Luke's to bid the priest be ready to come against you come
  with your appendix.   *Exit*
LUCENTIO I may and will, if she be so contented.   100
  She will be pleased – then wherefore should I doubt?
  Hap what hap may, I'll roundly go about her.
  It shall go hard if Cambio go without her.   *Exit*

[4.5] *Enter* PETRUCHIO, KATHERINA, HORTENSIO [*and* SERVANTS].

PETRUCHIO Come on, a God's name! Once more toward our
          father's.
  Good Lord, how bright and goodly shines the moon!
KATHERINA The moon? The sun! It is not moonlight now.
PETRUCHIO I say it is the moon that shines so bright.
KATHERINA I know it is the sun that shines so bright.   5
PETRUCHIO Now, by my mother's son – and that's myself –
  It shall be moon or star or what I list
  Or e'er I journey to your father's house.
  [*To Servants*] Go on and fetch our horses back again.
  Evermore crossed and crossed, nothing but crossed!   10
HORTENSIO Say as he says, or we shall never go.

Act 4, Scene 5   4.5] *Steevens; no scene division in* F   0 SD *and* SERVANTS] *Cam.; not in* F   9 SD *To Servants*] *Eds.;*
not in F   9 Go on] F; *Go one* Rann

96 parsley There is probably a joke here on the
reputation of parsley as a 'body opener' used in
herbal medicine.
98 against you come in preparation for your
coming.
99 appendix appendage, i.e. Bianca. Biondello
continues to use his metaphor from printing.
102 Hap...may Whatever may happen. Proverbial (Tilley C529).
102 roundly...her tackle her boldly, without
ceremony. A naval metaphor: compare 1.2.91.
103 Cambio Perhaps the fact that Lucentio calls
himself Cambio in soliloquy here is a further sign
of his confusion throughout this sequence.

Act 4, Scene 5
0 SD No act or scene division in F.
1 a in.
2 the moon In folklore versions of the shrew
story the husband usually makes absurd statements
about birds or animals seen on the journey (e.g. he

calls mares cows or doves ravens). Shakespeare
obviously had to alter this for dramatic purposes and
his invention of the sun/moon argument is
appropriate for the Elizabethan open-air theatre –
though not for the indoor setting envisaged in the
Induction. There is also some ironic play here on
the traditional association of the moon with
women's fickleness (see 20 and n.) and with
mutability in general, since this scene demonstrates
Katherina's transformation. Shakespeare develops
these associations again in *MND*.
  7 list please.
  8 Or e'er Before.
  9 The assumption is either that the characters
have just set out and are not mounted yet (Petruchio
asked for the horses to be brought to meet them at
'Long-lane end' at 4.3.179), or that they are in the
midst of the journey and are resting their horses by
walking a short distance. (Horses did not normally
appear on the Elizabethan stage.)
  10 crossed opposed, contradicted.

KATHERINA Forward, I pray, since we have come so far.
And be it moon or sun or what you please;
And if you please to call it a rush-candle,
Henceforth I vow it shall be so for me.   15
PETRUCHIO I say it is the moon.
KATHERINA   I know it is the moon.
PETRUCHIO Nay then you lie, it is the blessèd sun.
KATHERINA Then God be blessed, it is the blessèd sun.
But sun it is not, when you say it is not,
And the moon changes even as your mind.   20
What you will have it named, even that it is,
And so it shall be so for Katherine.
HORTENSIO [*Aside*] Petruchio, go thy ways. The field is won.
PETRUCHIO Well, forward, forward! Thus the bowl should run
And not unluckily against the bias.   25

Enter VINCENTIO.

But soft, company is coming here.
[*To Vincentio*] Good morrow, gentle mistress, where away?
Tell me, sweet Kate, and tell me truly too,
Hast thou beheld a fresher gentlewoman?
Such war of white and red within her cheeks!   30
What stars do spangle heaven with such beauty
As those two eyes become that heavenly face?
Fair lovely maid, once more good day to thee.
Sweet Kate, embrace her for her beauty's sake.
HORTENSIO [*Aside*] A will make the man mad, to make the woman of   35
him.

18 is] Q; in F   22 be so] F; be, so, *Rowe;* be, sir *Capell*   23 SD *Aside*] *Capell; not in* F   25 *Enter* VINCENTIO]
Follows 26 in F   26 soft, company] F; soft, some company *Pope;* soft, what company *Steevens*   27 SD *To Vincentio*]
Rowe; not in F   35 SD *Aside*] *Capell; not in* F   35 the woman] F, *Hibbard, Morris, Oliver;* a woman F2, *Bond, NS,*
Riverside

14 rush-candle Candle made from a rush dipped in grease (and hence giving a very feeble light).

20 moon...mind Even while submitting, Katherina gets her own back by implying that Petruchio is inconstant (in a feminine way) or even mad ('lunatic').

23 go thy ways well done, carry on.

24–5 bowl...bias A metaphor from lawn-bowls, a game which depends on the players exploiting the bias or weight which causes a ball to swerve. Petruchio is saying that Katherina is no longer perverting her own nature.

26 It is possible that a word has been dropped

from this line; Pope emends to 'some company', Steevens to 'what company'.

26 soft hush, wait a moment.

27 where away? where are you going?

29–32 The terms in which Petruchio describes the 'gentlewoman' are highly conventional, reminding us of the romantic rhetoric of the sub-plot.

29 fresher more youthful (and therefore radiant).

35 A He.

35 make the woman Thus F. F2 has 'a woman'. Perhaps the idiom 'to play the man' is a relevant analogy.

KATHERINA Young budding virgin, fair and fresh and sweet,
    Whither away, or where is thy abode?
    Happy the parents of so fair a child!
    Happier the man whom favourable stars   40
    Allots thee for his lovely bedfellow.

PETRUCHIO Why, how now, Kate! I hope thou art not mad.
    This is a man – old, wrinkled, faded, withered –
    And not a maiden, as thou say'st he is.

KATHERINA Pardon, old father, my mistaking eyes   45
    That have been so bedazzled with the sun
    That everything I look on seemeth green.
    Now I perceive thou art a reverend father.
    Pardon, I pray thee, for my mad mistaking.

PETRUCHIO Do, good old grandsire, and withal make known   50
    Which way thou travellest – if along with us
    We shall be joyful of thy company.

VINCENTIO Fair sir, and you, my merry mistress,
    That with your strange encounter much amazed me,
    My name is called Vincentio, my dwelling Pisa,   55
    And bound I am to Padua, there to visit
    A son of mine which long I have not seen.

PETRUCHIO What is his name?

VINCENTIO   Lucentio, gentle sir.

PETRUCHIO Happily met – the happier for thy son.
    And now by law as well as reverend age   60
    I may entitle thee my loving father.
    The sister to my wife, this gentlewoman,
    Thy son by this hath married. Wonder not,
    Nor be not grieved. She is of good esteem,
    Her dowry wealthy, and of worthy birth;   65
    Beside, so qualified as may beseem

---

38 or where] F2; or whether F

---

38 *where F's repetition of 'whether' here was probably due to scribal or compositorial error.

40–1 stars / Allots Another third-person plural in 's'; see 2.1.137 and n.

46 sun An allusion to the argument at the beginning of the scene which might be emphasised in performance. Katherina seems to be entering Petruchio's game with enthusiasm and skill here.

47 green fresh, youthful. Katherina's change of attitude seems to be accompanied by a change in the weather; compare 4.1.7–8 n.

54 encounter manner of greeting.

61 father Petruchio is extending the meaning of 'father-in-law' somewhat. (Compare his boldness in calling Baptista 'father' at 2.1.126.)

62–3 The sister...married Petruchio and Hortensio (who confirms his statement at 74) can hardly know this yet, and Hortensio ought to be surprised at the news, since he and 'Lucentio' (Tranio) forswore Bianca's love in 4.2. See Textual Analysis on 'loose ends' in the plot, pp. 161–4 below.

63 by this by now.

66 so qualified having such qualities.

66 beseem become.

The spouse of any noble gentleman.
Let me embrace with old Vincentio,
And wander we to see thy honest son,
Who will of thy arrival be full joyous.   70
VINCENTIO But is this true, or is it else your pleasure,
Like pleasant travellers, to break a jest
Upon the company you overtake?
HORTENSIO I do assure thee, father, so it is.
PETRUCHIO Come, go along and see the truth hereof,   75
For our first merriment hath made thee jealous.
                                        Exeunt [all but Hortensio]
HORTENSIO Well, Petruchio, this has put me in heart!
Have to my widow, and if she be froward,
Then hast thou taught Hortensio to be untoward.   *Exit*

[5.1] *Enter* BIONDELLO, LUCENTIO [*as himself*] *and* BIANCA.
GREMIO *is out before.*

BIONDELLO Softly and swiftly, sir, for the priest is ready.
LUCENTIO I fly, Biondello. But they may chance to need thee at home;
therefore leave us.
                                        Exit Lucentio [with Bianca]
BIONDELLO Nay, faith, I'll see the church a'your back, and then come
back to my master's as soon as I can.   *Exit*   5
GREMIO I marvel Cambio comes not all this while.

Enter PETRUCHIO, KATHERINA, VINCENTIO, GRUMIO, *with*
ATTENDANTS.

---

76 SD *Exeunt all but Hortensio*] *Warburton subst.; Exeunt.* F   78 she be froward] F2; *she froward* F   **Act 5, Scene 1**
5.1] *Warburton; no act or scene division in* F; *Act 5 / Theobald*   0 SD.1 *as himself*] *Hudson; not in* F   3 SD *Exit...Bianca*]
Capell; Exit F   5 master's] *Capell; mistris* F; *Master Theobald*   5 SD *Exit*] *Capell; not in* F

69–70 There is irony in the description of
Lucentio as 'honest' and in the idea that he will
rejoice at Vincentio's arrival.
  71 or...else or else is it.
  72 pleasant humorous.
  72 break a jest play a trick, make a joke.
  76 jealous suspicious.
  78 Have to Now I'll set about.
  78 froward difficult, perverse.
  79 untoward stubborn, unmannerly.

Act 5, Scene 1
  0 SD No act or scene division in F.
  0 SD.2 GREMIO...*before* Thus F, meaning

presumably that he comes on first. For a discussion
of 'irregular' stage directions, see Textual Analysis,
pp. 156–7 below.
  4 a' at; i.e. 'I'll see you safely married.'
  5 *master's* F reads 'mistris', emended by
Capell. See 1.2.18 and n. above and 42 below for
other possible misreadings of 'mrs.' in the copy.
  6 Presumably Lucentio is out of his disguise and
therefore not recognised by Gremio. It is not clear
why Gremio should be waiting for Cambio at this
point anyway, though he does seem to know about
the wedding plans which Baptista wanted to conceal
from him at 4.4.53. See Textual Analysis on 'loose
ends', p. 162 below.

PETRUCHIO Sir, here's the door, this is Lucentio's house.
My father's bears more toward the market-place;
Thither must I, and here I leave you, sir.

VINCENTIO You shall not choose but drink before you go.   10
I think I shall command your welcome here,
And by all likelihood some cheer is toward.

He knocks.

GREMIO They're busy within. You were best knock louder.

MERCHANT *looks out of the window.*

MERCHANT What's he that knocks as he would beat down the gate?

VINCENTIO Is Signor Lucentio within, sir?   15

MERCHANT He's within, sir, but not to be spoken withal.

VINCENTIO What if a man bring him a hundred pound or two to make
merry withal?

MERCHANT Keep your hundred pounds to yourself. He shall need none
so long as I live.   20

PETRUCHIO Nay, I told you your son was well beloved in Padua. Do
you hear, sir? To leave frivolous circumstances, I pray you tell
Signor Lucentio that his father is come from Pisa and is here at
the door to speak with him.

MERCHANT Thou liest. His father is come from Mantua and here   25
looking out at the window.

VINCENTIO Art thou his father?

MERCHANT Ay, sir, so his mother says, if I may believe her.

PETRUCHIO [*To Vincentio*] Why, how now, gentleman! Why, this is flat
knavery, to take upon you another man's name.   30

---

12 SD *He knocks*] Capell; *Knock.* F   25 from Mantua] *Capell, NS, Hibbard, Morris;* from Padua F, *Bond, Riverside, Oliver;* to Padua *Pope*   29 SD *To Vincentio*] Capell; not in F

7 This line indicates that, for this scene at least, one of the main doors onto the stage is seen as the entrance to Lucentio's house.

8 My...bears My father's (i.e. Baptista's) house lies.

12 some...toward some good entertainment can be expected.

12 SD *He knocks* F has *Knock*, an imperative stage direction like *Kneele* at 87 below and *Wind horns* and *Sound trumpets* in Induction 1.11 and 69. For the implications of this, see Textual Analysis, p. 157 below. The episode which follows, with a man being refused entry to his own or his son's house by another man who has assumed his identity, is also used by Shakespeare in *Err.* 3.1. He knew the version of it in Plautus's *Amphitruo* as well as that in Gascoigne's *Supposes* (4.3–7)

which is the obvious source here. See p. 14 above.

13 SD MERCHANT...*window* Presumably a window or gallery above the door being used as that of Lucentio's house; see 7 n. above. This piece of staging also comes directly from *Supposes* where Dalio, a servant of Erostrato (= Tranio) *commeth to the wyndowe, and there maketh answere* to the real father of the hero (4.3).

16 withal with, as in 18.

22 frivolous circumstances trivial details.

25 from Mantua F reads 'from Padua' here, which is clearly an error since we are in Padua. We cannot really know if Shakespeare intended the Merchant to give away his real residence (Mantua), to repeat 'from Pisa' after the true Vincentio, or even to claim that he has come 'to Padua'.

MERCHANT Lay hands on the villain. I believe a means to cozen
somebody in this city under my countenance.

Enter Biondello.

BIONDELLO [*Aside*] I have seen them in the church together – God send
'em good shipping! But who is here? Mine old master, Vincentio!
Now we are undone and brought to nothing!   35

VINCENTIO Come hither, crack-hemp.

BIONDELLO I hope I may choose, sir.

VINCENTIO Come hither, you rogue! What, have you forgot me?

BIONDELLO Forgot you? No, sir. I could not forget you, for I never
saw you before in all my life.   40

VINCENTIO What, you notorious villain! Didst thou never see thy
master's father, Vincentio?

BIONDELLO What, my old worshipful old master? Yes, marry, sir, see
where he looks out of the window.

VINCENTIO Is't so indeed?   45

He beats Biondello.

BIONDELLO Help! Help! Help! Here's a madman will murder me!

[Exit]

MERCHANT Help, son! Help, Signor Baptista! [*Exit from the window*]

PETRUCHIO Prithee, Kate, let's stand aside and see the end of this
controversy.

[They stand aside.]

Enter Merchant [below] with SERVANTS, BAPTISTA *and* TRANIO
[disguised as Lucentio].

TRANIO Sir, what are you that offer to beat my servant?   50

VINCENTIO What am I, sir? Nay, what are you, sir? O immortal gods!
O fine villain! A silken doublet, a velvet hose, a scarlet cloak, and

---

33 SD *Aside*] *Capell; not in* F   35 brought] Q; brough F   42 master's] F2; Mistris F   46 SD *Exit*] *Capell; not in* F
47 SD *Exit...window*] *Capell subst.; not in* F   49 SD.1 *They...aside*] *Theobald; not in* F   49 SD.2 *below*] *Capell;
not in* F   49 SD.3 *disguised as Lucentio*] *Pelican; not in* F

---

31 a he.

31 cozen cheat.

32 countenance name, identity.

34 shipping voyage, i.e. marriage. Another
nautical metaphor, as at 1.2.91 and 4.4.102.

34 old (1) elderly, (2) former.

35 undone ruined.

36 crack-hemp rogue, villain (literally, one who
will stretch or break the rope with which he is
hanged).

37 choose (1) please myself, (2) choose my
master.

42 *master's F has 'Mistris' here; see 5 n.

47 SD F has no stage direction here, but such
staging is implied by the direction after 49. In
Supposes we find *Dalio draweth his hed in at the
wyndowe, the Scenese* [= Merchant] *commeth out.*

48–9 For the first time our principals, Petruchio
and Katherina, become the audience for someone
else's 'show'. See p. 31 above for a general
discussion of *The Shrew*'s use of stage audiences.

50 offer dare attempt.

52 fine richly dressed.

a copatain hat! O I am undone, I am undone! While I play the good
husband at home my son and my servant spend all at the university.

TRANIO How now, what's the matter?   55

BAPTISTA What, is the man lunatic?

TRANIO Sir, you seem a sober ancient gentleman by your habit, but your
words show you a madman. Why, sir, what 'cerns it you if I wear
pearl and gold? I thank my good father, I am able to maintain it.

VINCENTIO Thy father? O villain! He is a sail-maker in Bergamo.   60

BAPTISTA You mistake, sir; you mistake, sir. Pray, what do you think
is his name?

VINCENTIO His name? As if I knew not his name! I have brought him
up ever since he was three years old, and his name is Tranio.

MERCHANT Away, away, mad ass! His name is Lucentio and he is mine   65
only son, and heir to the lands of me, Signor Vincentio.

VINCENTIO Lucentio? O, he hath murdered his master! Lay hold on
him, I charge you in the Duke's name. O my son, my son! Tell
me, thou villain, where is my son Lucentio?

TRANIO Call forth an officer.   70

                    [*Enter an* OFFICER.]

Carry this mad knave to the jail. Father Baptista, I charge you see
that he be forthcoming.

VINCENTIO Carry me to the jail?

GREMIO Stay, officer. He shall not go to prison.

BAPTISTA Talk not, Signor Gremio. I say he shall go to prison.   75

GREMIO Take heed, Signor Baptista, lest you be cony-catched in this
business. I dare swear this is the right Vincentio.

MERCHANT Swear, if thou dar'st.

GREMIO Nay, I dare not swear it.

---

58 'cerns] *Collier;* cernes F; concerns F2, *Rowe*   64 Tranio] F2; Tronio F   70 SD *Enter an* OFFICER] *Capell subst.;*
not in F

---

53 **copatain hat** a high-crowned hat in the form
of a sugar-loaf, fashionable in the sixteenth century
and apparently regarded as ostentatious on the
evidence of this passage and one in Act 4 of *Soliman
and Perseda* where Erastus refuses to wear the 'high
Sugar-loafe hat' and 'gilded gowne' the Emperor
Soliman has given him. See illustration 6 (p. 33
above).

54 **husband** manager, housekeeper.

57 **habit** dress. Tranio mischievously picks up
Vincentio's emphasis on clothing.

58 **what...you** what concern is it of yours.

59 **maintain** afford.

60 **Bergamo** Another inland town which is
apparently thought of as a port (see 1.1.42 n.).

Hibbard points out that it is appropriate as Tranio's
birthplace since it was the traditional home of the
Harlequin, the facetious servant of the Italian
Commedia dell'arte, and Maurice Hussey refers to
reports that it did indeed have a sail-making
industry despite its location (*The World of
Shakespeare and his Contemporaries*, 1971, p. 95).

72 **forthcoming** available for trial.

74–79 Gremio's contribution to the action here
is paralleled in *A Shrew*, where it is Christopher Sly
who attempts to intervene with 'I say wele have no
sending to prison'; see Appendix 1, pp. 176–7
below.

76 **cony-catched** deceived, tricked. See 4.1.30 n.

TRANIO Then thou wert best say that I am not Lucentio.   80
GREMIO Yes, I know thee to be Signor Lucentio.
BAPTISTA Away with the dotard, to the jail with him!
VINCENTIO Thus strangers may be haled and abused. O monstrous
　　villain!

　　　　　Enter Biondello, Lucentio and Bianca.

BIONDELLO O, we are spoiled, and yonder he is! Deny him, forswear   85
　　him, or else we are all undone.

　　　Exeunt Biondello, Tranio and Merchant, as fast as may be
LUCENTIO Pardon, sweet father.

　　　　　Lucentio and Bianca kneel.
VINCENTIO　　　　　　　　　　Lives my sweet son?
BIANCA Pardon, dear father.
BAPTISTA　　　　　　　　　How hast thou offended?
　　Where is Lucentio?
LUCENTIO　　　　　　　　Here's Lucentio,
　　Right son to the right Vincentio,   90
　　That have by marriage made thy daughter mine
　　While counterfeit supposes bleared thine eyne.
GREMIO Here's packing, with a witness, to deceive us all!
VINCENTIO Where is that damnèd villain, Tranio,
　　That faced and braved me in this matter so?   95
BAPTISTA Why, tell me, is not this my Cambio?
BIANCA Cambio is changed into Lucentio.
LUCENTIO Love wrought these miracles. Bianca's love
　　Made me exchange my state with Tranio
　　While he did bear my countenance in the town,   100
　　And happily I have arrived at the last
　　Unto the wishèd haven of my bliss.

---

83 haled] F3 (hal'd); haild F   84 SD *Enter...Bianca*] *Follows 83 in* F   87 SD *Lucentio...kneel*] *Capell; Kneele.* F
87–9 Pardon...Lucentio?] *Set as one complete line for each speaker in* F   101 at the last] F, *Bond, Riverside, Morris,*
Oliver; at last F2, NS, *Hibbard*

83 **haled** unceremoniously dragged about (by the
officer). F's 'haild', possibly meaning 'greeted',
'verbally welcomed', was changed to 'hal'd' in F3.
　85 **spoiled** ruined.
　87 SD F has *Kneele;* see 12 SD n.
　92 **supposes** Another allusion to Gascoigne's
play; see 2.1.396–7 n. and pp. 14–15 above.
　92 **eyne** eyes; an archaic plural. The rhymed
couplet helps to ritualise the lovers' kneeling for
forgiveness.
　93 **packing...witness** downright plotting,
deliberate deception.

　95 **faced and braved** outfaced and defied. The
words occur together at 4.3.121–4 and seem to have
been a common formula, perhaps a modernisation
of the older expression 'to face and brace', which
had the same meaning (*OED* Brace *v²*).
　98 **Love...miracles** Lucentio's claim seems
facile and premature in the light of 5.2.
　100 **bear my countenance** assume my identity.
　101–2 Lucentio's use of the nautical metaphor is,
characteristically, more conventional and refined
than the earlier examples at 1.2.91, 4.4.102 and
5.1.34.

What Tranio did, myself enforced him to;
Then pardon him, sweet father, for my sake.

VINCENTIO I'll slit the villain's nose that would have sent me to the   105
jail!

BAPTISTA But do you hear, sir? Have you married my daughter without
asking my good will?

VINCENTIO Fear not, Baptista, we will content you. Go to. But I will
in to be revenged for this villainy.   *Exit*   110

BAPTISTA And I, to sound the depth of this knavery.   *Exit*

LUCENTIO Look not pale, Bianca, thy father will not frown.
                         Exeunt [Lucentio and Bianca]

GREMIO My cake is dough, but I'll in among the rest,
Out of hope of all but my share of the feast.   *[Exit]*

KATHERINA Husband, let's follow, to see the end of this ado.   115

PETRUCHIO First kiss me, Kate, and we will.

KATHERINA What, in the midst of the street?

PETRUCHIO What, art thou ashamed of me?

KATHERINA No sir, God forbid – but ashamed to kiss.

PETRUCHIO Why then, let's home again.   120
  [To Grumio] Come, sirrah, let's away.

KATHERINA Nay, I will give thee a kiss.
                [She kisses him.]
Now pray thee, love, stay.

PETRUCHIO Is not this well? Come, my sweet Kate,
Better once than never, for never too late.   125
                         Exeunt

---

112 SD *Exeunt...Bianca] Capell; Exeunt.* F   114 SD *Exit] Rowe; not in* F   119 No] Q; Mo F
120–3 Why...stay] *As four verse lines, Hibbard; as two verse lines divided after* awaie, F   121 SD *To Grumio] Pelican;
not in* F   122 SD *She kisses him] Capell; not in* F   125 once] F; late *Hanmer*

105 slit...nose As a form of revenge. Compare
Oth. 4.1.142–3.

107 do you hear listen to me.

109 Go to Keep calm, don't worry.

110–14 The stage swiftly clears as the 'show'
dissolves, leaving the stage audience, Petruchio and
Katherina, to enact their own scene before they too
go off.

113 My...dough My project has failed. See
1.1.107–8 n.

122–3 Nay...stay Katherina calls Petruchio
'love' for the first time and completes his rhyme,
perhaps indicating a real willingness to form a
partnership, not just a grudging submission.

125 Better...late Petruchio combines two
proverbs, 'Better late than never' and 'It is never
too late to mend' (Tilley L85 and M875
respectively).

[5.2] *Enter* BAPTISTA, VINCENTIO, GREMIO, *the* MERCHANT,
LUCENTIO *and* BIANCA, [HORTENSIO] *and the* WIDOW, [PETRUCHIO
and KATHERINA], TRANIO, BIONDELLO *and* GRUMIO *with*
SERVINGMEN *bringing in a banquet.*

LUCENTIO At last, though long, our jarring notes agree,
    And time it is when raging war is done
    To smile at scapes and perils overblown.
    My fair Bianca, bid my father welcome,
    While I with selfsame kindness welcome thine.   5
    Brother Petruchio, sister Katherina,
    And thou Hortensio, with thy loving widow,
    Feast with the best, and welcome to my house.
    My banquet is to close our stomachs up
    After our great good cheer. Pray you, sit down,   10
    For now we sit to chat as well as eat.
PETRUCHIO Nothing but sit and sit, and eat and eat!
BAPTISTA Padua affords this kindness, son Petruchio.
PETRUCHIO Padua affords nothing but what is kind.
HORTENSIO For both our sakes I would that word were true.   15
PETRUCHIO Now, for my life, Hortensio fears his widow!
WIDOW Then never trust me if I be afeard.
PETRUCHIO You are very sensible, and yet you miss my sense:
    I mean Hortensio is afeard of you.

Act 5, Scene 2   5.2] *Steevens; Actus Quintus.* F   0 SD *Enter…banquet*] *Rowe subst.;* F *omits Hortensio, Petruchio and
Katherina, places the Widow after Grumio and mentions Tranio twice*   2 done] *Rowe;* come F

Act 5, Scene 2

0 SD F heads this scene *Actus Quintus.* The stage
direction in F omits Hortensio, Petruchio and
Katherina, although Lucentio greets them all by
name in his opening speech. It also gives Tranio's
name twice. There is some awkwardness moreover
in the fact that Petruchio and Katherina must exit
from the previous scene and re-enter immediately
(a situation Shakespeare normally avoids) although
we must suppose enough time has passed for a feast
at Baptista's house. Altogether it seems likely that
there is a problem with the copy here; see Appendix
1 and Textual Analysis, pp. 172–3 below.

0 SD.4 *banquet* desert of fruits, sweetmeats, etc.

1 **jarring notes** A reminiscence of the 'lesson'
scene, 3.1.

2–3 Lucentio's language suggests a dig at
Petruchio's courtship (see 2.1.126–33) and claims
(again prematurely) to bring all the nautical and
military metaphors to a satisfactory climax.

3 **scapes** escapes, dangerous moments.

9 **close…up** (1) finish our meal satisfactorily, (2)

put an end to any lingering irritability. After the
disruption of the wedding-feast for Petruchio and
Katherina in 3.2 and the taming of Katherina
through starvation in 4.1 and 4.3, it is particularly
appropriate that the play should end with such
lavish banqueting.

10 **our…cheer** i.e. the feast at Baptista's house.

13 **affords** (1) offers, provides, (2) has the
substance to provide.

13 **this kindness** this natural hospitality.

14 **kind** (1) natural, (2) affectionate. Petruchio
deliberately alludes to Katherina, and Hortensio
takes him up. It is surprising that Hortensio seems
unaware of the change in Katherina, given that he
was a witness in 4.5, but this is one of the many
inconsistencies in his role; see Textual Analysis,
pp. 161–4 below.

16 **fears** (1) is afraid of, (2) (as the Widow takes
it) frightens. See 1.2.204 for the same play on the
word.

18 **sensible** (1) sensitive, (2) alert to different
senses or meanings.

WIDOW He that is giddy thinks the world turns round.   20
PETRUCHIO Roundly replied.
KATHERINA   Mistress, how mean you that?
WIDOW Thus I conceive by him.
PETRUCHIO Conceives by me! How likes Hortensio that?
HORTENSIO My widow says, thus she conceives her tale.
PETRUCHIO Very well mended. Kiss him for that, good widow.   25
KATHERINA 'He that is giddy thinks the world turns round.'
          I pray you tell me what you meant by that.
WIDOW Your husband, being troubled with a shrew,
          Measures my husband's sorrow by his woe –
          And now you know my meaning.   30
KATHERINA A very mean meaning.
WIDOW   Right, I mean you.
KATHERINA And I am mean indeed, respecting you.
PETRUCHIO To her, Kate!
HORTENSIO To her, widow!
PETRUCHIO A hundred marks my Kate does put her down.   35
HORTENSIO That's my office.
PETRUCHIO Spoke like an officer. Ha' to thee, lad.
                    He drinks to Hortensio.
BAPTISTA How likes Gremio these quick-witted folks?
GREMIO Believe me, sir, they butt together well.
BIANCA Head and butt! An hasty-witted body   40
          Would say your head and butt were head and horn.

37 thee] Q; the F   39 butt] F (But); butt heads *Rowe*³   40 butt] *Theobald*; But F

20 He...round Proverbial (Tilley W870).
21 Roundly Boldly, outspokenly.
22 conceive (1) understand, (2) become pregnant.
The Widow means 'That is what I see as being
behind Petruchio's accusation: his own fears';
Petruchio takes up sense (2).
24 conceives her tale understands (i.e. intends)
her statement. Hortensio adds to the sexual
innuendos by his use of the word 'tale' ('tail' =
'genital organs'; see 2.1.211 and n.).
29 Judges or estimates my husband's problems
by his own unhappy state.
31 mean petty, ignoble.
32 And...you (1) My behaviour is moderate
compared with yours, (2) I am prepared to be petty
where you are concerned.
33–4 To her In an allusion to yet another game,
the men sound as if they are encouraging fighting
cocks; see pp. 36–7 above.
35 put her down defeat her (in argument).
36 office job. Hortensio puns on 'put her down'

in the sense of 'make her experience sexual
intercourse'.
37 like an officer like one who does what he
should.
37 Ha' Here's (i.e. I drink this to you).
39 butt butt their heads together. Some editors
unnecessarily emend to 'butt heads together' in
order to prepare for Bianca's reply.
40–8 Bianca's skill in bawdy repartee is out of key
with her image as the stereotype romantic heroine
('I saw her coral lips to move, / And with her breath
she did perfume the air', 1.1.165–6), but helps to
prepare us for her subsequent behaviour. The
change in her accompanies the more general shift
here from the urbane tone of a Paduan dinner-party
to the less sophisticated climax which is straight out
of folklore.
40 butt tail, bottom.
41 your...horn your butting head was a horned
head (a reference to cuckoldry; compare earlier
aspersions on Katherina's chastity at 1.1.55 and

VINCENTIO Ay, mistress bride, hath that awakened you?

BIANCA Ay, but not frighted me; therefore I'll sleep again.

PETRUCHIO Nay, that you shall not. Since you have begun,
Have at you for a bitter jest or two.   45

BIANCA Am I your bird? I mean to shift my bush,
And then pursue me as you draw your bow.
You are welcome all.

Exeunt Bianca, [Katherina and Widow]

PETRUCHIO She hath prevented me. Here, Signor Tranio,
This bird you aimed at, though you hit her not –   50
Therefore a health to all that shot and missed.

TRANIO O sir, Lucentio slipped me like his greyhound,
Which runs himself and catches for his master.

PETRUCHIO A good swift simile, but something currish.

TRANIO 'Tis well, sir, that you hunted for yourself –   55
'Tis thought your deer does hold you at a bay.

BAPTISTA O, O, Petruchio! Tranio hits you now.

LUCENTIO I thank thee for that gird, good Tranio.

HORTENSIO Confess! Confess! Hath he not hit you here?

PETRUCHIO A has a little galled me, I confess,   60
And as the jest did glance away from me,
'Tis ten to one it maimed you two outright.

BAPTISTA Now in good sadness, son Petruchio,
I think thou hast the veriest shrew of all.

PETRUCHIO Well, I say no, and therefore, Sir Assurance,   65

---

44 not. Since] *Pope* (not, since); not since F   45 bitter] *Capell, conj. Theobald;* better F, *Oliver*   48 SD *Exeunt...Widow*]
Rowe; Exit Bianca. F   62 you two] *Rowe;* you too F   65 Sir Assurance] *This edn;* sir assurance F; for assurance F2,
Bond, NS, Hibbard, Riverside, Morris, Oliver

2.1.283). It is not clear why Gremio has deserved
this gibe.

45 *bitter F has 'better', emended by Capell. It
means 'shrewd' or 'sharp' rather than 'ill-natured';
compare 3.2.13: 'Hiding his bitter jests in blunt
behaviour'.

46 bird i.e. target. The metaphor Bianca
develops is from the Elizabethan sport of killing
sitting birds with bow and arrow. There may be a
reference to Cupid (compare Beatrice's mention of
Cupid's 'burbolt' or bird-bolt at *Ado* 1.1.39–42)
and obscene undertones to 'bush' (= pubic hair)
and – by implication – Petruchio's 'arrow'.

52 slipped unleashed.

54 swift quick, apt.

56 deer...bay deer (dear) is fighting you and
holding you off. (An image from hunting, like that
of the greyhound.)

58 gird gibe.

59 here Perhaps Hortensio indicates the head,
repeating the 'horn' joke.

60 A He.

60 galled scratched, chafed.

63 good sadness proper seriousness.

65 Sir Assurance An ironic form of address to
the over-confident Baptista or Lucentio, depending
on the idiom used at 3.2.148, 'Sir Lucentio', and
4.2.105, 'Sir Vincentio'. Compare the similar
personification of 'Sir Smile' in *WT* 1.2.196, and
'Sir Prudence' (Gonzalo) in *Temp.* 2.1.286. F has
'sir assurance' but most editors prefer F2's reading,
'for assurance', on the grounds that 'for' and 'sir'
(with a long 's') could easily be confused in
Secretary hand.

> Let's each one send unto his wife,
> And he whose wife is most obedient
> To come at first when he doth send for her
> Shall win the wager which we will propose.

HORTENSIO Content. What's the wager?

LUCENTIO   Twenty crowns.   70

PETRUCHIO Twenty crowns?
> I'll venture so much of my hawk or hound,
> But twenty times so much upon my wife.

LUCENTIO A hundred then.

HORTENSIO   Content.

PETRUCHIO   A match! 'Tis done.

HORTENSIO Who shall begin?

LUCENTIO   That will I.   75
> Go Biondello, bid your mistress come to me.

BIONDELLO I go.   *Exit*

BAPTISTA Son, I'll be your half Bianca comes.

LUCENTIO I'll have no halves; I'll bear it all myself.

Enter Biondello.

> How now, what news?

BIONDELLO   Sir, my mistress sends you word   80
> That she is busy, and she cannot come.

PETRUCHIO How? 'She's busy and she cannot come'!
> Is that an answer?

GREMIO   Ay, and a kind one too.
> Pray God, sir, your wife send you not a worse.

PETRUCHIO I hope better.   85

HORTENSIO Sirrah Biondello, go and entreat my wife
> To come to me forthwith.

Exit Biondello

PETRUCHIO   O ho, 'entreat' her!
> Nay then, she must needs come.

HORTENSIO   I am afraid, sir,
> Do what you can, yours will not be entreated.

Enter Biondello.

82–3 How...answer] *As verse, Capell; as prose,* F   87–8 O...come] *As verse, Capell; as prose,* F   89 SD *Enter Biondello*]
Follows Do what you can *in* F

72 of on.
78 **I'll...half** I'll pay half the stake (and take half
the winnings).

83 **kind** (1) natural, appropriate, (2) (relatively)
affectionate.
85 i.e. I hope (she will send a) better (answer).

Now, where's my wife?   90

BIONDELLO She says you have some goodly jest in hand.
    She will not come. She bids you come to her.
PETRUCHIO Worse and worse! 'She will not come'! O vile,
    Intolerable, not to be endured!
    Sirrah Grumio, go to your mistress.   95
    Say I command her come to me.

                                  Exit [Grumio]

HORTENSIO I know her answer.
PETRUCHIO   What?
HORTENSIO   She will not.
PETRUCHIO The fouler fortune mine, and there an end.

                     Enter Katherina.

BAPTISTA Now, by my holidame, here comes Katherina!
KATHERINA What is your will, sir, that you send for me?   100
PETRUCHIO Where is your sister, and Hortensio's wife?
KATHERINA They sit conferring by the parlour fire.
PETRUCHIO Go fetch them hither. If they deny to come,
    Swinge me them soundly forth unto their husbands.
    Away, I say, and bring them hither straight.   105

                      [Exit Katherina]

LUCENTIO Here is a wonder, if you talk of a wonder.
HORTENSIO And so it is. I wonder what it bodes.
PETRUCHIO Marry, peace it bodes, and love, and quiet life,
    An awful rule and right supremacy
    And, to be short, what not that's sweet and happy.   110
BAPTISTA Now fair befall thee, good Petruchio!
    The wager thou hast won, and I will add
    Unto their losses twenty thousand crowns,
    Another dowry to another daughter,
    For she is changed, as she had never been.   115
PETRUCHIO Nay, I will win my wager better yet,
    And show more sign of her obedience –

93–4 Worse...endured] *Divided after* come *in* F   96 SD *Grumio*] *Rowe; not in* F   105 SD *Exit Katherina*] *Rowe; not in* F

91 goodly Often used ironically, as at 2.1.252.

99 holidame Spelt 'hollidam' in F, revealing the popular but erroneous etymology ('holy dame' = Virgin Mary). 'Halidom' meaning a holy place or thing (and hence one's honour) is what is meant.

104 Swinge me Beat on my behalf. For the archaic dative 'me' see 1.2.8 and n.

104 soundly thoroughly, effectively.

107 Hortensio refers facetiously to the belief that preternatural events were portents.

109 awful inspiring awe or respect.

110 what not i.e. everything.

111 fair...thee good fortune to you.

115 as...been as if she had never existed before.

Her new-built virtue and obedience.

Enter Katherina, Bianca and Widow.

See where she comes, and brings your froward wives
As prisoners to her womanly persuasion.   120
Katherine, that cap of yours becomes you not:
Off with that bauble – throw it underfoot!
                    [*She obeys.*]
WIDOW Lord, let me never have a cause to sigh
       Till I be brought to such a silly pass!
BIANCA Fie, what a foolish duty call you this?   125
LUCENTIO I would your duty were as foolish too.
       The wisdom of your duty, fair Bianca,
       Hath cost me a hundred crowns since supper-time.
BIANCA The more fool you for laying on my duty.
PETRUCHIO Katherine, I charge thee, tell these headstrong women   130
       What duty they do owe their lords and husbands.
WIDOW Come, come, you're mocking. We will have no telling.
PETRUCHIO Come on, I say, and first begin with her.
WIDOW She shall not.
PETRUCHIO I say she shall. And first begin with her.   135
KATHERINA Fie, fie, unknit that threatening unkind brow,
       And dart not scornful glances from those eyes
       To wound thy lord, thy king, thy governor.
       It blots thy beauty as frosts do bite the meads,
       Confounds thy fame as whirlwinds shake fair buds,   140
       And in no sense is meet or amiable.
       A woman moved is like a fountain troubled,

---

122 SD *She obeys*] *Rowe subst.; not in* F   128 a hundred] *Capell;* five hundred F; an hundred *Rowe*
130–1 Katherine...husbands] *As verse, Rowe³; as prose,* F   132 you're] F3; your F

118 SD The stage direction in *A Shrew* at this point reads *Enter Kate thrusting Phylema and Emelia before her, and makes them come unto their husbands call.*

119 **froward** disobedient, perverse.

121 **that cap** On stage it is often the case that in this scene Katherina wears the very cap and gown denied her in 4.3.

128 ***a hundred** F has 'five hundred' which is not consistent with the terms agreed at 74. Sisson has conjectured that an 'a' in the manuscript was misread as a 'v' (*New Readings*, pp. 166–7). Most editors therefore adopt Capell's emendation.

129 **laying** laying money, betting.

136–79 Katherina's speech is of course full of Elizabethan commonplaces, many of which can be found in the marriage service and in the homily 'Of the State of Matrimony'. Shakespeare, however, unlike the author of *A Shrew*, gives a purely secular account of the relationship between man and woman, omitting the theological arguments which were commonly used in this context. For a fuller discussion of this speech, see pp. 28–30 and 38–41 above.

136 **unkind** unnatural, hostile.

139 **blots** disfigures.

140 **Confounds thy fame** Destroys your reputation.

141 **meet** appropriate.

142 **moved** i.e. angry, disagreeable.

Muddy, ill-seeming, thick, bereft of beauty,
And while it is so, none so dry or thirsty
Will deign to sip, or touch one drop of it.　145
Thy husband is thy lord, thy life, thy keeper,
Thy head, thy sovereign; one that cares for thee
And for thy maintenance; commits his body
To painful labour both by sea and land,
To watch the night in storms, the day in cold,　150
Whilst thou li'st warm at home, secure and safe,
And craves no other tribute at thy hands
But love, fair looks and true obedience –
Too little payment for so great a debt.
Such duty as the subject owes the prince,　155
Even such a woman oweth to her husband.
And when she is froward, peevish, sullen, sour,
And not obedient to his honest will,
What is she but a foul contending rebel
And graceless traitor to her loving lord?　160
I am ashamed that women are so simple
To offer war where they should kneel for peace,
Or seek for rule, supremacy and sway,
When they are bound to serve, love and obey.
Why are our bodies soft, and weak, and smooth,　165
Unapt to toil and trouble in the world,
But that our soft conditions and our hearts
Should well agree with our external parts?
Come, come, you froward and unable worms,
My mind hath been as big as one of yours,　170
My heart as great, my reason haply more,
To bandy word for word and frown for frown.
But now I see our lances are but straws,
Our strength as weak, our weakness past compare,
That seeming to be most which we indeed least are.　175

148 maintenance; commits] *Collier, Hibbard, Riverside, Morris, Oliver;* maintenance. Commits F *;* maintenance commits
Cam., Bond, NS

150 **watch** stay awake during.
158 **honest** honourable; i.e. rightfully exerted;
see p. 29 above.
161 **simple** foolish.
167 **conditions** qualities.
169 **unable worms** feeble creatures.

170 **big** proud.
171 **heart** courage, temper.
174 **as weak** i.e. as weak as straws.
175 Seeming to be most that which we in fact are
least.

Then vail your stomachs, for it is no boot,
And place your hands below your husband's foot.
In token of which duty, if he please,
My hand is ready, may it do him ease.
PETRUCHIO Why, there's a wench! Come on and kiss me, Kate.   180
LUCENTIO Well, go thy ways, old lad, for thou shall ha't.
VINCENTIO 'Tis a good hearing when children are toward.
LUCENTIO But a harsh hearing when women are froward.
PETRUCHIO Come, Kate, we'll to bed.
We three are married, but you two are sped.   185
[*To Lucentio*] 'Twas I won the wager, though you hit the
white,
And being a winner, God give you good night.
Exeunt Petruchio [and Katherina]
HORTENSIO Now, go thy ways; thou hast tamed a curst shrew.
LUCENTIO 'Tis a wonder, by your leave, she will be tamed so.
[*Exeunt*]

186 SD *To Lucentio*] Malone; *not in* F   187 SD *Exeunt...Katherina*] Rowe; *Exit Petruchio* F   189 SD *Exeunt*]
Rowe; FINIS *centred and within rules,* F

176 **vail your stomachs** suppress your pride,
calm your tempers.
176 **no boot** no use, no good.
180 As at 5.1.116–25, the kiss confirms Katherina
and Petruchio's new partnership.
181 **go thy ways** well done.
181 **old lad** An affectionate form of address,
meaning roughly 'good old Petruchio'. (Grumio is
addressed as 'old lad' by his fellow-servant
Nathaniel at 4.1.84.)
182 **good hearing** good thing to hear.
182 **toward** docile, obedient (opposite of
'froward' and 'untoward').
184 **we'll to bed** Given the reference to
Petruchio's 'sermon of continency' on his wedding-
night (4.1.154) and his policy of depriving
Katherina of food, sleep and other physical
gratifications, we must assume that the marriage is
now about to be consummated. See also 3.2.235 n.
on the question of interrupted and delayed rituals.
185 **sped** taken care of (in a bad sense), done for.

Shakespeare uses the same rhyme in the poem found
by the Prince of Arragon along with the fool's head
in the silver casket: 'Take what wife you will to
bed, / I will ever be your head. / So be gone, you
are sped' (*MV* 2.9.70–2).
186 **hit the white** hit the centre of the target, i.e.
won Bianca whose name means 'white' in Italian.
187 **being a winner** i.e. while I'm still ahead.
188–9 Compare 4.1.181–2 for the identical
rhyme.
189 **wonder** Compare the quibble on 'wonder'
at 106–7. Lucentio could be expressing doubts
about whether Katherina really has been tamed, but
it is also possible (and appropriate after his glib
'Love wrought these miracles' at 5.1.98) that he
should be genuinely amazed at the transformation;
see p. 39 above. Even so, it is a rather feeble
couplet to end the play on and it is attractive to
assume that there was once another Sly scene after
this; see Appendix 1, pp. 177–8 below.

TEXTUAL ANALYSIS

The sole authority for the text of *The Taming of the Shrew* is the First Folio of 1623 (referred to throughout this edition as F). A quarto text (referred to as Q) was printed in 1631 and the Folio was reprinted three times during the seventeenth century, in 1632 (F2), 1663–4 (F3) and 1685 (F4). All these later texts offer minor corrections, some of which have been adopted here (as specified in the collation), but they derive from F and have no independent authority. Consequently, the text in the present edition follows F as closely as possible, emending only in cases where F seems clearly erroneous or (as, for example, in the case of stage directions) inadequate. Most of the emendations follow standard editorial practice, relying heavily on the work of eighteenth-century editors, especially Rowe, Theobald and Capell.

The Taming of the Shrew is the eleventh play in F, appearing amongst the comedies after *As You Like It* and before *All's Well That Ends Well*. It occupies twenty-two folio pages from sig. s2ᵛ to sig. v1 (pp. 208–29). Charlton Hinman's analysis of the printing procedures for F revealed that three compositors (a not unusual number) worked on the play and that their shares of the text were as follows:[1]

Sig. s2ᵛ–s6ᵛ	(up to 2.1.250 in this text)	Compositor B
Sig. T1–T2ᵛ	(2.1.251–4.1.11)	Compositor C
Sig. T3–T4ᵛ	(4.1.11–4.3.186)	Compositor B
Sig. T5–T6ᵛ	(4.3.187–5.2.131)	Compositor A
Sig. v1	(5.2.132 to the end)	Compositor B

Later scholarship has confirmed these findings with the exception of the four pages assigned to Compositor A, which have been reassigned[2] to Compositor D. The consensus is that fourteen out of the twenty-two pages were set by B, interspersed with brief four-page stints from C and D. The text is a relatively clean one with an average sprinkling of minor errors and misprints. There is no indication of any particular difficulty about the setting or printing of the play. Verse is occasionally set as prose by all three compositors (for example, 3.2.157–73 is the work of Compositor C, 4.1.154–8 is the work of B and 5.2.80–8 is the work of D), and prose is set as verse once, by Compositor B, at 2.1.75–83. It is not clear why this should have happened as distribution of space on the pages concerned does not seem to be a factor.

There has been much discussion of the relationship between the play printed in F in 1623 as *The Taming of the Shrew* and a play printed in quarto in 1594 with the title *A Pleasant Conceited Historie, called The taming of a Shrew* (referred to throughout this edition as *A Shrew*). This play was reprinted in 1596 and 1607 but

---

[1] Hinman, II, pp. 446–62.
[2] See T. H. Howard-Hill, 'The compositors of Shakespeare's Folio comedies', *SB* 26 (1973), 61–106, and John O'Connor, 'Compositors D and F of the Shakespeare First Folio', *SB* 28 (1975), 81–117.

on no occasion was it ascribed to Shakespeare, although it clearly has much in common with the Folio play. It was formerly assumed that *A Shrew* was the direct source of *The Shrew* but modern scholars have on the whole rejected this theory in favour of the belief that it is some kind of 'bad' quarto, either of Shakespeare's *The Shrew* as we know it or of a lost play (possibly Shakespearean) which was the source of *The Shrew*. In any case the two plays are so different on the level of verbal detail that *A Shrew* is of no direct use in establishing an authoritative text for *The Shrew*. It becomes significant, however, when one comes to consider whether the text we have of *The Shrew* is revised or incomplete.

The nature of the copy and its transmission

W. W. Greg thought that the Folio text of *The Shrew* was printed from Shakespeare's own manuscript (or 'foul papers', to use the technical term), but that that manuscript had been annotated for the theatre, probably by the book-keeper during the process of reading and casting.[1] Many scholars and editors have agreed with this basic assumption about the copy but the evidence is not entirely convincing. The main argument for the authorial origin of the manuscript rests on a number of minor peculiarities in the text, especially in stage directions and speech headings, which are careless and confused to the point that the Folio text as it stands could not have been used in the theatre. On several occasions, for example, no entrance is marked in the Folio for characters who clearly need to be on stage, as in the case of Hortensio at 2.1.38, Lucentio at the beginning of 3.2, and three important characters, Petruchio, Katherina and Hortensio, at the beginning of 5.2. At times the speech headings are inconsistent, as when the servingmen in Induction 2 are first labelled 1.*Ser.*, 2.*Ser.*, etc. and then become 3.*Man.*, 2.*Man.*, 2.*M.*, and on two occasions odd names appear which seem to refer to the actors rather than their parts, *Sincklo* at Induction 1.84 and *Nicke* at 3.1.79. Stage directions which are over-explicit, like *Enter Baptista with his two daughters, Katerina and Bianca, Gremio a Pantelowne, Hortensio sister* [suitor] *to Bianca* at 1.1.45, are more typical of an authorial manuscript than of a prompt-book, and so are those which are vague or 'permissive' like *Enter foure or fiue seruingmen* at 4.1.79: the book-keeper in the theatre does not need to be told that Katherina is Baptista's daughter but he does need to know how many servingmen should go on. Brian Morris's recent discovery of Shakespearean spellings in the Folio text adds to the impression that it was printed from Shakespeare's own manuscript, or from something very close to it.[2] He demonstrates that several words such as 'dogges', 'warre', 'affoords' and 'obay' are spelt in the same way in the Folio *Shrew* and in the three pages in the *Sir Thomas More* play generally believed to be written in Shakespeare's own hand.

On the other hand, it looks as if some notes have been added to the stage directions in an attempt to clarify them and make the text more useful in the theatre. In the

---

[1] Greg, pp. 212–15. Greg identifies the features which indicate that a text was printed from the author's foul papers on p. 142.

[2] Morris, pp. 8–9.

very first stage direction in Induction 1, for example, *Enter Begger and Hostes, Christophero Sly*, we have a redundancy which is probably the result of interference by a second hand: *Begger* or *Beg.* is the designation used throughout for Sly by the author, though it is clear from Induction 2.15 that his full name is Christopher Sly. What seems to have happened is that someone else looking through the text for the beggar's name came first upon his swaggering, mock-Spanish declaration 'I am *Christophero Sly*' at Induction 2.5 and so added that to the original stage direction. The repetition of the Merchant's (or Pedant's) entrance in 4.4 (at the beginning of the scene and at 17) and the odd *Gremio is out before* at the beginning of 5.1 may also suggest annotation by a later non-authorial hand, and the brief imperative directions, *Winde hornes* and *Sound trumpets* in Induction 1 (11, 69) and *Knock* and *Kneele* in 5.1 (12, 87) are typical of those usually found in texts set from theatrical transcripts. Greg thought these were all notes added by a book-keeper in the theatre and did not allow them to challenge his theory that the text was printed directly from Shakespeare's manuscript. Doubts about this were nevertheless raised in NS (1928), and have been revived in Hibbard (1968) and Morris (1981). All these editions have supposed that the text was printed from a scribal transcript rather than from foul papers. (This view is, however, not yet unanimous; Oliver (1982, pp. 4–13) reasserts the older opinion that the text was printed from Shakespeare's manuscript.)

Quiller-Couch and Dover Wilson in NS did take the stage directions to be evidence of a second, non-authorial hand in the text, not necessarily that of the book-keeper. They drew attention to the odd fact that the name 'Tranio' is always spelt correctly in the dialogue (apart from the single misprint 'Tronio' at 5.1.64) but appears as 'Triano' and 'Trayno' in the stage directions, and they argued that the confused speech headings at 3.1.45–55 and 4.2.4–8 could have arisen from careless transcription of the text: on both occasions the confusion involves Lucentio and Hortensio, and since the latter is disguised as Litio (or Licio) it is likely that Shakespeare's manuscript had *Luc.* and *Lit.* (or *Lic.*) as speech headings, which could easily be misread by a scribe.[1] Further evidence of ignorant transcription might be found in the mysterious and unnecessary speech heading *Par.* which is prefixed to the last line of Tranio's speech at 4.2.67–71. Greg suggested this might be the name of the actor about to play the Merchant (or Pedant) which was written in the margin and then mistakenly included in the text, but the identification with William Parr, who first appears in the plot of the play called *1 Tamar Cam* in 1602 (a decade later), seems to me doubtful.[2] It is just as likely that the word *Par.* relates to the confusion about the identity of the character who is about to speak the next line and who has been described by Biondello as 'a marcantant, or a pedant' (4.2.63). From the dialogue it is obvious that he is a merchant but all editors follow the Folio in calling him a pedant. It might be that the copyist was undecided which one to pick, put off perhaps by the unfamiliarity of the unique word 'marcantant', and first wrote *Mar.*, tried correcting

---

[1] NS, pp. 97–102.

[2] This might, however, be seen as a scrap of evidence for supposing that the transcript might have been made, not in the early 1590s, but in the first decade of the seventeenth century. I have not found any other evidence to support this possibility.

it to *Ped.* but found that too messy, abandoned the resulting *Par.* and wrote *Ped.* immediately beneath it. The compositor then set both. In any case the contradiction between the character as he exists in the dialogue and the *Pedant* label he is given in stage directions and speech headings reinforces the argument that someone other than the author intervened in the transmission of the text.

The principal objection to the theory that the entire copy for the Folio text of *The Shrew* was a scribal transcript has been the assumption that the reason for making such a transcript would be to produce a prompt-book for the theatre and the resulting version of *The Shrew* would not have been adequate to that purpose. It does bear some signs of theatrical annotation, as described above, but the job has not been done with anything like the necessary thoroughness and consistency. In support of his conviction that the text was printed from a scribal transcript, G. R. Hibbard argues round this by saying that this particular transcript might have been prepared 'hurriedly and carelessly', since the play dates from a period of great turmoil and change in the Elizabethan theatre when the prolonged ravages of plague in London kept the theatres closed and caused the acting companies to tour the provinces, sometimes splitting up into smaller groups and losing their former identity altogether. As he says,

Among these latter were the Earl of Pembroke's men, for whom this play seems to have been written. A company that was breaking up into two different groups might well need hurried transcripts of the most popular plays in its repertory, so that each group could act them.[1]

In this case we would assume that the transcript was made from Shakespeare's 'foul papers' with just a few theatrical annotations included and that the prompt-book for the original version of *The Shrew* acted in London was lost and either had not been found or was for some reason ignored in 1623 when Heminge and Condell needed a copy for the Folio. The implication that *The Shrew* as we have it represents an inferior and possibly incomplete version of the original could be supported by evidence from *A Shrew* that a fuller version containing more Christopher Sly scenes did once exist. It would be convenient to believe that the transcription and the cutting were both done at the same time and for the same reasons of theatrical exigency, since the reduction in casting requirements resulting from cutting the additional Sly scenes could be seen as a necessary change for a smaller company of actors on tour, although admittedly this might save only two or three actors.[2] Before embarking on the complex question of the relationship between *The Shrew* and *A Shrew* it is, however, necessary to complete the examination of the nature of the Folio text as it stands.

The most important evidence supporting the theory that the copy was a 'hurried transcript' lies in the number of small words or parts of words which have been omitted in the Folio and which have to be supplied by editors. In this respect the Folio text is unusual: the number of errors is uncommonly high in *The Shrew* when we compare it with other plays. It seems unlikely that these omissions originated in the

[1] Hibbard, pp. 245–8. The theatrical context of the play is discussed more fully at pp. 1–3 above.
[2] See the casting analysis in Karl P. Wentersdorf, 'The original ending of *The Taming of the Shrew*: a reconsideration', *SEL* 18 (1978), 201–15.

printing-house because (1) Compositor B, who set a large part of the First Folio as a whole as well as a large part of *The Shrew*, does not make so many errors of this kind elsewhere, and (2) the errors are found in the work of all three compositors, roughly in proportion to the amount of work they did on the play.[1] This suggests that the omissions are more likely to be a characteristic of the copy.

It has been claimed that these omissions make many lines unmetrical, which is perhaps an unfortunate argument as it depends on the dubious premise that all lines must conform to a single metrical ideal and it has been used to justify emendations which are debatable. I am not myself convinced of the need to emend the following lines, though many editors have added the words or syllables shown in square brackets (see collation for details):

Induction 2.69	And not a Tinker, nor Christopher[o] Slie
3.2.156	What said the wench when he rose [up] againe
4.2.120	Go with me [sir] to cloath you as becomes you
4.5.26	But soft, [what] Company is coming here

But there is still a significant number of lines where a single word or syllable needs to be added, not only for the metre but (more convincingly) for the sense. The following lines are ones I have emended in this way, with the word or syllable that is not in F again given in square brackets:

Induction 2.2	Wilt please your Lord[ship] drink a cup of sacke
1.2.115	And her with-holds from me [and]. Other more
2.1.8	Of all thy sutors heere I charge [thee] tel
2.1.77	Freely give vnto [you] this yong Scholler, that hath
3.2.29	Much more a shrew of [thy] impatient humour
3.2.118	But sir, [to] Love concerneth vs to adde
3.2.120	As [I] before imparted to your worship
4.3.81	Why thou saist true, it is [a] paltrie cap
4.3.88	What's this? a sleeue? 'tis like [a] demi cannon
4.5.78	Haue to my Widdow, and if she [be] froward

Moreover, most editors agree that the word 'old' must have dropped out of Biondello's (prose) line 'Master, master, newes, and such newes as you never heard of', to justify Baptista's reply 'Is it new and olde too?' (3.2.30–2) and that some word or words have been dropped from 3.2.16 where F reads 'Make friends, invite, and proclaime the banes'. The most commonly accepted emendation here is Dyce's 'Make feast, invite friends, and proclaim the banns.' Other short lines which cannot be emended without unjustifiable speculation are 2.1.105 'To my daughters, and tell them both', 3.1.4 'But wrangling pedant, that is', and 4.4.34 'Me shall you finde readie and willing'. In all these cases I think the theory that the copy was a 'hurried transcript' is a convincing explanation. It is of course possible that we could still be dealing with an authorial manuscript, if Shakespeare was a careless transcriber of his

---

[1] Of the ten lines quoted as ones I have emended on this page, for example, six fall into B's stint, three into C's and one into D's.

own work, but it seems more likely that such errors would have been made by a scribe than by the author who would have had the sense and metre of the lines more securely in his mind. One remarkable misreading, 'Butonios' for 'Antonios' at 1.2.184, possibly supports the view that the copy was not in Shakespeare's hand, since on the evidence of *Sir Thomas More*, where Doll conveniently refers to her Brother Arthur on fol. 8ᵛ, Shakespeare's Bs and As were quite distinct.

In conclusion, I think enough evidence has been collected to constitute a serious challenge to the earlier belief that the Folio text of *The Shrew* was printed directly from Shakespeare's own foul papers. The nature of some of the stage directions and speech headings seems telling, as does the number of monosyllabic omissions. At the .same time the nature of other stage directions and the survival of Shakespearean spellings indicate that we are certainly not dealing with a theatrical prompt-book. Some kind of transcription is involved, and it would be attractive to associate that transcription with the confused period of theatrical history in the early 1590s when the acting companies were in disarray and the curious text of *A Shrew* also appeared. But we cannot be certain of this, since the transcript could have been made at any time between the original writing of the play and its inclusion in the Folio in 1623.

Is the Folio text an incomplete or revised version?

There are three kinds of evidence for thinking that the Folio text of *The Shrew* represents an incomplete or revised version of Shakespeare's original play, rather than simply an annotated transcription:

1. The absence of the additional Christopher Sly material that we find in *A Shrew*.
2. Other loose ends and inconsistencies in the plot.
3. The presence of 'verse fossils' and other peculiarities of the language in some early scenes.

I shall deal with these problems in reverse order, finishing with a separate section on the whole question of the relationship of *The Shrew* to *A Shrew*.

It is not unusual to find rhymed couplets and other forms of heavily patterned language in Shakespeare's early plays but the odd thing about *The Shrew* is that almost all the instances occur in the third and fourth scenes of the play. We find couplets, for example, at 1.1.68–71 and 229–32, and at 1.2.11–14, 16–17, 22–5, 32–3, 123–4 and 213–30. In these scenes they seem to be embedded in the dialogue almost at random, whereas later in the play they are more obviously related to their context, as when they occur as exit lines or at the end of scenes (very frequently) or in Katherina's long formal speech in 5.2. They are accompanied in the early scenes by other examples of formal patterning which seem Lylyan in origin, like the repetition in Hortensio's prose speech, 'by helping *Baptista*'s eldest daughter to a husband wee set his yongest free for a husband' (1.1.130–1) or the structure of couplets like

> Counsaile me, *Tranio*, for I know thou canst:
> Assist me *Tranio*, for I know thou wilt. (1.1.148–9)

I am content to bee *Lucentio*,
Because so well I love *Lucentio*.   (1.1.207–8)

I come to wiue it wealthily in *Padua*:
If wealthily, then happily in *Padua*.   (1.2.72–3)

These instances are clearly part of a deliberate style; as Oliver argues (pp. 61–2), *The Shrew* offers many examples of experimentation in the use of rhyme and it would be unwise to treat all of them as evidence of revision or of different layers of composition.

I find a small group of repeated words in the Induction scenes more puzzling, since they do not have quite such an obvious stylistic effect. The following lines seem to draw attention to themselves:

What thinke you, if he were conuey'd to bed,
Wrap'd in sweet cloathes: Rings put vpon his fingers:
A most delicious banquet by his bed,   (Induction 1.33–5)

With soft lowe tongue, and lowly curtesie,   (Induction 1.110)

And Citherea all in sedges hid,
Which seeme to moue and wanton with her breath,
Euen as the wauing sedges play with winde.   (Induction 2.47–9)

It is difficult to tell whether the repetition of one word in these examples ('bed', 'lowe'/'lowly', 'sedges') is intentional on the part of the author or should be seen as further evidence of corruption in the transcription or composition of the text.

The existence of loose ends or inconsistencies in the plot of *The Shrew* has also been interpreted as evidence of corruption or revision in the text. Problems of this kind arise at the following points:

1. 1.1.218–24 Lucentio tells Biondello that he has changed clothes with Tranio to escape arrest for murder. This fiction is unmotivated and unsustained. It seems related to a possible gap in the text at 201–2: see note, p. 67 above.

2. 2.1.331 ff. Baptista, Gremio and Tranio (disguised as Lucentio) all seem to forget Hortensio's suit to Bianca and talk as if she had only two wooers.

3. 3.1.35 Although Hortensio is present (disguised as Litio) in this scene, Lucentio again seems unaware of his suit and claims that his own disguise (as Cambio) has been assumed to beguile only 'the old Pantalowne' (Gremio).

4. 3.2.21 ff. Tranio seems surprisingly intimate with Petruchio here and at 103 where he offers to lend him some clothes. Both speeches would seem more appropriate to Hortensio, Petruchio's 'best beloued and approued friend' (1.2.3).

5. 3.2.117–18 Tranio agrees with Baptista to try to persuade Petruchio to change his clothes but fails to follow the other characters off. After speaking to Baptista at 116 he seems to be in the middle of a conversation with Lucentio at 118; there may be a gap in the text here: see note, p. 106 above.

6. 4.1.122–3   Petruchio sends a servant to fetch his cousin Ferdinand whom he promises to introduce to Katherina. No more is heard of this.

7. 4.2.22   Tranio (disguised as Lucentio) says he has only 'heard of' Hortensio's suit to Bianca when he (a) had direct knowledge of it from Hortensio in 1.2 and (b) seemed totally ignorant of it in 2.1.

8. 4.2.54   Tranio claims that Hortensio has 'gone vnto the taming schoole' though (a) he has not stated any such intention and (b) it leaves him no time to woo his widow.

9. 4.4.1–17   The repeated entry of the Merchant (or Pedant) at the beginning of the scene and at 17 may imply two stages of composition, with lines 1–17 being written later.

10. 4.5.62–3   Petruchio tells Vincentio that the latter's son Lucentio has already married Bianca. He and Hortensio (who confirms his statement at 74 below) can hardly know this yet. Moreover, Hortensio ought to be surprised at the news since he and 'Lucentio' (Tranio) forswore Bianca's love in 4.2.

11. 5.1.6   Gremio seems to be waiting for Cambio (Lucentio) for some reason which has not been specified. Also, he clearly knows about the wedding plans, which Baptista intended to conceal from him at 4.4.53.

12. 5.2 *passim*   Although Hortensio witnessed the change in Katherina in 4.5, he seems to forget it here and is prepared to wager against her obedience.

Although most of these inconsistencies would pass unnoticed on stage and none of them constitutes a major challenge to the progress or outcome of either of the plots, there are so many of them that one hesitates to dismiss them as the normal results of rapid composition on Shakespeare's part. A few of them might be accounted for in this way but the sheer accumulation of examples has encouraged several scholars to suppose that the text represents an imperfectly revised version of some earlier lost play. It is remarkable that, apart from points 1, 6, 9 and 11 of the above list (which, as isolated instances of loose ends, would not attract much interest or speculation in themselves), all the points relate to the roles played in the sub-plot by Hortensio and Tranio: once Hortensio assumes his disguise as Litio, his original role as a wooer of Bianca is forgotten by all concerned (points 2, 3 and 7), his role as Petruchio's best friend in Padua is awkwardly assumed by Tranio (points 4 and 5), and his role in the concluding stages of the plot is handled in a perfunctory and inconsistent manner (points 8, 10 and 12).

G. I. Duthie, building on earlier work by P. A. Daniel, argued that all becomes explicable if we assume that there was an earlier version of the play in which Hortensio did not disguise himself, and that the confusion arose when this new element (clearly desirable for the comic effect of a scene like 3.1) was inserted into the plot without due care being taken over the resulting inconsistencies.[1] He also claimed that *A Shrew*

---

[1] G. I. Duthie, '*The Taming of a Shrew* and *The Taming of the Shrew*', RES 19 (1943), 337–56.

is free of these problems because Polidor (the character who is equivalent to Hortensio) does not disguise himself in any way. It is certainly the case that some inconsistencies in *The Shrew* are not found in *A Shrew*; in the equivalent of 3.2, for example, Polidor who really is the friend of Ferando (as Hortensio is of Petruchio) is given the speeches corresponding to the ones which in *The Shrew* (point 4 above) come awkwardly from Tranio, and later on Polidor (unlike Hortensio) declares his intention of going to visit Ferando and Kate (point 8 above). It would be possible to conclude from this evidence that the author of *A Shrew*, working from *The Shrew*, noticed the inconsistencies and tidied them up, but Duthie thought this degree of care unlikely in view of other inconsistencies and weaknesses in *A Shrew* and concluded instead that both the extant Shrew plays were derived (independently of each other) from a lost play in which the Hortensio/Polidor character did not assume a disguise. Since he also maintained that in some passages at least *A Shrew* is a memorial reconstruction dependent upon *The Shrew* 'or upon a text very close indeed to that of *The Shrew*',[1] he thought that the lost play was Shakespeare's own earlier version in which 'the Sly material and the main plot were in or near their final state' (i.e. the state existing in the Folio text of *The Shrew*) but that the sub-plot was less complicated and indeed very close to the sub-plot of *A Shrew*.

This difficult argument postulating a lost play and a two-stage composition of *The Shrew* was understandably not popular with subsequent scholars, though H. J. Oliver, the play's most recent editor, is inclined to favour the hypothesis that *A Shrew* was based on an earlier Shakespearean version in which Hortensio was not disguised (Oliver, pp. 22–8). E. A. J. Honigmann considered the question in 1954 and dismissed the evidence, saying 'Duthie's argument on behalf of a lost Shrew play comes to grief...because he overlooked the extant source-play, the *Supposes*.'[2] This is not strictly true (Duthie spent three pages discussing the *Supposes*), though one can see the attractions of cutting the Gordian knot by arguing, as Honigmann did, that Duthie's 'lost play' is simply the *Supposes*.[3] He attributed the inconsistencies in *The Shrew* to the fact that there is no character equivalent to Hortensio in the *Supposes*, so that the role had to be invented by Shakespeare, and he claimed that 'Shakespeare's elaboration of a plot which was already involved...seems sufficient excuse for loose ends.'[4] In fact the whole tangled question of the roles of Hortensio and Tranio is something which worries editors more than it does audiences or readers, who are often surprised when the supposedly glaring inconsistencies are pointed out to them. In an unpublished paper Gary Taylor has offered an explanation for this:

Once Hortensio disguises himself as Licio, Lucentio as Cambio, and Tranio as Lucentio, the subplot quest for Bianca falls into a neat pattern of symmetrical oppositions: Tranio against Gremio in the public wooing, Lucentio against Hortensio in the secret wooing. The whole intrigue is clearly seen, by an audience, from Lucentio's viewpoint; there can be no doubt

---

[1] See pp. 168–70 below for a discussion of Duthie's arguments on this point.

[2] E. A. J. Honigmann, 'Shakespeare's "lost source-plays"', *MLR* 49 (1954), 293–307.

[3] See pp. 14–15 above for a discussion of *Supposes* as a source for *The Shrew*.

[4] Further arguments against the existence of an Ur-Shrew have been put forward in Hosley, 'Sources and analogues', pp. 289–308, and J. C. Maxwell, '*The Shrew* and *A Shrew*: the suitors and the sisters', *N&Q* n.s. 15 (1968), 130–1.

about which suitor we expect to succeed. In keeping with this emphasis, only Lucentio is allowed to compete (in disguise, and through his agent Tranio) on both levels. In order to achieve the strict consistency called for by Duthie and other critics, Shakespeare would have had to make Hortensio a rival in both the public and private approaches, which would not only have upset the neat symmetry of the present arrangement (and possibly created difficulties in coordinating Hortensio's movements), but also would have made Hortensio himself and his double disappointment bulk too large in the subplot of the play. Moreover, in the public bidding between Gremio and Tranio, Shakespeare can exploit the discrepancy between the wooers' ages to good comic effect; Hortensio – who, except in disguise, is a 'straight' character – as a third bidder could have contributed nothing to the dramatic effectiveness of the scene. He would simply have been in the way. For all these reasons, the disregard of Hortensio's status as a public wooer seems to me perfectly logical and acceptable dramatically.

This seems entirely convincing and will perhaps allow us to set aside some of the loose ends and inconsistencies as problems which are more apparent (especially to the editor) than real, but it seems important to differentiate between these confusions in the sub-plot on the one hand and the disappearance of Christopher Sly on the other. It is by no means necessary to suppose that the two problems go together: if we do take them together we are more likely to suppose that the whole play was revised, whereas if we take the Sly question on its own we might conclude rather that the Folio text is merely an incomplete version of a lost original.

The relationship of *The Shrew* and *A Shrew*

The Taming of a Shrew is a text of considerable interest and merit whose bearing on *The Taming of the Shrew* has long vexed editors of the play and other scholars of Shakespearean textual problems. It contains all three of the main plot elements of *The Shrew*: the framing plot with the abduction and deception of Sly, the hasty courtship, wedding and taming of Katherina or Kate the shrew, and the courtship of her more conventional sister (in *A Shrew* Kate has two sisters). There are, however, marked dissimilarities as well as similarities in the treatment of all three plots:

(1) *The Sly frame*. The two opening scenes in *A Shrew* are similar in general outline to those of *The Shrew* but only half the length. A few sentences are the same, notably the unusual threat 'I'll feeze you', but in other respects the language is quite different, as for example in the Lord's first speech which begins with the lines

> Now that the gloomie shaddow of the night,
> Longing to view Orions drisling lookes,
> Leapes from th' antarticke World unto the skie
> And dims the Welkin with her pitchie breath,   (i, 10–13)[1]

before he establishes himself as one returning home from a day's hunting and proceeds to discover Sly. There are some differences in personnel: Sly is being ejected by a

---

[1] These lines are of course from *Dr Faustus* (1.3.1–4) and represent one of *A Shrew*'s many 'borrowings' from Marlowe. For a full list of the parallel passages, see Appendix 1 of *The Taming of a Shrew*, ed. F. S. Boas, 1908, pp. 91–8. Quotations from *A Shrew* below are from the old-spelling text printed in Bullough, *Sources*, 1, 69–108.

Tapster in *A Shrew* rather than by the Hostess of *The Shrew*, the Lord instructs one
of the players (not his own page) to dress up as Sly's 'wife', and the chief spokesman
for the players is given the speech heading *San.* which seems to identify him with
Sander or Saunder, the principal comic role in the main play and the equivalent of
The Shrew's Grumio. The second of the two opening scenes is apparently not set
'above' as it is in *The Shrew*, since it begins with a straightforward stage direction
Enter two with a table and a banquet on it... and ends with Sly telling the Lord 'stand
by Me and weele flout the plaiers out of their cotes', indicating that they simply move
to the side of the stage. Most significantly, Sly does not disappear at an early stage
as he does in *The Shrew* but clearly remains on stage and continues to comment. At
the end he is returned to his original position 'underneath the alehouse side' and has
a scene in which he wakes up and begins to recount his 'dream' (i.e. the play) to the
Tapster, claiming that he will get the better of his own wife when he goes home since
he now knows how to tame a shrew.[1]

(2) *The taming plot.* The whole of the main plot in *A Shrew* is set in Athens and
the names, apart from Katherina's, are different: her father is called Alfonso, the
Petruchio character is Ferando and his servant is Sander. Scene by scene the progress
of the plot is very similar, with some particularly close parallels in the actual 'taming'
scenes: the arrival at Ferando's house, the episode with the Tailor, and the argument
about the sun and the moon. Some aspects of the plot are handled slightly differently
in *A Shrew*; for example, we actually see Kate's music lesson (which is reported to
us in *The Shrew*), but there is no incident without a parallel apart from a comic scene
between Sander and another servant which takes place while the wedding of Ferando
and Kate is supposedly happening off stage.[2] All the scenes in *A Shrew* are shorter
than their equivalents in *The Shrew* despite the fact that the characters are far more
given to stating the motives for their actions: at the end of Ferando's outrageous
courtship, for example, Katherina has rather a clumsy aside (SD *She turnes aside and
speakes*):

> But yet I will consent and marrie him,
> For I methinkes have livde too long a maid,
> And match him too, or else his manhoods good.   (v, 40–2)

Later Ferando explains that it is because of his wife's temper that he has arrived for
his wedding 'baselie attired':

> Shees such a shrew, if we should once fal out,
> Sheele pul my costlie sutes over mine eares,
> And therefore am I thus attired awhile,   (vii, 30–2)

In general the plot is much more explicitly pointed out, explained and predicted in
A Shrew: at the end of the wedding scene, for example, we are told that Ferando
and Kate will return 'ere long' for her sister's wedding and that Polidor (the

---

[1] See Appendix 1 below for a complete text of these additional Sly passages.
[2] This scene (viii, 1–61) is quoted in Appendix 1 below. See also 3.2.117–18 n. above.

equivalent of Hortensio) intends to visit them before that. Polidor comments on Kate's shrewish behaviour but adds inconsequentially

> And yet it may be she will be reclaimed
> For she is verie patient grone of late. (viii, 108–9)

None of this rather explicit articulation of the plot is present in *The Shrew*. Another notable difference between the two plays occurs in Kate's speech of submission: in *A Shrew* she relies exclusively on the traditional theological argument that woman was created to be inferior to man.

(3) *The courtship of the shrew's sister(s)*. This is where we find the largest number of differences between the two plays. Katherina in *A Shrew* has two sisters, Philema and Emelia, who are courted by two young gentlemen, Aurelius (son of the Duke of Sestos) and Polidor. There is no equivalent of Gremio and no element of rivalry in the courtship, though there is some use of disguise in so far as Aurelius decides (for no very obvious reason) to court Philema in the guise of a 'Marchants sonne of Cestus' while his servant Valeria pretends to be the Duke's son, and later Valeria is disguised as a music master to occupy Kate while her two sisters 'steele abrode' to meet their lovers. Aurelius (like Tranio in *The Shrew*) proceeds in his courtship to the point where he needs someone to pose as his father and prevails on one 'Phylotus, the Marchant'. Meanwhile his real father is on his way to Athens and (like Vincentio in *The Shrew*) meets and is teased by Kate and Ferando on the road. The eventual confrontation of father and son and the unravelling of the deception is briefer and more perfunctory than it is in *The Shrew*. Apart from the element of the music lesson, this sub-plot, like that of *The Shrew*, derives from George Gascoigne's *Supposes* (1566, printed 1575), itself a prose translation of Ariosto's *I Suppositi* (1509). The version in *A Shrew* lacks dramatic tension and is rather verbose, padded out with scenes in which the lovers straightforwardly court one another, partly in lines stolen from Marlowe. As in *The Shrew* the two plots come together in the wager on the wives' obedience which is the climax of the play.

In *A Shrew* as in *The Shrew* the three elements in the plot are linked thematically since they all contain discussion of the relationship between the sexes in marriage and provide a range of different types of couples, rather like a miniature version of the 'marriage group' in *The Canterbury Tales*. The Sly material is more explicitly linked to this theme in *A Shrew* than it is in *The Shrew*: in both versions he is given a 'wife' who must specifically refuse to go to bed with him but in *A Shrew* there are two further links. First, the Lord asks the players the title of the comedy they have offered to perform and is told 'Marrie, my lord, tis calde *The taming of a shrew*: Tis a good lesson for us my lord, for us yt are married men.' Then we come back to this point at the end of the play when Sly wakes up and tells the Tapster 'I know now how to tame a shrew, / I dreamt upon it all this night till now.'

The combination of the three plots is a remarkably sophisticated example of dramatic structure for the early 1590s and the detailed execution of parts of the play is also very impressive. R. Warwick Bond said of *A Shrew*, 'I feel the Induction to be so vigorous and natural a piece of imaginative work, and the conception of Kate and Ferando so powerful and humorous that one knows not to whom to attribute these creations if not to Shakespeare.'[1] Yet he went on to support the conventional view of his time that *A Shrew* was the original (anonymous) play, reworked by Shakespeare as *The Shrew*.

A major reason for hesitating to assign *A Shrew* to Shakespeare as it stands has always been the sheer number of lines in it that are directly 'borrowed' from other plays. In his edition of the play, F. S. Boas cites sixteen separate instances, a total of forty-eight lines, where the author of *A Shrew* virtually quotes from Marlowe's *Tamburlaine* and *Dr Faustus*. A couple of typical examples are:

> O might I see the center of my soule
> Whose sacred beauty hath inchanted me,
> More faire than was the Grecian *Helena*
> For whose sweet sake so many princes dide,
> That came with thousand shippes to *Tenedos*,   (*A Shrew* iv, 52–6)

>   ...pale and ghastly death:
> Whose darts do pierce the Center of my soule.
> Her sacred beauty hath enchaunted heauen,
> And had she liu'd before the siege of *Troy*,
> *Hellen*, whose beauty sommond Greece to armes,
> And drew a thousand ships to *Tenedos*,
> Had not bene nam'd in *Homers* Iliads.   (*2 Tamburlaine* 3051–7)[2]

> Eternal heaven sooner be dissolvde,
> And all that pearseth Phebus silver eie,
> Before such hap befall to *Polidor*.   (*A Shrew* vi, 67–9)

> Eternall heauen sooner be dissolu'd,
> And all that pierceth *Phebus* siluer eie,
> Before such hap fall to *Zenocrate*.   (*1 Tamburlaine* 1003–5)

This is of course not at all like Shakespeare's regular way of using other authors. Most of these instances occur in the sub-plot relating to the courtship of the shrew's sisters, which is by far the weakest part of the play, but one cannot comfortably resort to a theory of collaborative authorship since there are two instances in the Induction and five in the taming plot, which would otherwise seem the more Shakespearean parts of the play.

The modern student can choose between three distinct theories as to how to define the relationship between the two plays: (1) *A Shrew* is the original play and the direct source of *The Shrew*; (2) *The Shrew* is the original play and *A Shrew* is a 'bad' quarto of it; (3) both *The Shrew* and *A Shrew* derive from a lost original which was Shakespeare's first version of the play. The first theory was for a long time the standard view of the matter; when Thomas Amyot edited *A Shrew* for the Shakespeare Society in 1844 he described it on the title page as 'The old *Taming of a Shrew*, upon which Shakespeare founded his comedy' and F. S. Boas followed suit with his title page in

---

[1] Bond (rev. edn, 1929), p. xlii.
[2] Quotations from Marlowe are from C. F. Tucker Brooke (ed.), *The Works of Christopher Marlowe*, 1910.

1908 which reads '*The Taming of a Shrew* being the original of Shakespeare's *Taming of the Shrew*'.

It is easy to see why this theory was so plausible for so long, since in most respects *The Shrew* gives a fuller and more polished version of the material and it is natural to suppose that the shorter and cruder version came first. But a query had been raised as early as 1850 by Samuel Hickson,[1] who declared he could 'show grounds for the assertion that *The Taming of the Shrew*, by Shakespeare, is the original play, and that *The Taming of A Shrew*...is a *later* work, and an imitation' (p. 345). What he did was to compare a number of passages in *The Shrew* with similar passages in *A Shrew*, claiming in each case that the passage in *The Shrew* was good sense and good poetry while that in *A Shrew* was garbled and inferior, hence *A Shrew* must be the work of a pirate or imitator. He cited for example, the point in 4.3 of *The Shrew* where Kate tries on a cap:

> *Kate.* Ile haue no bigger, this doth fit the time,
> And Gentlewomen weare such caps as these.
> *Pet.* When you are gentle, you shall haue one too,
> And not till then.　　　　　　　　　　　　　　　(4.3.69–72)

In the parallel scene in *A Shrew* we find the following dialogue:

> *Kate.* Thou shalt not keepe me nor feede me as thou list,
> For I will home againe unto my fathers house.
> *Feran.* I, when you'r meeke and gentell but not
> Before,　　　　　　　　　　　　　　　　　　　(xi, 41–4)

Hickson noted that in *The Shrew* Katherina's 'Gentlewomen' suggested Petruchio's 'gentle', whereas in *A Shrew* 'the reply is evidently imitated, but with the absence of the suggestive cue' (p. 346).

This view did not win many followers at the time, but it was revived and elaborated in the 1920s by a number of scholars, notably Peter Alexander, John Dover Wilson and B. A. P. van Dam.[2] It gradually became the orthodox opinion, and the seal was set on this development in 1943, when G. I. Duthie published his influential article, '*The Taming of a Shrew* and *The Taming of the Shrew*'.[3] He quoted Hickson's parallel passages and added new evidence of his own for believing that 'at any rate in certain passages, *A Shrew* may represent an attempt at memorial reconstruction of the text of *The Shrew* or a text closely resembling it' (p. 338). He was able to draw on work that had recently been done on the 'bad' quartos of *Romeo and Juliet* and *Hamlet* to describe the typical operation of the memorial reconstructor who 'remembering the thought but forgetting most of the phrasing of the original, produces blank verse of his own, arranging in new combinations the words which he does recollect from the original, and eking out these recollections with his invention and sometimes with reminiscences of passages in other plays' (pp. 338–9). An example of this in *A Shrew*

---

[1] 'The Taming of the Shrew', *N&Q* 22 (1850), 345–7.
[2] Alexander, '*The Taming of a Shrew*', *TLS* 16 Sept. 1926, 614; NS, pp. 97–126; van Dam, '*The Taming of a Shrew* and *The Taming of the Shrew*', *ES* 10 (1928), 97–106.
[3] *RES* 19 (1943), 337–56.

is Ferando's soliloquy explaining his methods of taming his wife at the end of scene
ix:

> This humor must I hold me to a while,
> To bridle and hold backe my headstrong wife,
> With curbes of hunger: ease: and want of sleepe,
> Nor sleepe nor meate shall she injoie to night,
> Ile mew her up as men do mew their hawkes,
> And make her gentlie come unto the lure,
> Were she as stuborne or as full of strength
> As were the *Thracian* horse *Alcides* tamde,
> That King *Egeus* fed with flesh of men,
> Yet would I pull her downe and make her come
> As hungry hawkes do flie unto there lure.   (ix, 42–52)

The speech as a whole is clearly related to Petruchio's soliloquy at the same point
in the plot in 4.1 of *The Shrew*:

> Thus haue I politckely begun my reigne,
> And 'tis my hope to end successefully:
> My Faulcon now is sharpe, and passing emptie,
> And til she stoope, she must not be full gorg'd,
> For then she neuer lookes vpon her lure.
> Another way I haue to man my Haggard,
> To make her come, and know her Keepers call:
> That is, to watch her, as we watch these Kites,
> That baite, and beate, and will not be obedient:
> She eate no meate to day, nor none shall eate.
> Last night she slept not, nor to night she shall not:
> As with the meate, some vndeserued fault
> Ile finde about the making of the bed,
> And heere Ile fling the pillow, there the boulster,
> This way the Couerlet, another way the sheets:
> I, and amid this hurlie I intend,
> That all is done in reuerend care of her,
> And in conclusion, she shal watch all night,
> And if she chance to nod, Ile raile and brawle,
> And with the clamor keepe her stil awake:
> This is a way to kil a Wife with kindnesse,
> And thus Ile curbe her mad and headstrong humor:
> He that knowes better how to tame a shrew,
> Now let him speake, 'tis charity to shew.   (4.1.159–82)

Duthie pointed out that the standard of writing in the speech from *A Shrew* is
generally low; the word 'ease' does not make sense in 44, there is repetition in 46–7
and 51–2, the metaphors from subduing horses and hawks are badly mixed and there
is garbled borrowing from *Tamburlaine* in 48–50, the original being Tamburlaine's
comparison of the Kings of Trebizon and Soria to

> The headstrong Iades of *Thrace*, *Alcides* tam'd,
> That King *Egeus* fed with humaine flesh,
> And made so wanton that they knew their strengths.   (*2 Tamburlaine* 3991–3)

There are several verbal parallels between the two speeches, notably between 42–4 of the *A Shrew* version and 179–80 of the *The Shrew* version where the words 'wife', 'curb', 'headstrong' and 'humour' occur in both. Similarly, the word 'lure' occurs at the end of 163 in *The Shrew* and at the end of two lines, 47 and 52, in *A Shrew*. Duthie claimed that the condition of Ferando's speech can best be explained by assuming that the author had Petruchio's speech in mind and eked out his memory of it with the lines from Marlowe. He further noted that the version in *A Shrew* contains phrases from other scenes in *The Shrew*, as for example in 46, 'Ile mew her up as men do mew their hawkes', which combines Petruchio's plan 'to watch her, as we watch these Kites' (166) with the line describing Baptista's treatment of Bianca much earlier in the play, 'And therefore has he closely meu'd her vp' (1.1.174). This combination of echoes from different parts of a play is characteristic of memorial reconstruction – and the author of *A Shrew* is further damned in Duthie's eyes since he introduces a technical error: hawks are mewed up when they are moulting and not as part of the training process.

Most subsequent scholars have been convinced by Duthie's arguments, with the exception of John W. Shroeder, who argued in 1958 that the case was not completely cut and dried and that it was still possible to see *A Shrew* as the earlier play.[1] In any event it is not easy to see *A Shrew* as an ordinary 'bad' quarto since in some ways it is so strikingly different from *The Shrew*, and moreover it is not, objectively considered, a bad play in its own right – a point Shroeder argues well. Duthie himself pointed out a problem with his own argument, namely that 'practically all the verbal parallelism is to be found in the Sly material and in the main plot. There is almost none in the sub-plot' (p. 346). This caused him to move on from theory (2) of the three possibilities outlined on p. 167 above to theory (3), i.e. that *A Shrew* does not derive directly from *The Shrew* as we have it but from an earlier version (also Shakespearean) in which the sub-plot was more like that of *A Shrew*. The same conclusion was reached independently by R. A. Houk, who used different and rather less reliable evidence from the supposedly 'obscured' chronology and 'deranged' order of scenes in *A Shrew*.[2]

Duthie's objection has, however, been met by Harold Brooks who has made an extensive study of the verbal detail of the sub-plot scenes in *The Shrew* and *A Shrew* and has discovered a large number of parallel passages which indicate a greater degree of dependence than has hitherto been supposed.[3] A group of parallels from a short passage in scene v of *A Shrew* will serve as examples: Polidor tells his servant Valeria that Alfonso (the father of the three girls)

spoke to me

To helpe him to some cunning Musition. (v, 142–3)

[1] '*The Taming of a Shrew* and *The Taming of the Shrew*: a case reopened', *JEGP* 57 (1958), 424–43.
[2] 'The evolution of *The Taming of the Shrew*', *PMLA* 57 (1942), 1009–38.
[3] These findings have not been published but are summarised in Morris, pp. 27–31.

This echoes Hortensio's response to Gremio's 'discovery' of the tutor Lucentio/
Cambio in *The Shrew*:

> 'Tis well: and I have met a Gentleman
> Hath promist me to helpe [me] to another,
> A fine Musitian to instruct our Mistris.   (1.2.165–7)

Lucentio has talked of 'cunning Schoolemasters' at 1.1.178 and Hortensio/Litio is
described as 'Cunning in Musicke, and the Mathematickes' at 2.1.55. In *A Shrew*
Polidor goes on to tell Valeria 'thou I know will fit his turne' (v, 145), echoing
Gremio's description of Lucentio/Cambio as 'Fit for her [Bianca's] turne' at 1.2.163,
and he explains his purpose with the words

> Now sweet *Aurelius* by this devise
> Shall we have leisure for to courte our loves.   (v, 149–50)

recalling Hortensio's request to Petruchio

> That so I may by this deuice at least
> Haue leaue and leisure to make loue to her,
> And vnsuspected court her by her selfe.   (1.2.129–31)

Thus in the space of ten lines the sub-plot of *A Shrew* reveals close verbal links with
that of *The Shrew* even though there are many differences in the larger pattern of
the narrative. Given the sheer complication and confusion of *The Shrew*'s sub-plot,
it would not be surprising if the actor or actors who were trying to reconstruct the
play from memory had given up the attempt and decided to go back to the *Supposes*
(clearly signalled as the source in *The Shrew* itself at 2.1.396–7 and 5.1.92) and rewrite
the sub-plot from there, padding it out with passages from Marlowe. He or they then
decided to drop the rivalry theme altogether and pair off the spare young man with
a newly invented third sister, since three women are required for the highly traditional
(and memorable) climax. Brian Morris has recently argued that the actor who played
Grumio in *The Shrew* and went on to play Sander in *A Shrew* was largely responsible
for the memorial reconstruction of the text.[1] This would also help to explain the
greater differences between the two sub-plots, since Grumio would not have been on
stage for most of the relevant scenes.

But the difference between the two sub-plots is only one reason (and to my mind
a weak one) for thinking that *A Shrew* derives from a version of *The Shrew* which
was not quite the same as the one we now have. There is better evidence in the
additional Sly material in *A Shrew*, but it is important to remember that this evidence
implies merely that our text of *The Shrew* is incomplete: it does not necessarily follow
that the rest of the play has been revised. Duthie and Houk, however, gave the Sly
problem secondary importance; they argued for authorial revision in terms of the
sub-plot and then went on to assume that Shakespeare decided to drop Sly at the
end of 1.1 in the course of that revision. There might have been a practical reason

---

[1] Morris, pp. 46–50.

for doing this since it would cut down the number of actors needed to perform the play and such a reduction might have been necessary if, as suggested above, the text that we have represents a 'hurried transcript' prepared for an acting company which was splitting up to tour the provinces. This view was argued by Peter Alexander in 1969, and he therefore concluded that 'the original ending of Shakespeare's play is to be found, very imperfectly reported,...in the final scene of [*A Shrew*]'.[1] On the other hand, Richard Hosley had maintained (without committing himself to any particular opinion on the relationship between *The Shrew* and *A Shrew*) that the dropping of Sly and the lack of an 'epilogue' could be seen as deliberate authorial decisions made for aesthetic reasons as well as practical ones.[2]

Hosley pointed out that the situation in *The Shrew* is not unusual in so far as, out of forty-five plays of the period that begin with an Induction, nineteen end with an epilogue returning the audience to the Induction characters while twenty-six do not. These statistics are, however, somewhat dubious since they include plays like Jonson's *Bartholomew Fair* where the Induction concerning the Stage-Keeper, Book-Holder and Scrivener is completely self-contained and there is no need for an epilogue of the kind that seems implied by the incomplete narrative of Sly. Hosley also argued that a return to Sly would have constituted an anti-climax after 5.2 and that Shakespeare would have been unwilling to point the shrew-taming moral in an overtly didactic ending. These aesthetic arguments are interesting but the actual ending of the Folio text with the somewhat equivocal triumph of Petruchio and Katherina and the discomfiting of the other couples is so unlike the generally joyful endings of Shakespeare's other comedies that it is hard to see it as 'more characteristic' of the author than an epilogue would have been. Moreover it remains difficult to interpret the stage direction *They sit and marke* after Sly's final comment at 1.1.243 to mean, as Hosley would have it, that the 'presenters' get up and leave almost immediately.

The most recent contribution to the debate, that of Karl P. Wentersdorf, offers new grounds for believing that Shakespeare originally did intend that Sly and his companions should remain on stage and comment on the action from time to time as they do in *A Shrew*.[3] He points out that the absence of a Sly episode between 5.1 and 5.2 of *The Shrew* creates a real problem since (a) Petruchio and Katherina are forced to break the Shakespearean 'law of re-entry' by coming back onto the stage immediately after leaving it, and (b) there is no dramatic time during which we can imagine that the marriage feast at Baptista's house has taken place. The 'law of re-entry' was first described by Irwin Smith, who explained that Shakespeare almost always avoided having a character enter at the beginning of a scene if he had been on stage at the end of the preceding one.[4] This was because there were no intermissions in the public playhouse, and when an actor left the stage he would do so in order to accomplish some purpose. His immediate re-entry would deny that any time had

---

[1] 'The original ending of *The Taming of the Shrew*', *SQ* 20 (1969), 111–16.
[2] 'Was there a dramatic epilogue to *The Taming of the Shrew*?', *SEL* 1 (1961), 17–34. Hosley's arguments are supported and extended in Oliver, pp. 40–3; Oliver believes that Shakespeare had very good reasons for dropping Sly at an early stage though it may not be possible to prove that this decision was authorial.
[3] Wentersdorf, 'Original ending'.
[4] Irwin Smith, 'Their exits and re-entrances', *SQ* 18 (1967), 7–16.

elapsed and would thus also deny that he had performed what he intended to do when he left. Smith finds that out of approximately seven hundred and fifty scenes in the Shakespearean canon only sixteen break this 'law' and that in most of those cases it can be argued that the characters do not really leave the stage at all. This is his solution to the problem at 5.1/5.2 of *The Shrew*, but Wentersdorf argues convincingly that the circumstances here lead one to suspect that something has been omitted from the text. Since it is emphasised at the end of 5.1 that Petruchio and Katherina are 'in the midst of the street' and that they have not yet completed their journey to Baptista's house, it would be confusing for the audience, and quite uncharacteristic of Shakespeare, if they simply remain on stage and we have to suppose that they are now in Lucentio's lodgings for a final 'banquet' after the main celebrations at Baptista's. When we observe that there is a Sly episode in *A Shrew* at just this point, it begins to seem very likely that a similar episode also once existed in *The Shrew* and, since it is the episode in which the Lord tells his men to put Sly back where they found him, its existence would imply the existence of a final scene (or 'epilogue') in which he wakes up as he does in *A Shrew*.

Conclusions

It is not easy to produce satisfactory answers to the questions raised by the nature of the Folio text of *The Taming of the Shrew*, but my conclusions can be summarised as follows:

1   It is no longer possible to believe that the Folio text was printed directly from Shakespeare's manuscript. Some kind of transcription intervened, and the play *may* have been cut at the same time. Both transcription and cutting could have been necessitated by the difficult theatrical conditions of the early 1590s, though they could also have occurred at any time before 1623.

2   The internal evidence for major revision is weak. The 'verse fossils' may be simply stylistic or they may at most indicate different stages in the composition of a single text. The loose ends and inconsistencies surrounding the role of Hortensio have probably been overemphasised by editors and textual scholars. It does not seem necessary to follow Duthie in positing an earlier Shakespearean version of the play in which the sub-plot was entirely different, especially as the differences between the sub-plots of *The Shrew* and *A Shrew* can be accounted for in other ways.

3   The evidence for the incompleteness of the Folio text is strong though not conclusive. The additional Sly episodes in *A Shrew* provide good grounds for believing that the Folio text is a cut version of a longer play. The assumption that similar episodes have been omitted from *The Shrew* both answers the common feeling that the Induction is incomplete and explains specific problems in the existing text at 3.2.117–18 and 5.1/5.2. Thus if there was an earlier Shakespearean version of the play it would have been simply an uncut version of the play that we have, not a radically different version in any other respect.

4   *A Shrew* should be seen as a 'bad' quarto in the sense that it is a derivative text dependent on *The Shrew*, but the original has been handled more freely and rewritten more extensively (especially in the sub-plot) than is usually the case with memorially reconstructed texts. It may preserve hints of the original staging (see, for example, my notes at Induction 1.0 SD, 4.1.148 and 4.3.63) and it is of course valuable for the additional Sly material.

Appendix 1: Passages from *The Taming of a Shrew*

In the 1594 quarto of *A Pleasant Conceited Historie, called The taming of a Shrew*, the action of the play involves Christopher Sly on five occasions after the end of 1.1 where he disappears from the Folio text of *The Taming of the Shrew*. Although the language of these passages in their present state is not particularly Shakespearean (any more than is that of the remainder of *A Shrew*) it seems highly likely that there was some equivalent for them in Shakespeare's original version of the play. Pope actually inserted them into the text of his edition of *The Shrew* but in at least one instance the context in *A Shrew* is so different (and so problematic in itself) that it is not possible to be certain where to place the passage in the Folio text. After the Sly passages printed below I have included the text of a non-Sly comic scene from *A Shrew* which I believe may similarly relate to a Shakespearean scene missing from the Folio text. For a full discussion of the relationship between the two versions, see Textual Analysis, pp. 164–74 above.

A facsimile of the unique copy of the 1594 quarto of *A Shrew* was prepared by Charles Praetorius for the Shakespeare Society in 1886 and this is the source of the passages printed below. A modern-spelling edition of the play by F. S. Boas appeared in the *Shakespeare Classics* series in 1908 and a complete old-spelling text is given by Geoffrey Bullough in *Narrative and Dramatic Sources of Shakespeare*, 8 vols., 1957–75, I, 69–108. Praetorius and Boas divided the play into acts as well as scenes but they did not agree on the divisions, which are difficult to decide. Bullough simply numbered the scenes and I have used his system below, as well as folio references to the facsimile.

The additional Sly material

1. At the end of Bullough's scene v of *A Shrew* is the following brief dialogue between Sly and his fellow-spectator the Lord (who has told Sly in scene ii that his name is Simon):

[*Exit Polidor*]

Then Slie speakes

Slie. Sim, when will the foole come againe?
Lord. Heele come againe my Lord anon.
Slie. Gis some more drinke here, souns wheres
　　The Tapster, here *Sim* eate some of these things.
Lord. So I doo my Lord.
Slie. Here *Sim*, I drinke to thee.
Lord. My Lord heere come the plaiers againe,
Slie. O brave, heers two fine gentlewomen.

Enter Valeria with a Lute and Kate with him　　[Sig. CI, scene v]

The 'fool' to whom Sly refers here and in his next comment is Sander, Ferando's servant, who is roughly equivalent to the Folio's Grumio. This episode is difficult to place in relation to the Folio text since it comes at the end of a sub-plot scene in *A Shrew* for which there is no exact equivalent, though it covers some of the material of 2.1 of *The Shrew*, specifically the presentation of a man disguised as a music master to the father of the heroines. The scene which follows in *A Shrew* (Bullough's scene vi) is indeed Kate's music lesson, which is not staged in *The Shrew* but reported by Hortensio at 2.1.141–55.

The placing of the episode in *A Shrew* itself has aroused some suspicion, since Sly's announcement 'heers two fine gentlewomen' is not consistent with the entry of Kate and Valeria which follows, since Valeria is Polidor's male servant disguised as a music master. Sly, who is drunk, could simply be making a mistake here, but Raymond Houk argued for a considerable rearrangement of the scenes in *A Shrew* to remove this and other inconsistencies (and to bring the order of scenes into line with that of *The Shrew*).[1] In reply, John W. Shroeder pointed out that it is more likely that the Sly episode itself has been misplaced (rather than the following scene) and that there is more than one other position where it could occur.[2]

2. At the end of Bullough's scene xiv of *A Shrew*, Sly speaks again:

[Exeunt Omnes]

Slie. Sim must they be married now?
Lord. I my Lord.

[Scene xv]

Enter Ferando and Kate and Sander

Slie. Looke *Sim* the foole is come againe now. [Sig. E4, scene xiv/xv]

The sub-plot characters, Polidor and Emelia, Aurelius and Philema, have indeed just gone off to be married. The nearest equivalent to scene xiv in *The Shrew* is 4.4, and the following scene in both plays (xv in *A Shrew*, 4.5 in *The Shrew*) presents the characters on the road on the way back to Kate's father's house and includes the argument about the sun and the moon. Grumio does not appear at all in 4.5 of *The Shrew* and Sander disappears from scene xv of *A Shrew* at line 4 having spoken one line, but of course Sly cannot be expected to predict this, though some critics (including Houk) have argued for the relocation of this episode in *A Shrew* on the grounds that Sly's enthusiasm for the reappearance of Sander is 'inconsistent' with the minimal nature of his actual part in the scene.

3. In the middle of Bullough's scene xvi, Sly actually tries to intervene in the main action of the play:

Phylotus and Valeria runnes away

Then Slie speakes

---

[1] 'The evolution of *The Taming of the Shrew*', *PMLA* 57 (1942), 1009–38.
[2] '*The Taming of a Shrew* and *The Taming of the Shrew*: a case reopened', *JEGP* 57 (1958), 424–43.

Slie. I say wele have no sending to prison.

Lord. My Lord this is but the play, theyre but in jest.

Slie. I tell thee *Sim* wele have no sending,
   To prison thats flat: why *Sim* am not I *Don Christo Vary?*
   Therefore I say they shall not go to prison.

Lord. No more they shall not my Lord,
   They be run away.

Slie. Are they run away *Sim?* thats well,
   Then gis some more drinke, and let them play againe.

Lord. Here, my Lord.

Slie drinkes and then falls asleepe   [Sig. F2, scene xvi]

This episode could be inserted at 5.1.86 of *The Shrew* which is the equivalent point in the action, where the Merchant (or Pedant) and Tranio (equivalent to Phylotus and Valeria) run away (with Biondello).

4. At the end of the same scene (xvi) in *A Shrew*, Sly is still asleep and is carried off stage:

Exeunt Omnes

Slie sleepes

Lord. Whose within there? come hither sirs my Lords
   Asleepe againe: go take him easily up,
   And put him in his one apparell againe,
   And lay him in the place where we did find him,
   Just underneath the alehouse side below,
   But see you wake him not in any case.

Boy. It shall be don my Lord come helpe to beare him hence.   [Sig. F3, scene xvi]

This episode could be inserted between 5.1 and 5.2 of *The Shrew*. Indeed, Karl P. Wentersdorf has argued convincingly that some such scene is needed here in order to prevent a violation of the Shakespearean 'law of re-entry' and to provide time for the wedding-feast to take place.[1] One problem about the episode is that it removes Sly surprisingly early and prevents him from witnessing the climax of the play with the public demonstration of Petruchio's triumph.

5. When the final scene of the play proper is over, *A Shrew* gives us this conclusion · to the framing action:

[Scene xix]

*Then enter two bearing of Slie in his
Owne apparrell againe, and leaves him
Where they found him and then goes out*

Then enter the Tapster

---

[1] 'The original ending of *The Taming of the Shrew*: a reconsideration', *SEL* 18 (1978), 201–15. See also 5.2.0 SD n. above.

Tapster. Now that the darkesome night is overpast,
    And dawning day apeares in cristall sky,
    Now must I hast abroad: but soft whose this?
    What *Slie* oh wondrous hath he laine here allnight,
    Ile wake him, I thinke he's starved by this,
    But that his belly was so stuft with ale,
    What how *Slie*, Awake for shame.
Slie. Sim gis some more wine: whats all the
    Plaiers gon: am not I a Lord?
Tapster. A Lord with a murrin: come art thou dronken still?
Slie. Whose this? *Tapster*, oh Lord sirra, I have had
    The bravest dreame to night, that ever thou
    Hardest in all thy life.
Tapster. I marry but you had best get you home,
    For your wife will course you for dreming here to night,
Slie. Will she? I know now how to tame a shrew,
    I dreamt upon it all this night till now,
    And thou hast wakt me out of the best dreame
    That ever I had in my life, but Ile to my
    Wife presently and tame her too
    And if she anger me.
Tapster. Nay tarry *Slie* for Ile go home with thee,
    And heare the rest that thou hast dreamt to night.

                    Exeunt Omnes   [Sig. G2–G2ᵛ, scene xix]

Sly's lines, 'I have had / The bravest dreame to night, that ever thou / Hardest in all thy life' have reminded some critics of Bottom saying 'I have had a most rare vision. I have had a dream, past the wit of man to say what dream it was', etc. (*MND* 4.1.204 ff.), but apart from the question of whether we have an echo of a genuine Shakespearean line here, many directors have felt the need to use this episode or some equivalent of it in order to round off the play satisfactorily.

An additional scene

When Ferando and Kate have gone off stage to be married in Bullough's scene vii, *A Shrew* gives us the following comic scene between Polidor's servant (roughly equivalent to Biondello) and Sander (Grumio):

[*Scene viii*]

Enter Polidors boy and Sander

Boy. Come hither sirha boy
San. Boy; oh disgrace to my person, souns boy
    Of your face, you have many boies with such
    Pickadeuantes I am sure, souns would you
    Not have a bloudie nose for this?
Boy. Come, come, I did but jest, where is that
    Same peece of pie that I gave thee to keepe.
San. The pie? I you have more minde of your bellie
    Then to go see what your maister dooes.

Boy. Tush tis no matter man I prethe give it me,
     I am verie hungry I promise thee.
San. Why you may take it and the devill burst
     You with it, one cannot save a bit after supper,
     But you are alwaies readie to munch it vp.
Boy. Why come man, we shall have good cheere
     Anon at the bridehouse, for your maisters gone to
     Church to be married alreadie, and thears
     Such cheere as passeth.
San. O brave, I would I had eate no meat this week,
     For I have never a corner left in my bellie
     To put a venison pastie in, I thinke I shall burst my selfe
     With eating, for Ile so cram me downe the tarts
     And the marchpaines, out of all crie.
Boy. I, but how wilt thou doo now thy maisters
     Married, thy mistresse is such a devill, as sheele make
     Thee forget thy eating quickly, sheele beat thee so.
San. Let my maister alone with hir for that, for
     Heele make hir tame wel inough ere longe I warent thee
     For he's such a churle waxen now of late that and he be
     Never so little angry he thums me out of all crie,
     But in my minde sirra the yongest is a verie
     Prettie wench, and if I thought thy maister would
     Not have her Ide have a flinge at hir
     My selfe, Ile see soone whether twill be a match
     Or no: and it will not Ile set the matter
     Hard for my selfe I warrant thee.
Boy. Sounes you slave will you be a Rivall with
     My maister in his love, speake but such
     Another worde and Ile cut off one of thy legges.
San. Oh, cruell judgement, nay then sirra,
     My tongue shall talke no more to you, marry my
     Timber shall tell the trustie message of his maister,
     Even on the very forehead of thee, thou abusious
     Villaine, therefore prepare thy selfe.
Boy. Come hither thou Imperfecksious slave in
     Regard of thy beggery, holde thee theres
     Twoshillings for thee? to pay for the
     Healing of thy left legge which I meane
     Furiously to invade or to maime at the least.
San. O supernodicall foule? well Ile take your
     two shillinges but Ile barre striking at legges.
Boy. Not I, for Ile strike any where.
San. Here here take your two shillings again
     Ile see thee hangd ere Ile fight with thee,
     I gat a broken shin the other day,
     Tis not, whole yet and therefore Ile not fight
     Come come why should we fall out?
Boy. Well sirray your faire words hath something
     Alaied my Coller: I am content for this once

To put it vp and be frends with thee,
But soft see where they come all from church,
Belike they be Married allredy.

Enter *Ferando and Kate and Alfonso and Polidor*
and Emelia and Aurelius and Philema.   [Sig. C4^v–D1^v, scene viii]

There are two reasons for thinking that a scene like this might have been present in Shakespeare's original version of *The Shrew*. Firstly, there is a conspicuously awkward moment in the Folio text at just this point, where a scene seems to be missing (see 3.2.117–18 n. above), and if we take *A Shrew* to be some kind of reported text of *The Shrew* it might be argued that this scene is as likely to represent a reported version of a Shakespearean scene as the Sly material quoted above.

Secondly, there may be evidence of a Shakespearean original in the offer made by Polidor's servant, 'theres / Twoshillings for thee? to pay for the / Healing of thy left legge which I meane / Furiously to invade or to maime at the least'. This is interesting because it is very common in folklore versions of the shrew-taming story for the husband to offer his wife money in exactly this threatening way, according to J. H. Brunvand, who proves moreover that a significant difference between *The Shrew* and *A Shrew* is that 'the author of *The Shrew* must have had closer contact with the folklore tradition than did the author of *A Shrew*'.[1] He points out that *The Shrew* as printed in the Folio contains at least six traits or narrative elements which are not found in *A Shrew* but which are common in folklore versions of the story. Some of them are treated at length, such as Grumio's description of the journey to Petruchio's house after the wedding. Here, as in many folklore versions, the taming process begins – in this case, when the couple fall into the mud. Elsewhere Shakespeare shows his familiarity with the folklore tradition by a brief reference, such as when Curtis asks Grumio whether both Petruchio and Katherina were riding on one horse (see 4.1.50 n. above). The reference to the folklore tradition in the words of Polidor's servant here is of the latter kind, and it does seem characteristic of Shakespeare's handling of the material. It is in fact difficult to believe that the author of *A Shrew* was capable of inventing this line, or that he was sufficiently familiar with the folklore tradition to add it on his own initiative, since elsewhere (apart from the single trait of using three sisters instead of two) his version is further away from the tradition.

If a scene like this did exist in Shakespeare's original version of the play it is not clear why it should have been dropped, since unlike the Sly scenes it would not economise on personnel. Two possible reasons suggest themselves, both of which take us back to the author: (1) Shakespeare may have felt that this kind of banter between servants was no longer funny or had simply gone out of fashion (in general, he seems to have dropped it after his very earliest comedies). (2) At the point when the decision was taken to put Hortensio into disguise and generally complicate the sub-plot, there may have been a need to cut down the number and length of existing scenes slightly and this is one of the few which are expendable.

[1] '*The Taming of the Shrew*: A Comparative Study of Oral and Literary Versions', unpublished Ph.D. thesis, Indiana University, 1961, p. 287.

Appendix 2: The staging of Induction 2

There is no problem about the staging of the opening scene of *The Taming of the Shrew* (designated 'Induction 1' since Pope); it clearly takes place on the main stage. After line 134 however, the Folio text, which does not specify a change of scene at this point, does indicate a change of location with the stage direction

Enter aloft the drunkard with attendants, some with apparel, Bason and Ewer, & other appurtenances, & Lord.

The implication is that the whole of the action for the next 141 lines (the scene called 'Induction 2' in this and all other modern editions) takes place 'aloft' and that the main stage is not used again until the entry of Lucentio and Tranio at the point where modern editors begin Act 1, Scene 1 of the play proper (although again there is no scene division in F).

'Aloft' is a specific and quite common direction in Elizabethan and Jacobean play texts which usually refers to an upper acting-area which formed a kind of gallery or balcony at the back of the main stage. Shakespeare used this upper area in twenty of his thirty-eight plays,[1] the most familiar examples being the balcony scene in *Romeo and Juliet* (2.2) and the scene at Cleopatra's tomb where the dying Antony is heaved aloft by Cleopatra and her women (*Antony and Cleopatra*, 4.15). Scenes played 'aloft' are quite common in the earliest plays: *The Two Gentlemen of Verona* and *3 Henry VI* both require a gallery twice, for example, and *2 Henry VI* and *Titus Andronicus* require one three times each, while *1 Henry VI* requires one no less than six times.[2] It is apparent, then, that some kind of upper acting-area was available to whatever company Shakespeare was writing for around 1590, though scholars have put forward different theories about its precise nature. Some have assumed that a gallery must have been a permanent feature of most of the buildings used for theatrical performances, but C. Walter Hodges has suggested, relying heavily on the evidence of this particular scene, that some theatres may have been able to enlarge their space 'aloft' by the use of a 'temporary porch-like booth' attached to the existing gallery or tiring-house.[3] This solution is favoured by both Hibbard and Morris in their recent editions of the play,[4] but it is, as Hodges says, pure conjecture. Even with the help of some temporary structure the space 'aloft' would have been restricted in size compared with the main stage and, naturally, more remote from the audience. There

[1] Statistics are from Richard Hosley, 'Shakespeare's use of a gallery over the stage', *S.Sur.* 10 (1957), 77–89.
[2] The relevant scenes are: *TGV* 4.2, 4.3; *3H6* 4.7, 5.1; *2H6* 1.4, 4.5, 4.9; *Tit.* 1.1 (three separate occasions); *1H6* 1.6, 2.1, 3.2 (two separate occasions), 4.2, 5.3.
[3] *The Globe Restored*, 1953, pp. 56 ff.
[4] Hibbard (1968) and Morris (1981) respectively. Oliver (1982) also thinks that one way or another the scene must be set 'aloft'.

are, moreover, further problems about accepting the Folio's 'aloft' in the case of Induction 2 of *The Shrew*, since this scene is exceptional, indeed unique, in the following ways:

1. The number of actors involved is much larger than in any other scene staged 'aloft'. Usually the gallery is used by a single actor, as when Silvia appears 'at her window' in *The Two Gentlemen of Verona*, or by a small group of actors, as in the many appearances of characters 'on the walls' of a castle or town in the history plays. Richard Hosley has calculated that the average number of actors who are actually 'aloft' across the whole range of Shakespeare's thirty-five gallery scenes is three, but in Induction 2 we find a minimum of nine if we follow the Folio's directions: we begin with Sly, the Lord and an unspecified number of 'attendants', three of whom have speaking parts, then at line 93 the stage direction says *Enter Lady with Attendants*, implying a minimum of two additional attendants, and at line 123 there is a further direction, *Enter a Messenger*. From line 31 'Wilt thou have music? Hark, Apollo plays', and its accompanying stage direction, '*Musick*', we might deduce the additional presence of one or more musicians, though these could be doubled by the attendants, or they might be placed under the gallery as in illustration 1 (p. 4 above). It is, however, clear from the text of the play as a whole that the Folio's stage directions are far from being definitive, and it would be possible to perform a version of this scene with only six actors 'aloft' at any one time if we cut out the (non-speaking) 'Attendants' who enter with the 'Lady' and allow one of the original three servingmen (or even the Lord himself, as in Hibbard's edition) to double as the 'Messenger' after leaving in obedience to Sly's command, 'Servants, leave me and her alone' at line 112.

2. The scene is considerably longer and more elaborate than any other 'aloft' sequence. The average length of most of Shakespeare's gallery scenes is under fifty lines whereas Induction 2 is three times this length. It also has some quite elaborate 'business' with the various items that are offered to Sly (sack, conserves, raiment, the basin to wash his hands in), and the knot of actors around Sly have to regroup when new characters arrive. All this would be difficult for the actors to manage and for the audience to see if the acting-area 'aloft' was a small one with restricted sight-lines. The fact that the scene is entirely an interior one, taking place in the Lord's 'fairest chamber' (Induction 1.42), is also exceptional since Shakespeare normally uses the gallery to represent some part of a building overlooking an outdoor location.

3. There is no interaction between the gallery and the main stage, and the latter remains unlocalised until the end of the scene, when it becomes the Paduan street necessitated by the main action. Usually an action 'above' will be closely related to an action 'below', as when characters who are presumed to be at a window or on the walls of a building communicate with those on the ground outside. There are only two instances in the entire Shakespearean canon where the main stage is left empty during an action 'aloft', this scene and one in *I Henry VI*. In the latter case, Joan, the Dauphin, Reignier, Alencon and Soldiers appear on the walls of Orleans for the space of thirty lines, and although no one appears below, it is clear that the main stage represents a place beneath the walls. Leaving the main stage not only empty but unlocalised would seem puzzling to an audience and wasteful to a director, especially

as the sheer size of the main stage in an Elizabethan theatre would emphasise the remoteness of a long scene played exclusively in the gallery. If we accept the notion that a 'temporary booth' would be available, it would help to open out the gallery space into the main theatre but it would not entirely solve the problem.

In purely theatrical terms, then, it seems on the whole unlikely that this scene would really have been played 'aloft', since it is a unique example of a long, elaborate interior sequence involving a large number of actors using the gallery without reference to the main stage. The stage direction with which it opens is a vague one which may have originated with the author rather than in the theatre, like several other directions in this text:[1] it fails to specify how many attendants are needed, for example, and anyone actually staging the play would need to know that the 'other appurtenances' brought on must include food, drink and musical instruments. One wonders if Shakespeare could have originally intended to set this scene 'aloft' and neglected to cross out the direction when it became too long and elaborate for this to be practical. Or perhaps the unstable conditions of theatrical production at the time meant that he wrote the play for a playing-area rather different from the kind that became standard later on.

The attempt to unravel Shakespeare's intentions about the staging of this scene is of course linked to the whole question of what he intended to do with Christopher Sly afterwards. In the Folio text as it stands, Sly presumably remains visible during 1.1, as he makes a brief comment at the end of it. The stage direction then says of him and his companions that *They sit and marke*, implying that they continue to be present and perhaps even prepare for further comment, but no more is heard of them and no exit is given. Any director of the play has to make his own decision about when and how to get these characters off stage. If Induction 2 has indeed been played 'aloft' it might be possible to draw a curtain across them at some early point when the audience's attention has been diverted to the main action, or if Induction 2 has been played on the main stage with Sly and his companions moving to the side of the stage for the beginning of the play proper, they may just exit silently as soon as they can. If we assume on the evidence of *A Shrew* that Shakespeare did originally write further material for Sly so that he continues to watch and comment on the action throughout,[2] a further problem arises in 5.1 if Sly is still 'aloft' when the false Vincentio needs to use the gallery for his scene 'at the window': does he appear in the same gallery as Sly? Altogether it would be easier if Sly moved to the side after playing the first two scenes on the main stage. In doing this he would be setting the pattern for the large number of 'standings aside' that are to follow, from the moment in the next scene when Lucentio and Tranio 'stand by' to watch the 'show' of Baptista, his daughters and Bianca's suitors to the moment in 5.1 when Petruchio and Katherina 'stand aside' to watch the dénouement of the sub-plot.[3] Although many scenes in the play proper contain on-stage audiences in this way, there is never more than one small group (usually consisting of two or at most three characters) 'standing

[1] See Textual Analysis, pp. 156–8 above.
[2] See Textual Analysis, pp. 164–74 above and Appendix 1.
[3] See p. 31 above for further discussion of the play's use of on-stage audiences.

aside' together, so it would always be possible for Sly and his companion(s) to be on one side of the stage while the second on-stage audience was on the other.

This seems to be what happens in *A Shrew* which may, as a reported text, preserve some details of the original staging of *The Shrew*. The stage direction at the beginning of the scene which is equivalent to Induction 2 makes no mention of 'aloft' but simply says

Enter two with a table and a banquet on it, and two other, with Slie asleepe in a chaire, richlie apparelled, & the musick plaieng.

This indicates that Sly is carried onto the main stage. It is interesting that his being asleep is specifically mentioned, as in both plays the audience has been prepared to enjoy the moment of Sly's awakening, and his first line of dialogue works best when delivered as if he is just regaining consciousness. It has sometimes been assumed that a gallery (with a curtain) is necessary to present this moment effectively, but *A Shrew* shows us how it can be done on the main stage. As for the chair, *The Shrew* has the Lord order that Sly be 'conveyed to bed', but *A Shrew* substitutes 'set him at the Table in a chair' which would certainly make for easier staging, since a bed would take up too much room later (either 'aloft' or at the side of the stage) or else would have to be carried off at some point, whereas a chair could remain to the end without any trouble.[1] At the end of this scene in *A Shrew* it is suggested that the characters simply move to the side when Sly says to the Lord (whose name is Simon in this version)

> Come *Sim*, where be the plaiers? *Sim* stand by
> Me and weele flout the plaiers out of their cotes.

There were certainly no rigid conventions about the staging of Inductions or the positioning of 'presenters', as several contemporary texts (including *The Shrew* at 1.1.238 SD) call actors representing spectators who are outside the main action of the play and who comment upon it. If we look at some other plays written around 1590 we find a mixture of methods. In Greene and Lodge's *Looking Glass for London and England* the gallery is apparently used for the prophet Oseas, who is *brought in by an Angell...and set downe over the stage in a Throne*, from which position he makes comments after various scenes. In Greene's *James IV*, on the other hand, the Induction characters – Bohan the disaffected Scottish courtier and Oberon, King of the Faeries – begin their action on the main stage but move aloft after about a hundred lines of dialogue when Bohan says he will tell Oberon a story from Scottish history to parallel his own misanthropy and invites him to 'Gang with me to the gallery, and I'll show thee the same in action.' At the end of each act they come onto the main stage to comment but always retreat again to the gallery, variously referred to as 'our harbour' and 'our cell'. There are no such indications of another location in Kyd's *Spanish Tragedy* where Revenge and the Ghost of Andrea perform a similar choric function at the end of each act, implying probably that they sit at the side of the main stage throughout, simply moving into the centre when they are needed.

---

[1] Despite the Lord's order in *The Shrew*, it is apparent that Sly is not in bed in Induction 2 since he is told he will be taken to a 'couch' (presumably elsewhere) if he wishes to sleep (35–7).

Presumably Shakespeare, like the other playwrights, would make his decision about staging taking into account the resources of the actual theatre he was writing for, the length and elaboration of the scene, the number of actors involved and, perhaps, the degree of intimacy or distance he wished to establish between the Induction and the main action. Even then his decision would be a provisional one, since he would probably expect his play to be adapted to the circumstances of different theatres, indoor and outdoor, at different times. An edited modern text tends to assume an 'ideal' and consistent manner of theatrical presentation but plays of this period were clearly very adjustable in practice and Shakespeare took no interest in publishing his plays, let alone in establishing a 'definitive' text complete with stage directions.[1]

[1] See illustrations 1 and 2 (pp. 4 and 5 above) for sketches illustrating the staging of Induction 2 with and without a gallery.

Appendix 3: Music in the play and Hortensio's gamut (3.1.64–75)

The Taming of the Shrew contains a number of references to music, of which Hortensio's gamut in Act 3, Scene 1 is the most detailed and technical.[1] In the Induction, music is one of the refined entertainments that the Lord proposes to offer to Sly: 'Procure me music ready when he wakes / To make a dulcet and a heavenly sound' (Induction 1.46–7), but the elevated terms in which it is described – 'Wilt thou have music? Hark, Apollo plays, / And twenty cagèd nightingales do sing' (Induction 2.31–2) – are ridiculously inappropriate to Sly's likely experience and taste, even if he does not, like Bottom in a similar situation, put in a request for 'the tongs and the bones' (*MND* 4.1.29). In the main plot the snatches of ballads and folk-songs give Petruchio's courtship something of the air of a 'wooing dance', as he puts it (1.2.65), and the taming process is seen through musical metaphors as the harmonising of the discordant Katherina, bringing her from the point where she destroys Hortensio's lute in 2.1 to the end when Lucentio can say 'At last, though long, our jarring notes agree' (5.2.1).[2] The sub-plot, however, contains the majority of the play's references to music, which is seen in Paduan society as an important part of the 'good bringing up' which Baptista wants for his daughters.[3] Hortensio duly disguises himself as a music teacher and Tranio, playing his master's role, offers a lute as a present to ingratiate himself.

In 3.1, Lucentio and Hortensio begin by arguing for precedence in terms of the respective merits of music and philosophy, though the latter term is used very loosely, since Lucentio's lesson consists, on the surface, of a reading from Ovid's *Heroides*, a set of verse epistles supposed to be written by ladies abandoned by their lovers. Both teachers are of course fraudulent and they use their lessons as a cover for their courtship of Bianca. Lucentio's false translations are obvious enough, but Hortensio's gamut involves some ingenious double meanings which depend on a knowledge of the Elizabethan system of musical notation.

'Gamut' itself was the term given to the written hexachord series, consisting of the first six notes of the major scale. It was important as a tool for teaching pupils to sight-read music; hence in this scene Bianca must *read* it – and perhaps learn to 'read' her teacher at the same time. As today in phrases like 'to run the gamut', the

---

[1] The quantity, quality and overall consistency of the musical allusions in *The Shrew* were used to support the argument for Shakespeare's sole authorship by Tommy Ruth Waldo and T. W. Herbert, 'Musical terms in *The Taming of the Shrew*: evidence of single authorship', *SQ* 10 (1959), 185–99.

[2] For further discussion of these musical allusions in the main plot see pp. 13 and 16–17 above and 1.2.52 and 2.1.198 nn. above.

[3] There is some discrimination between the sexes here: Tranio advises his master 'Music and poesy use to quicken you' (1.1.36), implying they are to be the lighter side of his studies, but they seem to constitute Bianca's entire educational programme.

word 'gamut' could also be used in a more general sense to mean the whole range or compass of a thing.

Each hexachord or six-note scale overlaps three notes with the next hexachord, three being the perfect number in medieval music systems as in theology (compare George Herbert's 'Easter': 'All music is but three parts vied / And multiplied'). Two hexachords are used in this passage, the one beginning with G which was known as the 'hard' hexachord and the one beginning with C which was the 'natural' hexachord. Where the two hexachords overlap (73–5), each note is given two titles, D for example being the fifth note (sol) of the G hexachord and the second note (re) of the C hexachord. The titles for the notes originated with Guido d'Arezzo (*fl.* 1024), who based them on the first syllables of the lines of the hymn for St John the Baptist's day, 'Ut queant laxis', since each line began on the subsequent note up the hexachord from the last. Thus ut, re, mi, fa, sol, la came to represent the notes of a hexachord at whatever pitch.[1] Hortensio's playful exploitation of this system needs to be analysed line by line:

70   '*Gamut* I am, the ground of all accord:'
     G (Gamma ut) is the lowest note of this hexachord, the 'ground' or basis of all harmony or 'accord', both in the musical sense and perhaps in relation to Hortensio and Bianca's love.

71   '*A re* to plead Hortensio's passion;'
     It has been pointed out by Harry Colin Miller, 'A Shakespearean music lesson', *N&Q* 165 (1933), 255–7, that the two names given to the note here make up the word 'array'; hence Hortensio is calling on the notes of the gamut to arrange themselves so as to plead his passion eloquently.

72   '*B mi*, Bianca, take him for thy lord;'
     The Folio has 'Beeme' here, emended by Pope. Either way the meaning seems to be 'Be my Bianca.'

73   '*C fa ut*, that loves with all affection;'
     Miller hears '*C fa ut*' as 'Assay fate' which may be a little over-ingenious. It is perhaps more important that the two hexachords begin to overlap here producing two harmonic sets, hence 'affective' music in a double sense (as Hortensio goes on to explain in the next line). There may be a reference to the fact that the 'hard' hexachord G has been 'softened' or 'affected' by the combination with C, and of course Hortensio alludes hopefully to the 'affection' which can draw two people, like two hexachords, into harmony.

74   '*D sol re*, one clef, two notes have I;'
     'Clef' is ambiguous: it could refer to the clef sign (as in modern musical terminology) but Morley also uses 'clef' to refer to the letter (D) designating both note sound and clef. Hence 'one clef, two notes' could mean that the note D has two titles, sol and re, according to the two hexachords, and thus has not

[1] See Thomas Morley, *A Plain and Easy Introduction to Practical Music* (1597), for a contemporary explanation of this system. I have also made use of the entries under 'gamut' and 'hexachord' in Stanley Sadie (ed.), *The New Grove Dictionary of Music and Musicians*, 20 vols., 1980, vols. 7 and 8.

only two names but two existences as it functions in both systems simultaneously. The allusion to Hortensio's disguise is obvious, and it may be intended as a joke that he stumbles into obscenity here since 'clef' or 'cliff' could also mean 'female genitals' as in *Tro.* 5.2.10–11 where Thersites says of Cressida 'any man may sing her, if he can take her cliff; she's noted'.

75 '*E la mi*, show pity or I die.'

Miller's interpretation based on sound (*E la mi* – Ill am I) seems more plausible here than the one in line 73. Also, Hortensio has come to the end of his gamut, so his 'life' as a suitor now rests on Bianca's mercy. Musical cadences were spoken of as small 'deaths' (compare George Herbert's 'Vertue': 'My musick shows ye have your closes, / And all must die'), and there may again be an obscene undertone since 'to die' could mean 'to experience orgasm'.

It is difficult to imagine how all of this could ever have been conveyed on stage, but an audience with a reasonable general knowledge of music would at least have been able to make more sense of these lines than most of us can today.

READING LIST

This list includes details of books and articles referred to in the Introduction or Commentary, and may serve as a guide to those who wish to undertake further study of the play.

Baskervill, C. R. *The Elizabethan Jig and Related Song Drama*, 1929

Berry, Ralph. *Shakespeare's Comedies*, 1972

Bradbrook, M. C. 'Dramatic role as social image: a study of *The Taming of the Shrew*', *SJ* 94 (1958), 132–50

Brunvand, Jan Harold. 'The folktale origin of *The Taming of the Shrew*', *SQ* 17 (1966), 345–59

   '*The Taming of the Shrew*: A Comparative Study of Oral and Literary Versions', unpublished Ph.D. thesis, Indiana University, 1961

Cooper, Marilyn M. 'Implicature, convention and *The Taming of the Shrew*', *Poetics* 10 (1981), 1–14

Dusinberre, Juliet. *Shakespeare and the Nature of Women*, 1975

Duthie, G. I. '*The Taming of a Shrew* and *The Taming of the Shrew*', *RES* 19 (1943), 337–56

Greenfield, Thelma N. *The Induction in Elizabethan Drama*, 1969

Heilman, Robert B. 'The *Taming* untamed, or the return of the shrew', *MLQ* 27 (1966), 147–61

Hibbard, G. R. *The Making of Shakespeare's Dramatic Poetry*, 1981

Hosley, Richard. 'The formal influence of Plautus and Terence', in J. R. Brown and B. Harris (eds.), *Elizabethan Theatre*, 1966, 131–45.

   'Shakespeare's use of a gallery over the stage', *S.Sur.* 10 (1957), 77–89

   'Sources and analogues of *The Taming of the Shrew*', *HLQ* 27 (1963–4), 289–308. Reprinted in the Signet *Shrew*, ed. R. B. Heilman, 1966, 186–208

   'Was there a dramatic epilogue to *The Taming of the Shrew*?', *SEL* 1 (1961), 17–34

Kahn, Coppélia. *Man's Estate: Masculine Identity in Shakespeare*, 1981

Leggatt, Alexander. *Shakespeare's Comedy of Love*, 1974

Lenz, Carolyn Ruth Swift *et al.* (eds.), *The Woman's Part: Feminist Criticism of Shakespeare*, 1980

McMillin, Scott. 'Casting for Pembroke's Men: the *Henry 6* quartos and *The Taming of a Shrew*', *SQ* 23 (1972), 141–59

Mincoff, M. 'The dating of *The Taming of the Shrew*', *ES* 54 (1973), 554–65

Nevo, Ruth. *Comic Transformations in Shakespeare*, 1980

Novy, Marianne L. 'Patriarchy and play in *The Taming of the Shrew*', *ELR* 9 (1979), 264–80

Pinciss, G. M. 'Shakespeare, Her Majesty's Players, and Pembroke's Men', *S.Sur.* 27 (1974), 129–36

Praz, Mario. 'Shakespeare's Italy', *S.Sur.* 7 (1954), 95–106

Righter, Anne. *Shakespeare and the Idea of the Play*, 1962

Salingar, Leo. *Shakespeare and the Traditions of Comedy*, 1974

Seronsy, Cecil C. '"Supposes" as the unifying theme in *The Taming of the Shrew*', *SQ* 14 (1963), 15–30

Stone, Lawrence. *The Family, Sex and Marriage in England 1500–1800*, 1977

Wentersdorf, Karl P. 'The origin and personnel of the Pembroke company', *Theatre Research International* 5 (1980), 45–68

'The original ending of *The Taming of the Shrew*: a reconsideration', *SEL* 18 (1978), 201–15